Birds of PREY

Birds of PREY

Written by

PHILIP BURTON

Illustrated by

TREVOR BOYER

MALCOLM ELLIS

DAVID THELWELL

GALLERY BOOKS
An Imprint of W. H. Smith Publishers Inc.
112 Madison Avenue
New York City 10016

Acknowledgements

The author wishes to acknowledge with thanks the invaluable help of Peter Colston and Tim Parmenter in the provision of reference material, and the assistance of Derek Read in the preparation and editing of the text.

On behalf of the artists, sincere thanks are due also to the following individuals and organizations for help with photographic reference and access to live specimens of many of the species illustrated.

Ken & Shaun Smith,
Bird of Prey Conservation Centre, Hornsea Potteries, North Humberside.
John Metcalf, Christopher Marler, Colin Bradshaw, Howard Roberts, Brian Simpson, Donald Ideson.
Graham Cowles, British Museum, Tring.
The Falconry Centre, Gloucester.
Michael Bryant, Eddie Mills, Derek Wood, Steve Madge, Richard Meyer

This edition first published in the United States in 1989 by
Gallery Books, an imprint of W.H. Smith Publishers, Inc.,
112 Madison Avenue, New York 10016.

Designer: Tom Deas
Editor: Martyn Bramwell
Editorial Assistant: Diana Steedman
Managing Editor: Pippa Rubinstein

Published in England by Dragon's World Ltd, Limpsfield and London

ISBN 0 8317 6381 7

Printed and bound in Spain by
Grupo Nerecan - Tonsa, San Sebastian

Contents

Foreword

The Rt.Hon. The Lord Tweedsmuir, C.B.E., C.D.
President of The Hawk Trust

Birds of prey have been allies of man for many centuries. They have been his companions in the chase, providing him with sport as well as food. References to them are common in our everyday language, in phrases such as "an eye like a hawk". They are also part of our literary heritage, as in these splendid lines from Shakespeare's *Macbeth*:

> "A falcon, towering in her pride of place,
> Was by a mousing owl hawk'd at and kill'd."

Their links with man go back further still. No wonder they have become the emblems of some of the most important countries in the world and have given their names to some of the most prestigious orders of chivalry, including the Order of the Condor of the Andes, the Icelandic Falcon and the White Eagle of Serbia.

In the Middle Ages you kept a hawk according to your social rank; the Kestrel was reserved for the knave. Living largely on mice and sparrows, it could hardly be regarded as a provider. I started my falconry as a schoolboy and my first bird was a Kestrel. Then I flew a Peregrine and later on a female Goshawk. Her name was Jezebel and she was probably the finest Goshawk in the country in her day. I ended up by training a Sparrowhawk, a tiny creature with all the dash and courage in the world.

Since boyhood my recollections have nearly always had raptorial birds as their central figures. I left England to start a career in Africa, and from then onwards followed a nomadic course including a year in the Arctic with the Eskimos and several years during the Second World War in the Mediterranean. I remember in Africa going through a burnt forest and seeing a rock, and on the top of the rock there appeared to be an old man sitting with his back to me. I crept forward with great curiosity and, as if by magic, the figure spread two enormous wings and floated away above the trees. It was a Martial Eagle.

I saw my first Bald Eagle on a wonderful summer's day in British Columbia, in a canyon through which the river threaded its way, its pools shining green as emeralds in the bright sunlight. I have only once seen a Gyr Falcon and that was on Baffin Island in the Arctic. The frozen stillness of the winter had given way to sunshine, the coming of vivid rock plants, and above all the noise of literally thousands of birds.

In 1945 I had to go on military duty to Texel in the Friesian Islands where the German Army had mined almost all the flat fields behind the sand-dunes. The place was full of rare birds. I have never seen so many Montagu's Harriers in one place. I went back there forty years later. The mines had all gone. So had the Montagu's Harriers.

In the Northern Hemisphere birds of prey have suffered greatly at the hands of man. During the last century their numbers were greatly reduced, in many cases by hunting; and then, in this century, pollution came to take its toll. Ospreys and Peregrines were badly affected and great inroads were made into Bald Eagle populations. In the 1960s it was discovered that widespread use of the pesticide DDT, which was supposed to be a tremendous blessing, had proved to be the most tremendous curse. In California, Bald Eagles were virtually wiped out by the 1970s. Today, re-introduction is being tried with considerable success.

The 1960s and 1970s were bad times for Peregrines. Their eggshells became too thin to withstand the pressures put upon them during incubation. Although Peregrine numbers in Britain fell steeply, the birds were not as badly hit as in some other European countries where the species almost disappeared. In the United States scores of Peregrines have now been reared in captivity, and use of the traditional falconry technique of "hacking" (feeding young birds until they are able to kill prey for themselves) has enabled many to be returned successfully to the wild.

In Scotland, where the Osprey was extinct as a breeding bird for forty years, a healthy population now exists largely as a result of the work of dedicated volunteer nest watchers. Steps are now being taken to protect the few breeding pairs of White-tailed Sea Eagles successfully reintroduced to Scotland in recent years by the Nature Conservancy Council.

Among the roughly 290 bird of prey species there is every possible variety, as reflected in their names. Africa has its Chanting Goshawks and the Grasshopper Buzzard. There is a bird called a Changeable Hawk-eagle which is found from India to Indo-China, and the Laughing Falcon of the South American rainforests. Some of these species have names that seem to have come straight from fairyland; which is fitting since there is a lot of magic in birds of prey. I have mentioned only a few of them, but I am all too aware that many other species, like the Philippine Eagle, are very much under threat. It is our duty to manage their habitats wisely to ensure that their magic continues to enrich our lives.

Tweedsmuir

The Rt.Hon. The Lord Tweedsmuir, C.B.E., C.D.

Introduction

American Kestrel

From the earliest times, birds of prey have occupied a special place in man's feelings towards the natural world. At times his attitudes have appeared favourable, and the aerial hunters have been seen as symbolizing freedom, power and nobility. Conversely, birds of prey have equally often been perceived as a threat, and have been persecuted mercilessly as a result. Neither attitude really does the birds justice, however, and only now are they coming to be valued for their own sake, as superbly adapted living creatures, often endowed with great beauty, and with fascinating ways of life. If this book helps to foster a true appreciation of them, coupled with a concern for their future, then it will have achieved its object.

Classifying the Birds of Prey

Hopefully it should be possible to open this book anywhere and find interesting reading coupled with fine illustrations, but in order to understand its scope and arrangement more fully it is helpful to have a working knowledge of how birds and other living things are classified and named. First of all, terms such as "bird of prey" and "raptor" need to be

Grey-headed Fishing Eagle

explained. In the broadest sense, any bird that takes animal food, be it the tiniest insect, could be described as a bird of prey, but in practice the term is usually reserved for those that capture prey that is large in proportion to their own size. Usually this will be vertebrate prey – chiefly reptiles, mammals and other birds, but sometimes also fish and amphibians. Even here a difficulty arises because some other groups of birds, such as herons, gulls and crows, take similar animals. All these, however, capture and kill their prey with the bill. True birds of prey have the feet and claws developed into formidable talons to perform these tasks; in most species the intimidating hooked bill is for tearing up food rather than for killing it in the first place.

Following these criteria then, the term "birds of prey" is normally understood to include the hawks, eagles, vultures, falcons and allies, and the owls. The first set are grouped together in a single Order called the Falconiformes; these are the day-active birds of prey, also called "raptors", with which this book is concerned. The owls, the nocturnal birds of prey, are classified in a separate Order, Strigiformes. This implies that the two are not considered closely related, and that their similar features have evolved independently. Such judgements about relationships are based on very detailed studies of anatomy, behaviour and biochemistry which try to chart the course taken by evolution. The various levels of grouping therefore aim to reflect ancestry rather than merely overall similarity of features.

Below the level of Order, the next main unit of classification is the Family. Within the Order Falconiformes, five families are recognized – the Cathartidae, Pandionidae, Accipitridae, Sagittariidae and Falconidae. Two of these – the Pandionidae and Sagittariidae – contain just one species each. Surprising as this might seem at first, it is necessary in order to recognize the many unique and fundamental features which set them apart from the larger families. Continuing down the scale of classification, the next main level of grouping is the Genus, and this leads us into a consideration of nomenclature, as the name of the genus is also the first part of the scientific name of each species. A genus may include only one species if it has no close relatives, or it may include a large number of species. The largest genus in this book, for example, is *Accipiter*, which contains 47 species, all sharing a very similar body plan and way of life. Each species is given a scientific name consisting of the genus name first, followed by the species name; the whole usually being printed in italics. Thus, the Sparrowhawk of Eurasia is called *Accipiter nisus*, while a similar species in North America, the Sharp-shinned Hawk, bears the name *Accipiter striatus*. When several species of a genus are listed following one another, the full genus name is usually given only for the first, and subsequently contracted to the initial letter, thus: *A. striatus*.

Scientific names may appear intimidating, but they are necessary because they provide stability, and enable ornithologists to know with certainty which bird they are talking about. By contrast, vernacular or common names are frequently varied or changed by different authors, despite the existence of various semi-official regional lists. Stability is especially important for species names because the species is the basic unit of classification. The word is frequently misused in everyday speech, and is sometimes employed interchangeably with such words as "breed" and "variety", each of which has its own distinct and precise meaning. Strictly speaking, a species is a population whose members are capable of interbreeding, and which is reproductively isolated from other populations. Very occasionally species may interbreed (especially in captivity), but the resulting hybrids, even if fertile, have little chance of perpetuating themselves under natural conditions.

Species may, however, show considerable geographic variation, and localized forms called subspecies or races are sometimes given names made up by adding a third word to the species name. They have not been given undue prominence in this book, but they are an important feature of many widely distributed birds of prey, and a potential source of confusion in identification. Closely related forms scattered over many small islands in an archipelago create the greatest difficulty in the classification of birds of prey as it is difficult – sometimes impossible – to test the species criteria in practice, and opinions may vary as to whether some birds should be regarded as races or full species.

The Species Checklist

Species are dealt with generally in the same order as that followed in the important monograph on brids of prey by the American authors Brown and Amadon (see Bibliography). However, to accommodate varying sizes of plate, and to permit a smooth flow of text, this order has been varied in places. The conventional order is shown in the species checklist at the end of the book. This list also gives various measurements, which are intended to give some idea of the general size of the species, and the range of size variation if this is considerable. Two types of measurement are given. Length is that of the bird on its back, from bill tip to tail tip, a condition normally only attainable with a dead specimen. As it is prone to subjective error in measuring it is not available for all species, but it does give some indication of general size. The other measure, wing length, is widely used in ornithology due to its greater precision. It refers to the distance from the wrist joint of the wing to the tip of the longest flight feather. Wing length should not be confused with wing-span, which is the distance between the two wing tips when the wings are fully stretched out. This is the measurement most people are interested in, but unfortunately it is even more prone to error than body length, and is consequently available only for a small proportion of species. Accordingly it has been ommitted here, but as a rough guide, the span of many large soaring birds of prey is about three times the wing length.

Merlin

Individuals vary in size in all species, but where this variation is not large, a single median value is given. For many species, however, it is necessary to give a size range. This may be due to geographical variation, but more usually it is due to size difference between the sexes. Interestingly,

Japanese Sparrowhawk

in most birds of prey it is the female that is the larger, and the difference is most marked in many bird-eating species. It is least marked in scavenging species, and in some vultures particularly, the males are somewhat larger, as in the majority of birds. It has been suggested that the usual greater size of females is necessary to enable them to establish the dominance that causes the males to bring food throughout incubation and much of the fledging period. The size difference may also have some safety value during courtship, so strong are the aggressive urges of the male.

The Flight Characteristics of Raptors

Important general features common to a group of birds (whether a family, a genus or a number of similar species within a genus) are discussed as far as possible in this book under the first member of the group to be introduced. Hence it is not necessary to dwell at length on group characteristics in this introduction. However, a few aspects deserve amplification.

Much interest is shown in the powrs of flight displayed by birds of prey, although there is often some misunderstanding on this topic. High speed, as demonstrated by falcons such as the Peregrine, for example, is not by any means a universal characteristic of raptors; indeed some are actually specialized for flying extremely slowly. Taking the group as a whole, the range of wing shapes and modes of flight is very wide indeed. In comparing them, key factors to be considered are wing loading, aspect ratio and the shape of the primaries or main flight feathers.

Wing loading is a simple enough concept; it is simply the relationship between body weight and wing area. Birds that have a large wing area relative to their weight are said to have low wing loading, and vice versa. Among birds of prey, harriers have the lowest wing loading at some 0.41 to 0.61 pounds per square foot (2.0 to 3.0 kilogrammes per square

Lammergeier

metre). Unspecialized birds of prey such as buzzards stand at around 0.82 to 0.90 pounds per square foot (4.0 to 4.5 kg/sq m); sparrowhawks and goshawks at about 1.1 pounds per square foot (5.5 kg/sq m), and large falcons at about 1.43 pounds per square foot (7.0 kg/sq m). In general, higher wing loadings are associated with more rapid flight, and this is especially true for birds such as falcons, which attain maximum speed in a dive. Highest loadings of all, however, are found in large eagles and vultures. Although their huge wings have a very large area, their bodies are proportionately heavier still, and wing loading can be as high as 2.46 pounds per square foot (12 kg/sq m). The very low wing loading of harriers is related to their method of hunting, which involves quartering a stretch of ground very slowly and systematically. As they do this they are not only looking for prey but also listening for it, as hearing is especially highly developed in this group.

Aspect ratio is the ratio of wing length to wing breadth: short, broad wings have low aspect ratios; long narrow ones have high aspect ratios. High aspect ratios are most suited to soaring and gliding, but in their most extreme form, as in albatrosses, they make take-off slow and difficult and cause proportionately more turbulence, so that a high air-speed is required. Soaring raptors such as vultures and some eagles have wings a good deal broader than this to permit slower flight with greater manoeuvrability, but a higher aspect

Letter-winged Kite

ratio is seen in the Bateleur, which covers large areas in high-speed gliding flight. Very low aspect ratios are typical of forest species, which may have to weave in and out of trees at high speed as they pursue their prey.

The shape and relative length of the primary flight feathers affects the whole appearance and functioning of the wing tip. Swift species such as the falcons have pointed wing tips, but in many species the shape is more rounded, and the feathers themselves may have a "cut-away" outline so that their tips appear widely separated, like splayed fingers. Particularly strongly marked in large soaring species, this feature helps smooth the air flow over the wing, a vital factor when air-speed is slow. The "alula", a bunch of feathers attached to the vestigial thumb of the wing skeleton, has a similar effect, and functions rather like the flaps that are deployed as an aircraft comes in to land.

Soaring species, when not migrating, are generally using their high vantage-point to look for ground-living prey or carrion. The same is generally true for those species that "still hunt", that is, watch for prey from a perch. Raptors that take their prey in flight have attracted particular interest, however, and careful studies of falconers' birds using high-speed cinematography have clarified the technique they employ. It is the large falcons and the accipiters (sparrowhawks and goshawks) that specialize most in this type of hunting, falcons typically attacking in a dive or "stoop", while accipiters generally attack in level flight. Both, especially the falcons, are travelling very fast when they overtake their prey, but this speed is primarily concerned with bringing them into a killing position. What then happens is that the pelvis and legs are swung at the prey, adding greatly to the force of the blow. Peregrines in fact level out and slow down somewhat as they strike, and in any case deliver only a glancing blow with the open feet.

Black-legged Falconet

This is still enough to cause instant death in most cases: were the strike any harder, the falcon would endanger its own limbs, to no good purpose. I have so far avoided being struck by a raptor, but have twice been the target for a Tawny Owl, which uses a similar technique. Such a blow feels like a direct hit from a brick, and one is astonished that it can have come from a bird weighing little more than a pound, or about half a kilogramme.

Threats to the Birds of Prey

Concern over environmental issues is now a prominent feature of current affairs, and birds of prey illustrate (very clearly) some of the key problems in conservation. The relationship between the numbers of prey and the number of predators is one of the most crucial of these. One of the chief reasons why birds of prey have so often been persecuted is their supposed depletion of stocks of game. This ignores the fact that under natural conditions it is the numbers of prey that control the numbers of predators, and not the other way about. Thus, if two grouse moors of equal size are hunted respectively by one pair of eagles and by two pairs, it can be confidently predicted that the moor with the extra eagles also has substantially *more* grouse, not less. The only exceptions to this occur when numbers of predators are maintained at an artificially high level by some human activity such as the disposal of offal or garbage, which provides a large supplementary food source. This type of problem occurs more commonly with such predators as gulls than with raptors.

Birds of prey are, indeed, much less numerous than most of the smaller species they feed on, but because they are relatively large and conspicuous this fact is often overlooked. It does, however make them much more vulnerable to persecution or environmental hazards. Where pollutants are concerned, an additional problem is that although the chemicals are initially widely dispersed, they accumulate in even greater concentrations as they move upwards through a food pyramid, and birds of prey which generally stand at the top of such pyramids may receive them in dangerous concentrations. For this reason, birds of prey can serve as valuable indicators of the health of our environment, and studies of their breeding success and ecology play a prominent role in monitoring the impact of modern technology on the world we live in.

Philippine Eagle

Family CATHARTIDAE
New World Vultures

Seven species in five genera

ANDEAN CONDOR

Fossil relatives of the Andean Condor (*Vultur gryphus*) would have dwarfed it in size, but today it is the largest of all birds of prey and arguably the largest flying bird. Weighing up to 26 pounds (12kg) and with a wing-span that may exceed 10 feet (3m) its majestic appearance outweighs its unpleasant feeding habits in popular appeal; indeed it figures in the national crests of four South American countries. Its role in mythology and folklore, however, occasionally operates to the bird's disadvantage, as in certain Andean villages which hold festivals in which a Condor's feet are sewn to the back of a bull, which is then released to rush about in pain until exhausted. Supposedly the Condor symbolizes the native Indian peoples, and the bull the Spanish *conquistadores.* If the Condor survives its enforced struggle it is released.

Such rituals, cruel though they may be, can have little effect on the Andean Condor's numbers, but in areas where stock-rearing encroaches into the bird's mountainous habitat, persecution may become more serious. Condors are frequently accused of attacks on young calves or other domestic animals, and they have been shot in large numbers. Additionally, dead Condors have some commercial value, especially for their huge primary wing quills which are made into cigarette-holders and are even employed to pluck the strings of harpsichords! Supposed eye-witness accounts of attacks on young animals can rarely be verified, but it seems that the bird may occasionally kill live prey. However, there is no doubt that the great bulk of the Condor's food consists of carrion. Essentially a bird of the Andes mountains, its original food no doubt included substantial numbers of native mammals such as llamas and guanacos, with seabirds and fur seals on the coast. As well as dead seabirds and nestlings, it will also take large numbers of eggs. With the introduction of horses, cattle and other Old World stock, its potential food supply was increased, but so was the intensity of persecution. However, the remoteness and inaccessibility of much of its habitat should ensure its continued survival in many areas.

The Condor locates its food in soaring flight, either by spotting it directly or by seeing other Condors or smaller carrion-eating birds descending to a corpse. It may wait patiently for a sickly animal to die, or for a large corpse to decompose to the point at which it can be opened up. Food is not easily found in this way, and this is no doubt why, when they do find food, the great birds often gorge so heavily that they are unable to take off from level ground.

Condors nest on cliffs, in hollows or on exposed ledges. In some areas, large numbers breed close together, while in others the birds are more solitary. A single white egg is laid, and is incubated by both male and female for about eight weeks. The young Condor is at first covered with pale grey down, later succeeded by darker down, and feathers only start to make their appearance at ten weeks. To judge from captive birds, the young one probably remains on its cliff ledge for some six months, and is attended by its parents well into its second year: consequently, Condors breed at most every alternate year. The comb-like structure on the head of the male is present at hatching, and males grow to a considerably larger size than females. In raptors that hunt live prey, the female is normally larger, but in less aggressive species such as the vultures, the sexes are the same size or, as in this case, the male is larger than the female.

NEW WORLD VULTURES

Although they resemble the vultures of the Old World in their scavenging habits and general appearance, these American birds are actually very different in anatomy, and are not at all related. Indeed, many ornithologists believe that the New World Vultures are unrelated to *any* other birds of prey, and that they have evolved similar attributes quite independently.

An important family characteristic is the keen sense of smell, which reaches its highest development in the Turkey Vulture (*Cathartes aura*). This is particularly valuable when seeking food above the canopy of tropical rainforest, where there is not the slightest chance of seeing a dead animal on the forest floor. Turkey Vultures are usually first on the scene at such sources of food, followed by Black Vultures or King Vultures that have been watching their movements. By contrast, Old World Vultures have only a feeble sense of smell, and can find food only in open country.

The Turkey Vulture is the most widely distributed member of its family, ranging from southern Canada right down to Tierra del Fuego, and occurring in all types of habitat. Part of the North American population, particularly in the arid west, is highly migratory and moves south through Central America each year to winter in South America. Its wide choice of habitat is matched by an equally catholic choice of food. Any type of carrion, large or small, fresh or putrid is accepted, and it will also feed on rotten fruit and vegetables where these are available. Although sometimes accused of attacking lambs or other livestock, it rarely attacks live prey, and then usually only small nestlings. Tidal beaches also provide food, and in recent times the lethal effects of motor traffic have added a new source of carrion in the form of road casualties.

Scarcely an attractive bird when at rest, the Turkey Vulture is the epitome of grace on the wing. Its buoyant, gliding flight makes full use of thermals and air currents to

Andean Condor
Symbolic of the wild, mountainous regions of South America, the Andean Condor, despite featuring in legend and folklore, is much persecuted – not only for its reputed attacks on domestic livestock, but also for its quills, which are much prized by musical instrument makers.
(*Map 1*)

New World Vultures:1
These medium-sized vultures, found only on the American continent, all have dark plumage and typical vulturine flight-habits. They are therefore most easily distinguished by the colour of the bare skin on the head.

In the Turkey Vulture (1) it is reddish, in the Yellow-headed Vulture (2) it is yellow to orange, occasionally mixed with red or blue, whilst in the Greater Yellow-headed Vulture (3) it is deep yellow, combined with a deep-blue crown.
(Maps 2–4)

keep flapping flight to a minimum – a valuable economy when the bird is migrating, as probably little or no food is consumed on the journey. As all the Turkey Vulture's migrations are made over land, the birds are most concentrated where the American continents are at their narrowest, in the Isthmus of Panama. Here, one observer estimated about 15,000 passing in an hour at the beginning of March.

Like other members of the family, Turkey Vultures make no nest but lay their two eggs on or near the ground in some dark hollow such as a cave or rotten tree stump. Male and female take equal shares in incubation, which lasts about forty days. The young remain ten to twelve weeks in the nest.

Two close relatives with more restricted distributions occur in tropical America. These are the Yellow-headed Vulture (*Cathartes burrovianus*) which occurs in Mexico, Panama and lowland areas of South America, and the Greater Yellow-headed Vulture (*Cathartes melambrotus*) which is found in several scattered regions of South America. As they share their range with the Turkey Vulture there are, presumably, differences in their habits that minimize competition, but it is not clear exactly what these are. In Panama, at least, the Yellow-headed Vulture appears to be more fond of marshy habitats than the Turkey Vulture, and it seems that fish may be more important in its diet. There is evidence that some of these may be taken alive, presumably when they become stranded in shallow water. The Greater Yellow-headed Vulture has only been known since 1964, and there is little information about its habits.

Teeming dark shapes around garbage-strewn docks or shanty towns in South American cities are almost certain to be Black Vultures (*Coragyps atratus*). The sheer numbers and boldness of these birds only serve to reinforce the sinister aura created by their appearance. Their readiness to exploit the squalid by-products of man's activities has been a major ingredient in their success, and they are considerably more numerous overall than the Turkey Vultures which sometimes consort with them.

In open country Black Vultures may soar to seek food, and often follow Turkey Vultures down to items they have located with their keener sense of smell. However, in towns they need do little more than perch on rooftops, sometimes with wings spread, waiting for the next batch of refuse to be jettisoned. Markets, slaughterhouses and garbage dumps all provide ample food, while in harbours they may be joined by Brown Pelicans and Frigate Birds, all foraging on human waste in different ways. To a larger extent than the Turkey Vulture, this species is prepared to attack live prey. Usually this means nestling birds or small mammals, though a group has been seen to kill a skunk. They also gather in great numbers on beaches where hatchling turtles are struggling out of the sand and towards the sea.

The Black Vulture's breeding sites are equally varied, and include caves and hollows in cliffs, hollow trees, dense vegetation and even cavities in tall buildings. The two eggs take about five weeks to hatch, producing young that are aggressive to intruders from an early age. They are fed by regurgitation by both parents, as in other members of the family, and can fly from about ten weeks old.

Substantially larger than Black or Turkey vultures is the King Vulture (*Sarcorhamphus papa*), a striking-looking bird clad in pinkish-white plumage with contrasting black flight feathers, and with the head and neck ornamented with brightly coloured wattles and bare skin. It is much more exclusively a forest bird than other New World Vultures, although in places it also occurs in savanna grasslands and cattle country. It spends much time soaring above the forest, but is also partial to resting on sandbanks in rivers, sometimes in company with other vultures. Due to its larger size, Black and Turkey vultures give way to it at a carcass, although they tend to be first on the scene. Having a considerably more powerful bill than the other two, it seems better equipped to deal with the tough skin of larger animals, and would probably be well able to deal with live prey. However, there are no well-corroborated reports of it doing so. As with many rainforest birds, there is a scarcity of information about the King Vulture's breeding habits. It is said to nest in a hollow stump or rock crevice, and to lay a single egg, and in captivity it has an incubation period of eight weeks.

Nearly as large as its Andean counterpart, the California Condor (*Gymnogyps californianus*) is the only member of the family confined to the North American continent. Unfortunately, it is on the verge of extinction even there. Formerly widespread in the west, from Washington State south to northern Baja California, Texas and New Mexico, the California Condor has been ruthlessly persecuted until only a handful remain. Not only were large numbers shot, in the mistaken belief that the birds killed young livestock, but many more were poisoned by bait left out for wolves and coyotes. A dwindling remnant population survived at the traditional California nesting cliffs until 1986, by which time there were only three birds left in the wild, with twenty-four others held in two zoos in California. Nesting only every second year, and requiring several years to reach sexual maturity, the wild birds' prospects were very bleak, and in 1987 they too were taken into captivity. Captive breeding now appears to be the only remaining hope for this magnificent bird's survival.

New World Vultures:2
Each of these three American vultures is uniquely distinctive. The Black Vulture (1) is dull-coloured and slender-billed, the King Vulture (2) is almost grotesque with its large head-wattle and wrinkled facial skin, whilst the huge, orange-faced California Condor (3) now survives only in captivity.
(Maps 5–7)

Family PANDIONIDAE
Osprey

One species

LOCAL THREATS TO A GLOBAL SPECIES

Acclaimed as a conservation success story, the return of the Osprey (*Pandion haliaetus*) as a breeding bird in the British Isles has an ironic aspect, for this is actually one of the most widespread of all birds of prey worldwide. Yet unlike the Peregrine, which is even more widely distributed, it shows relatively little geographic variation in plumage or size.

Specialized for catching fish, the undersides of the Osprey's toes are covered with sharp spicules to aid in gripping slippery prey. In its internal anatomy, however, the bird shows numerous differences from other raptors, quite unconnected with its feeding habits. These indicate that it is only distantly related to most of them, and for this reason it is placed in a separate family of its own.

Despite its enormous range, the problems that have faced the Osprey over the past century cannot be taken lightly. Persecution was the first of these. Never popular with the water bailiffs and gamekeepers of nineteenth-century Britain, it was shot extensively, and as its numbers dwindled its eggs acquired rarity value to collectors. Its decline accelerated, and the last British pair was seen at Loch an Eilean in the Spey Valley in Scotland in 1902. Elsewhere in Europe the story was similar; the Mediterranean population dwindled to a few pairs, and the only reasonably healthy population left was that in Scandinavia. Fortunately, some of the Scandinavian birds continued to pass through Britain on migration to and from the Mediterranean and West Africa, and it was undoubtedly from this stock that a British breeding population was eventually re-established. This momentous event took place in 1954, and after a shaky start, troubled again by egg collectors, the birds commenced a steady expansion which is still continuing. One brilliant innovation in the early years was the decision by the Royal Society for the Protection of Birds (RSPB) to throw open to the public one of the nest sites, at Loch Garten. The effect of this was to create an army of extra wardens, making life far more difficult for egg collectors and other persecutors. A back-up public relations campaign, aimed especially at the proprietors of fisheries, helped ensure general goodwill towards the bird.

Problems still lay in store, however, but it was in North America that they first became a cause for serious concern. Like many other raptors, the Osprey was in danger of accumulating dangerous pesticides in its body, acquired by progressive concentration through the food chain. Its peril was particularly acute, however, due to the huge quantities of these chemicals draining from the land into lakes and waterways. From the early 1960s a decline associated with breeding failures was seen throughout the northeastern USA. Eventual curbs on agricultural insecticides have improved the situation, but efforts to encourage the birds continue in areas from which they have disappeared.

Generally tolerant of man, Ospreys will nest in surprisingly urbanized areas as long as they are in reach of good fishing. In some such places, nesting platforms on poles have been erected and successfully used; one technique for installing these on salt-marshes involves dropping pole and platform from a helicopter and allowing gravity to do the work.

Ospreys catch fish by seizing them in their talons after a spectacular crash dive in which they may become almost completely immersed. Fish of up to 4.5 pounds (2kg) may be carried, which is appreciably more than some adult birds weigh. Occasionally Ospreys drown through locking their talons in fish too big to lift. One fish, however, has evolved a means of escape; the Blowfish (*Spheroides maculatus*) can inflate itself like a football until the bird's talons lose their grip! Occasionally other prey such as snakes, frogs and small birds are also taken.

Owing to the publicity that has surrounded the Osprey, its nest may be one of the most familiar of all raptors' nests; a large structure of sticks, it is added to year after year, eventually becoming immense in some sites. Artificial platforms apart, trees are the most usual choice of nest site, but rocks and buildings may also be used. Three eggs are usually laid, and these are incubated for about five weeks, mainly by the female. The young fledge in about eight weeks, and those from northerly breeding areas will then migrate southwards. Some return next year to the vicinity of their birthplace, but they will not breed until they are three years old.

Osprey
A handsome and impressive fisher, successful in as many as 90 per cent of its sorties, the Osprey is unfortunately none too popular among trout and salmon breeders, whose fish-farms provide it with a relatively regular and easy food supply.
(*Map 8*)

Family Accipitridae

Kites, Vultures, Eagles and Hawks

Two hundred and seventeen species in sixty-four genera

Brahminy Kite

To ornithologists this bird is known as *Haliastur indus*, but to the Iban or Sea-Dayak people of Borneo it is Singalang Burong, earthly messenger of the god of the same name who holds a central place in their elaborate system of augury. A high god himself, Singalang Burong prefers to communicate with men via seven lesser gods, each of which has a particular bird as his messenger. These birds are regarded by the Iban as the principal way in which the gods communicate with men, and their calls, flight directions and behaviour are considered of great importance in deciding anything from making war to planting a rice crop. By contrast, the Kenyah people of the same island regard the Brahminy Kite itself as the main bird of augury, representing the god Bali Penyalong. Yet another Bornean group, the Dusun, consider it vital that no Brahminy Kite should land on a house while it is being built. This event, unlikely though it is, would be considered to doom the house to eventual destruction by fire.

Augury and ornithology seem worlds apart, but the distinction accorded to this species by Bornean peoples may not be too inappropriate. It is a handsome and widespread species, and a fitting one to introduce the diverse assemblage of kites, a group of birds considered to be close to the stem group from which more specialized predators such as hawks and eagles have evolved. Kites are for the most part scavengers, taking either carrion or relatively small prey such as rodents, reptiles, crabs and large insects. Their feet and talons are relatively small, and the sexes differ only slightly in size, a feature common to most of the less aggressive raptors. The Brahminy Kite exemplifies these attributes very well. It is particularly associated with wet places, especially coastal areas and rice paddies. In wilder areas it tends to be shy, which is why Dusun housebuilders have little to fear. However, it has learned to be tolerant of man in the vicinity of seaports, where floating offal and garbage provide a rich source of food. It is also well capable of catching live fish, rather in the manner of a sea eagle. Here it may well perch on half-constructed buildings, though the incidence of resulting fires has not been studied!

Brahminy Kites breed from India right through Southeast Asia and its islands to Northern Australia, New Guinea and the Solomon Islands. The nest is nearly always in a tree, anything from 26 to 165 feet (8 to 50 metres) above the ground, and generally near a river or lake. Basically made of sticks, and lined with green sprays like many raptor nests, it can also include a variety of refuse such as seaweed, paper and rags. Some nests have a lining of mud. In northern parts of the bird's range breeding commences in the early part of the year, but near the Equator or south of it may be as late as August. Two eggs are usually laid, sometimes up to four though occasionally only one. Incubation is largely by the female, fed by the male who may also occasionally assist her. The incubation period is thought to be a little less than four weeks. The roles of the sexes in caring for the young are typical of many birds of prey. At first, food is brought mainly by the male, while the female feeds it to the young and broods them. Later, as the young become able to tear up their own food and their appetites increase, both parents are obliged to forage to keep them supplied. The fledging period is some seven or eight weeks.

Newly fledged young lack the handsome rufous-and-white plumage of their parents, and their drab spotted colouring makes them more difficult than the adults to distinguish from other kites. As this is generally a sedentary species, most birds probably do not disperse far from their birthplace, but in Australia there seems to be some southward movement during the dry season.

Brahminy Kite
Monsoon rains bring rich feeding opportunities to this scavenger of coasts and waterways. As the floodwaters rise, land crabs leave their burrows and are picked off as they crowd together on patches of high ground. Winged termites are another flood-season food source – captured in flight as they are forced to take to the air.
(*Map 10*)

Honey Buzzard
Although not a true buzzard, the Honey Buzzard does, nevertheless, have a liking for honey, as well as for the occupants of bees' and wasps' nests. Remarkably, the bird appears to be impervious to the stings of these insects.
(*Map 9*)

THE HONEY BUZZARDS

Short stiff feathers covering the face are the only special feature protecting the Honey Buzzard (*Pernis apivorus*) from enraged bees or wasps as it digs out a nest to get at the honey and grubs inside. Its name is apt as far as the honey goes, but it is not closely related to true buzzards, despite the fact that it superficially resembles them. It is a highly successful species, with a range extending right across Eurasia from Spain to Japan, though it is only a scarce summer visitor to Britain. All the northern populations are strongly migratory, and Honey Buzzards can be seen in spectacular numbers in southern Sweden, Gibraltar and the Bosporus at the southern outlet of the Black Sea, where they are usually seen with other birds of prey and other large birds such as storks. The reason is that these are all soaring birds, which depend on thermal air-currents to make their journeys. As thermals form only over land, the birds keep sea crossings as short as possible by making them at very narrow straits such as those just mentioned.

Various foraging methods are used by the Honey Buzzard in its search for the nests of social insects. It may soar or hover, but it also perches to scan an area, and will frequently walk about on the ground. Having located a nest, it digs it out with the feet, slightly assisted by the bill, pulling out chunks of comb and skilfully seizing the adult insects in order to bite off their stings. Where wasps' nests are suspended beneath the eaves of a house, the bird will snatch them off in flight. It will also take small mammals and reptiles, and large insects such as grasshoppers, and such prey are probably more important in the winter quarters.

Broadleaved woodland, especially beech, is favoured as a breeding habitat, and the nest is placed fairly high up in a tree fork, often with an old nest of another bird as a foundation. It is built of sticks, with a lining of fresh green leaves. One to three eggs are laid, and they are incubated by

Long-tailed, Black, and Barred Honey Buzzards
Although sometimes thought to be a single species, the Long-tailed Honey Buzzard (1) of New Guinea and the Black Honey Buzzard (2) of New Britain are very different, in both plumage and size. The strongly-marked Barred Honey Buzzard (3) is found in the Philippines, and on Celebes, where it appears to be a mimic of the Celebes Hawk-eagle.
(Maps 11–13)

both sexes, hatching after about five weeks. The young are fed mainly on the nest, on the combs of bees and wasps, carried in the parents' crops and regurgitated. Fed by the parents at first, the young first learn to pick the larvae out of the combs, and later to tear up other prey. The nest soon becomes littered with empty combs, and the young make their first flights at about six weeks old, returning to the nest for a further two weeks or so to be fed.

Three relatives of the Honey Buzzard occur on islands in the Indo-Pacific area. The Barred Honey Buzzard (*Pernis celebensis*) is found on the island of Sulawesi (formerly Celebes) in Indonesia, and in the Philippines. Little is known about its habits, but honeycombs have been found in the stomachs of birds collected as specimens, so its way of life is probably similar to that of its more widespread relative. This species has a short crest, and with the strongly barred underparts this gives it an extraordinarily close resemblance to the Celebes Hawk-eagle (*Spizaetus lanceolatus*). With both species occurring on the same island, it is difficult to believe that the resemblance is due to chance, but so poorly are both species known that the reasons for it are at present a mystery. Several similar examples are found amongst other birds of prey, and are mentioned elsewhere in this book.

Two other relatives are placed in a separate genus, *Henicopernis*, recognizing the fact that they are less specialized birds, lacking the protective facial feathering of *Pernis*. These are the Long-tailed Honey Buzzard (*Henicopernis longicauda*) and the Black Honey Buzzard (*Henicopernis infuscata*); the former from New Guinea and its islands, and the latter from New Britain. The Long-tailed Honey Buzzard is known to take wasps' nests as well as a variety of other prey, despite its more vulnerable face, and it is assumed that the Black Honey Buzzard is similar in habits. Very little else is known about either.

BAZAS AND CUCKOO FALCONS

Five handsome and interesting birds of prey comprise the genus *Aviceda*, and these specialized small kites inhabit forest, forest edges and scrub in Africa, Asia and parts of Australia. Their appearance is distinctive, with a crest of varying length on the back of the head, boldly barred underparts, and a double-notched upper mandible. The wings are surprisingly long for a forest raptor, but their hunting habits hardly necessitate weaving in and out of trees at high speed like some hawks. The name Cuckoo Falcon is applied to the African and Madagascan species, but seems rather unfortunate as they are neither cuckoos nor falcons, nor even very much like either apart from the barring of the underparts.

One of the most widespread species is the Crested or Pacific Baza (*Aviceda subcristata*) which occurs from the Moluccas (Indonesia) east through numerous island chains to New Guinea, northeast Australia and the Solomon Islands. Island populations differ in size and in darkness of colouring, and sixteen races are recognized. By virtue of its occurrence in Australia, the Crested Baza is one of the best-known and most thoroughly studied species, and its foraging habits are probably typical of the genus. Subsisting mainly on insects and small vertebrates such as frogs, one of its techniques is to watch from a perch, moving on after a time if nothing is seen. When prey is spotted, the bird dives into the foliage below with talons extended to make its capture. It is recorded as hanging head-downwards at times, taking insects from the foliage. Some prey are recorded as being taken from the ground. At nests observed by bird photographer David Hollands in Queensland, the chief prey appeared to be the large stick insects that abound there.

The nests themselves are surprisingly flimsy structures for a bird of this size, and appear to be held together by the weight of their occupants, usually falling to pieces within a short time of being vacated. Made of sticks and green leaves, they are usually sited high in a forest tree. Nest-building is carried out by both sexes, and is preceded by a period of spectacular nuptial displays in which the birds soar, dive, tumble and roll to the accompaniment of much loud calling. Both sexes also appear to participate in incubation and care of the young, though the duration of each is uncertain. Outside the breeding season, Crested Bazas are rather sociable, and parties of up to thirty now regularly visit suburban areas on the outskirts of Brisbane.

Such venturesome behaviour is not a feature of the other species of *Aviceda*. More strictly confined to dense forest, or other inaccessible areas, their habits are generally much less well known.

The African Cuckoo Falcon (*Aviceda cuculoides*) forages in forest or second-growth woodland mixed with cultivation. It is constantly on the move, and takes an appreciable amount of prey from forest undergrowth or from grass. As well as insects and lizards, small birds are occasionally taken. The Madagascan species (*Aviceda madagascariensis*) shows a particular predilection for the chameleons that are so plentiful on that island.

Jerdons's Baza (*Aviceda jerdoni*) is another widely-distributed species, found from Sikkim through Southeast Asia and in Sri Lanka (Ceylon), Borneo and Sulawesi (Celebes). It also shows geographical variation, with five recognized races. It inhabits hill forest up to 2600 feet (800m) and also frequents tea plantations. Generally similar to other bazas in its habits, it is noted as being particularly active around evening and dusk. Possibly this is a more general feature of the genus than has been recognized, for the eyes are particularly well developed and prominent in all bazas. Another surprising note concerning Jerdon's Baza is that the nest is said usually to be sited low down.

Probably the most striking member of the group is the Black Baza (*Aviceda leuphotes*). As its name indicates, it is predominantly black, though barred below, and it has the longest crest of any bird in the genus. Breeding mainly in the foothills of the Himalayas, it migrates south in winter into India and Southeast Asia. It is also noted as being crepuscular, that is, active at dusk, and has curious roosting habits, assembling for the night in parties of up to twenty-five birds which huddle in a compact group in the middle of a tree.

Bazas and Cuckoo Falcons

These small to medium-sized kites, with nape-feathers typically elongated into a more-or-less distinct crest, are all boldly marked, and the African (1) and Madagascar (2) Cuckoo Falcons form a closely knit group with Jerdon's Baza (3) and the Crested Baza (4). The fifth species, the Black Baza (5), is very distinctive, with striking plumage and a prominent crest.
(Maps 14–18)

Red Kite
Once plentiful in many parts of its range, this beautiful bird is now sadly a dwindling species. It can easily be identified in flight by its long, deeply-forked tail, and by its long wings, which are angled back from the carpal joint.
(Map 19)

Red Kite and Black Kite

Similar though their habits are in many respects, these two species have fared very differently at the hands of man. The Red Kite (*Milvus milvus*) has dwindled alarmingly as a result of persecution, while the Black Kite (*Milvus migrans*) has learned to exploit man to its own advantage, and has fared much better as a result. Both are excellent fliers, seeking most of their food in flight whether it be live prey or carrion, and both are agile enough to seize small birds or insects in flight. Visitors to the Hawk Conservancy near Andover in southern England will have seen this dexterity impressively demonstrated when four or five birds are released together to take scraps of food shot into the air from catapults! The feet are relatively small and weak, but live prey are killed efficiently enough with the bill. The crucial difference as it affects the birds' survival is the way in which they exploit these gifts.

The Black Kite is a bold and daring species which has discovered that human cities, especially in warmer countries, can provide a rich source of food. These audacious birds are capable not merely of taking refuse, but of snatching food from market stalls or even from people's hands. Much derided and insulted as a result of their habits, they survive nonetheless. Only from the hygienic cities of Western Europe have they disappeared, but the species is still found there in gradually declining numbers, preferring open countryside in the vicinity of water. Elsewhere the Black Kite ranges over a huge area of Eurasia, Africa and Australasia.

Black Kite
One of the world's most successful birds of prey, the Black Kite is often surprisingly common over much of its extensive range. Closely associated with man in many areas, it is a bold and opportunistic feeder, almost to the point of foolhardiness, and is often found scavenging and stealing from street-stalls. (*Map 20*)

Red Kites apparently scavenged in English towns in the sixteenth century and earlier, and are still found in towns in one or two places such as the Cape Verde islands, but evidently the busier cities of today do not suit them. Consequently they are found mainly in open countryside with scattered patches of woodland. Here the familiar pattern of persecution for alleged interference with game preservation has taken a grievous toll. In Britain, the population has shrunk to a tiny remnant in mid-Wales. At one time it was as low as four pairs, but strict protection by the RSPB has built this up to over thirty. However, its status remains precarious, and there are continuing threats from egg collectors and concerns about the species' low breeding success. Confined mainly to Europe and a few parts of the Near East, the Red Kite has dwindled everywhere, even in its remaining strongholds of Iberia and Germany.

Welsh Red Kites are fairly sedentary, although some young birds move into England to pass their first winter before returning to the breeding area. Elsewhere, most northerly breeders are migratory, wintering mainly around the Mediterranean. A few ringed Continental birds have been recovered in Britain, giving hope that this relict population may occasionally receive infusions of fresh blood from outside. Black Kites are also migratory in the northern part of their much larger range, and share their habitat with resident birds in winter quarters. To Britain, however, they are only occasional accidental visitors.

Both species start the breeding season with similar courtship displays. Initial soaring and calling by the unmated male is followed by more spectacular aerobatics after pairing, in which the two birds circle together at a great height – criss-crossing each other's paths and concluding with a steep dive into the nesting wood. Talon-grappling and cartwheeling are part of the Black Kite's courtship display, though in the Red Kite such behaviour seems to occur between rival males. The Black Kite is at all times a more gregarious bird than the Red, and this is even shown during the breeding season, when nests may be grouped in loose colonies of up to thirty. By contrast, the Red Kite's nests are normally well dispersed, usually 2 to 3 miles (3 to 5 kilometres) apart in Wales. Both species prefer tree forks as a nest site, although cliff ledges are sometimes used. The nests are relatively small and compact for birds of prey of this size. That of the Black Kite is invariably decorated with sprays of green leaves and scraps of paper, plastic or other rubbish. Up to three eggs are laid by each species, and the incubation period seems to be 31 to 32 days in both cases. Black Kites evidently fledge about a week earlier on average than Red Kites, that is, at about six as opposed to seven weeks.

Black-breasted Buzzard Kite
Resembling the Bateleur of Africa in its high-speed gliding flight, the Black-breasted Buzzard Kite is often to be seen in pairs, wheeling high above open country in Australia.
(Map 21)

BLACK BREASTED BUZZARD KITE AND WHISTLING KITE

Australia is the home of these two very different kites. Often referred to simply as the Black-breasted Buzzard (*Hamirostra melanosternon*), the first is a rather scarce bird of northern and central Australia, most numerous in northern Queensland and Northern Territories. A powerful and striking-looking bird with long wings, short tail and a long bill, it looks almost eagle-like, and it has indeed been suggested that it is not a kite at all but a relative of the serpent eagles. In addition to its distinctive appearance it has a number of unique behavioural features ranging from mutual feeding to kidnapping!

Black-breasted Buzzard Kites have a characteristic flight action in which they sweep swiftly along, often gliding and rocking from side to side as they go. This type of flight somewhat resembles that of the African Bateleur and has been cited as further evidence of a relationship with the serpent eagles. Snakes and lizards do indeed form part of this bird's diet, and may have been more important to it before Australia was colonized by rabbits. A few birds are also taken, but all food is seized from the ground. This seems somewhat surprising in view of the bird's swift flight, as most other ground feeders either perch, hover, or fly very slowly when hunting. More surprising still, if true, are the unconfirmed Aborigine reports that it will drive emus off their nests, and then smash the eggs open with stones. Egg-breaking with stones is known in vultures, but not in combination with deliberate aggression. However, Buzzard Kites have certainly been seen eating broken eggs, so the Aborigines' accounts may well be correct.

However, it is various features of the species' breeding habits that have provided the greatest surprises. The nest is a large structure of sticks built in a tree fork, and two eggs are laid. In two nests that have been studied in the course of photography, the young hatched a good ten days apart, a quite exceptional gap for a small clutch. In both cases the young both fledged, and appeared to live peaceably together, contradicting earlier surmises that "Cain and Abel" battles occurred in this species, as they do in many

Whistling Kite
Although it is quite often wrongly called the Whistling Eagle, the long-winged, long-tailed Whistling Kite is in every respect a true kite. Despite being one of the most common birds of prey in Australia, with a preference for wet locations, mystery still surrounds much of its life history. *(Map 22)*

eagles. Another surprise in the course of these observations was that both parents sometimes turned up together at the nest and gave food to each other as well as to their young.

Greatest of all surprises, however, was the discovery in 1976 of a nest in which Black-breasted Buzzard Kites were rearing a brood of seven young Australian Kestrels! Apparently these had been taken from nearby Kestrel nests and brought back to the nest of the Buzzard Kites, whose own breeding attempt had failed for some reason. Kestrels sometimes fall prey to this species, and indeed some Kestrel remains were found at this nest. It is thought that perhaps the young Kestrels were brought back alive, initially as intended prey, but escaped this fate when they triggered the breeding urge of a frustrated female Buzzard Kite. Remarkably, the young Kestrels thrived, and when last seen, four had fledged and the others seemed set to do so too. Since then, an earlier and similar case has come to light, apparently involving the young of a Brown or Black Falcon.

Whistling Kites (*Haliastur sphenurus*) are close relatives of the Brahminy Kite (page 19), with which they overlap in northern Australia. The range of the Whistling Kite extends also into New Guinea and New Caledonia. Although sometimes called the Whistling Eagle, this species is very much a kite in its behaviour; much more so than the preceding species. It likes the vicinity of water, but is found in all types of open country where it feeds on small mammals, especially rabbits, reptiles, small birds and insects. It takes carrion freely, including fish, for which it is prepared to wade. It forages mainly in flight, although along some stretches of highway it is commonly seen perching on telegraph poles, probably on the lookout for road casualties. It is a gregarious species, and arrives in the breeding areas still in flocks, which then break up as nuptial behaviour proceeds. The nest is placed in a tree fork, and is often re-used for several years. Two or three eggs are laid, and the young are believed to fledge in about six weeks.

Black-shouldered Kite
When manoeuvring on the wing, the Black-shouldered Kite often turns into the wind with an unusual rapid wing-vibration, of up to 30 seconds' duration, followed by an up-raising of the wings, before plunging in a rapid descent on to its prey. (*Map 23*)

The Elegant *Elanus* Kites

Four beautiful and graceful small kites make up the genus *Elanus*, and between them they span most of the warmer regions of the world. All are birds of open country, taking a variety of small mammals, reptiles, birds and insects, and they share several features of hunting technique. Hovering is as characteristic of *Elanus* kites as it is of kestrels, though performed with a somewhat different wing action. Even more distinctive is their method of descending on to prey once it has been spotted. Rather than the swoop with half-closed wings used by a kestrel, these kites prefer a more controlled descent with the wings raised. The final drop is achieved by raising the wings vertically above the back. This method of losing height quickly is also seen in various facets of their display and social behaviour.

Birdwatchers in Europe know the Black-shouldered Kite (*Elanus caeruleus*) as an Iberian speciality, and it appears to be on the increase in Spain and Portugal. However, it also has an extensive breeding distribution in East Africa, parts of West Africa, and also the Indian subcontinent and Southeast Asia. Outside the breeding season, the small European population appears to be resident, but in the tropics the bird wanders widely at this time. Occasionally large invasions of Black-shouldered Kites appear in areas where they are normally rarely seen, only to disappear again after a year or two. Such nomadic behaviour, presumably influenced by fluctuations in prey numbers, is also seen in

Kites of Australia and the New World
Long-winged and rather small, these kites re all grey-and-white, with black shoulder markings. Large eyes indicate their fondness for hunting in twilight or at night. Whilst the White-tailed Kite (1) is confined to the New World, both the Australian Black-shouldered Kite (2) and the Letter-winged Kite (3) are found in Australia, where the distinctive underwing pattern of the latter is its best distinguishing field-mark. *(Maps 24–26)*

the two Australian species, and may well occur in the less well studied South American populations of the White-tailed Kite (*Elanus leucurus*).

Breeding behaviour is typical of all the species except the Letter-winged Kite (*Elanus scriptus*) of Australia. Male and female remain together the whole year round, but the breeding season starts with nuptial behaviour including circling at a height, various types of pursuit between male and female, and a more elaborate circling flight in which the members of a pair drift round and round with slow, exaggerated wing-beats, early in the morning. A less well understood ritual is the "perch-and-call" behaviour of the male at the start of the breeding season, when he may perch in one tree calling incessantly for most of the day and into the evening. The nest, built anew each year, is a rather flimsy stick platform sited at varying heights in a tree, often a thorny one or a pine. Three to five eggs are laid. They hatch after 26 days, and the young fledge in 30 to 35 days.

The White-tailed Kite of the New World appears to lead a similar lifestyle to the Black-shouldered Kite. It is marginally the largest of the genus, and its prey includes mammals up to the size of a small rabbit. Mice are important in some areas, and the kites settle in places where they are temporarily abundant and then move on when their numbers fall. Such small prey may be swallowed whole or in large pieces, and consequently the birds' pellets contain quite large bone fragments – a feature shared with the owls. The White-tail is often attracted to grass fires to seek prey driven into the open by the flames, and often gathers in some numbers along the fire's edge. A tendency to gregariousness, especially in roosting, is common to all *Elanus* kites, and in this species there is also a slight tendency to nest in loose colonies.

Courtship flights are rather similar to those of other *Elanus* kites, but one special feature is a performance in which the male raises his wings at 45 degrees and then beats them through a very narrow arc. Aerial battles between neighbouring pairs indicate that territory is still held and protected, even within a colony. All hunting is done by the male through-out the incubation and fledging period, and some of the food is passed to the female in flight. This is accomplished in a manner rather different from that of other raptors, such as harriers in which the male drops the food for the female to catch. Calling to his mate as he approaches, the male White-tail holds the prey with legs extended below his body. Closing from behind, the female swings into a vertical position to grasp the offering as the male checks momentarily in flight to assist the aerial hand-over.

Australia's Letter-winged Kite carries gregariousness to its extreme and is thoroughly colonial, with up to fifty pairs nesting together. It is also an extremist in two other ways. It is highly nomadic, and for that reason one of the most rarely seen Australian raptors; and it is nocturnal. The keys to all three features are found in its chief food, the Long-haired Rat (*Rattus villosissimus*), and the vagaries of the Australian climate. Also known as the Plague Rat, the rodent in question is one that appears in enormous numbers in desert areas that have recently been kindled into life by one of the rare periods of rain. Living in burrows by day, these potential prey can only really be exploited by nocturnal species, and the two birds that do so are the Letter-winged Kite and the Barn Owl (*Tyto alba*). The other three species of *Elanus* show a distinct tendency to be crepuscular, that is, more active in the evening, but this species is unique not only in the genus, but among all raptors, in being truly nocturnal. Its native relative the Australian Black-shouldered Kite (*Elanus notatus*) appears much more similar to the Eurasian species in general habits, but it shares with the Letter-wing (and probably the rest of the genus) an adaptation for pinpointing sound sources accurately. This is an asymmetrical placement of the ear openings, a feature otherwise seen mainly in owls.

KITES OF TROPICAL AMERICA

Tropical and sub-tropical forests of the southern USA, Central and South America are home to the varied group of kites considered here. The large and handsome Cayenne or Grey-headed Kite (*Leptodon cayanensis*) is unusual in having two different colour forms in the immature plumage, but not in the adult. It is thought to have some affinity with the Honey Buzzards, and certainly includes the nests, combs and larvae of wasps in its diet. Invertebrate animals in general form the bulk of its food, which consists of a great variety of large insects and molluscs. Ranging from Mexico south to northern Argentina and Paraguay, it is typically a bird of lowland rainforests, often found near forest edges or by water. When foraging it sometimes perches on an exposed vantage point, but at other times stays within the shelter of a tree canopy and clambers about looking for insects. When moving from one tree to another, the flight is leisurely, just a few flaps and a glide, but it has been seen to pursue a flying insect with great agility. As with many tropical raptors, nothing is known of its breeding habits.

By contrast, a good deal of information exists on the nesting of the Hook-billed Kite (*Chondrohierax uncinatus*) since it has on two occasions nested on the Santa Ana Wildlife Refuge in Texas. This area, right on the Mexican border, is the northern limit of the species' range, which extends south to northern Argentina and includes several islands in the Caribbean. It is a remarkable species in a number of ways, the most striking being the large and very strongly hooked bill. There is great individual variation in the size of this bill, and very considerable plumage variation as well. As might be expected, the unusual bill is an adaptation for unusual feeding habits. Like the Snail Kite and Slender-billed Kite (pages 38–39) it is a snail specialist, although the more massive form of the bill suggests that it must use a different extraction technique from those species. Frogs, salamanders and insects are also taken. The nest is a shallow cup of twigs, sited in a tree fork, and two or three eggs are laid.

Distinctive bills are also a feature of the two species of *Harpagus*, the Double-toothed Kite (*Harpagus bidentatus*) and the Rufous-thighed Kite (*Harpagus diodon*). With two strong notches, it resembles that of the bazas (*Aviceda* spp.) but a close relationship is thought unlikely. It is more likely that the bill form is an example of convergent evolution, which has been developed in both cases to aid in grasping and dismembering large insects and lizards. A curious feature of both species in this genus is their close resemblance to hawks of the genus *Accipiter*, which contains such fierce and dashing predators as the goshawks and sparrowhawks. These two kites even fly in a similar swift manner, although there seems no urgent need to do so when they are merely moving from tree to tree to hunt insects.

Small Kites: 1
The rather stout and strongly hooked bill of the Hook-billed Kite (1) is an obvious distinguishing field-mark, whilst the well-marked plumages of the Cayenne Kite (2), Double-toothed Kite (3) and Rufous-thighed Kite (4) make these species relatively easy to identify. *(Maps 27–30)*

Swallow-tailed Kite
Although quite common in several areas of the USA in the days of the famous bird artist John James Audubon, nowadays the Swallow-tailed Kite has a much reduced population and range. (*Map 31*)

Their usual foraging methods involve very little flight at all; they simply hop and scramble about on large branches, picking off prey.

The Double-toothed Kite is the better-known of the two species, ranging from southern Mexico to Bolivia. Observations have been made at a number of its nests, though mostly of a rather limited nature. One promising case in Panama was observed from nest building to the laying of the first egg, but came to grief when a pair of toucans frightened the kite from its nest and ate the egg. At a nest with two downy young in Costa Rica, the great delicacy and dexterity with which insects were divided up for the young was remarked on, but lizards, by contrast, were swallowed whole! All but one of the nests were at a great height in forest trees, and consisted of a simple stick platform. The breeding habits of the Rufous-thighed Kite are unknown except for a clutch of two eggs taken in Brazil from a nest said to be built of twigs and lined with leaves.

Both related, though somewhat distantly, to the *Elanus* kites, the Swallow-tailed Kite and the Pearl Kite of the New World have little else in common but beauty. The Swallow-tailed Kite (*Elanoides forficatus*) is by far the better-known, since the northern limit of its distribution extends into the USA. Formerly it could be found as far north as Minnesota, but now it is largely confined to Florida, though a few breed along the Atlantic coast to South Carolina. Outside the USA its range stretches south to northern Argentina. Cypress

Pearl Kite
Although originally thought to be a falcon, the small and brightly-coloured Pearl Kite has been proved by its wing-moult, bill-shape, proportions, and tarsal scutellations, to be closely related to the true kites of the genus *Elanus*.
(*Map 32*)

swamps are its characteristic habitat in the USA, though it inhabits pines in some areas and a variety of forested areas in South America.

The Swallow-tailed Kite is a master of the air, as graceful in the manner of its flight as in its appearance. The knife-blade wings carry it swiftly and buoyantly, with the deeply forked tail opening, closing and warping as it adjusts to the air-flow. It feeds entirely in the air, either on flying insects or on prey snatched from the ground, or from water or foliage. Insects are plucked out of the air with one foot and transferred to the bill. Lizards, snakes, pieces of wasp nest, and eggs or fledgling birds are taken from trees or grass. The bird never lands to consume its prey, and has been seen to seize a whole nest in passing, and to eat the contained fledglings one by one in flight. Drinking in flight, swallow-fashion, is another of its unusual habits, and it has been seen trying to snatch small fish from the water in the same way. Perching Swallow-tailed Kites are likely simply to be resting, rather than on the lookout for prey like many other raptors. These are rather sociable birds, sometimes seen feeding in small parties, and calling shrilly to one another. Sizeable flocks may be seen in the southern part of their range where the birds are migratory.

The breeding season starts in March in the USA. Courtship flights occur at this time, but have not been described in detail, possibly because the species is capable of such aerobatic feats at all times that it is difficult to identify those with special significance. The nests are sited in the very tops of tall, slender trees, pines being favoured in Florida. Twigs for the nest are broken off in flight, then transferred to the bill for the task of construction. The nest is lined with the long wispy strands of Spanish moss which adorn the branches of the swamp cypresses, and this material too is gathered in flight. Both sexes participate in building, and continue to add to the moss lining during incubation, often when the male brings food to the nest or takes a turn at brooding the eggs. The finished nest is a well-made structure by the standards of most raptors, with a well-formed cup about 6 inches (15cm) wide and 4 inches (10cm) deep. Two or three eggs are usually laid. They hatch after 28 days, and the young fledge in 36 to 42 days.

At one time the Pearl Kite (*Gampsonyx swainsonii*) was classified with the falcon family, and indeed its striking plumage does recall that of the Old World falconets, which it also resembles in its small size. Pointed wings are another feature in which it resembles falcons rather than kites. Nevertheless, detailed features of anatomy and moult pattern show that it does truly belong to the hawk family, and has clear affinities with *Elanus*. Frequenting savanna country in South America south to Argentina, the Pearl

Kite hunts by perching on a branch or post from which it makes sallies to seize prey. This comprises chiefly insects and lizards, but small birds are taken as well. A small neat nest of twigs is built in a scrubby savanna tree or bush. It is said sometimes to nest in small colonies. One nest described held two small young and a hatching egg, but there is a lack of detailed information about its breeding habits.

SMALL KITES FROM FOUR CONTINENTS

Appearing sometimes more like a tern than a bird of prey, the African Swallow-tailed Kite (*Chelictinia riocourii*) is scarcely less graceful than its American namesake. However, it is more closely related to the *Elanus* kites, and this is evident in its hunting methods and several other aspects of its behaviour. It is a gregarious species, usually roosting and hunting in small parties. A bird of arid semi-desert country, it hovers repeatedly in its search for prey, which is usually taken from the ground. However, it is also capable of catching insects in flight, and is on the wing most of the day. Grass fires attract it, due to the prey they disturb. Insects are its main food in the dry season, but small mammals and reptiles are more important during the rains, when the bird usually breeds. Distributed in a narrow band across Africa just south of the Sahara, it performs somewhat irregular north-south movements. It is a colonial breeder, nesting in groups of ten to twenty pairs in the tops of thorny trees or bushes, and seems to have a predilection for establishing a colony around the nest of a larger bird of prey. Nests are of sticks, lined with grass, and four eggs are laid, timed to coincide with the height of the rainy season.

Quite as aerial as the American Swallow-tailed Kite are two other American species comprising the genus *Ictinia*. Central and South America south to Argentina is the range of the Plumbeous Kite (*Ictinia plumbea*), while the closely similar Mississippi Kite (*Ictinia misisippiensis*) is found in the central and southern USA. Inevitably the latter is the better-known of the two, although its total population is probably much smaller, and nowhere can it be called really common. Though less conspicuously graceful on the wing than the Swallow-tailed Kite, its flight is easy and buoyant as it drifts about catching aerial insects with leisurely ease. Occasionally, when pursuing dragonflies, it is obliged to show a turn of speed, although its attacks are not invariably successful. A party of Mississippi Kites has been seen to gather at dusk by a cave entrance from which bats were emerging, so presumably these too become prey on occasions. A Chimney Swift is also recorded being brought to young at a nest. The Mississippi Kite forages above forest canopies and across open ground, and lizards are sometimes snatched from treetops.

A sociable bird at all times, it often nests in scattered colonies, and groups of individuals are often seen perching around a nest. Already paired up when they arrive at the breeding place, the birds commence nesting with little in the way of preliminary courtship. Nest sites range in height from 80 feet (25m) in tall forest trees to as little as 10 feet (3m) in the scrub oaks of Oklahoma. Twigs with a lining of green leaves form the nest, which is sometimes distinctly flimsy. Two eggs are usually laid, and both parents incubate for 31 to 32 days, the young departing after a further 34 days.

Resembling its northern relative closely in most ways, the Plumbeous Kite is also mainly an aerial insect hunter. Prey are usually snatched with the feet by both species, but a dead Plumbeous Kite has been found with its crop packed with tiny insects, so small they must have been scooped into the bill in the manner of a swallow. In the southern part of its range the bird is migratory, travelling in flocks of forty or so, sometimes in company with Swallow-tailed Kites. The few recorded observations of breeding behaviour refer to single nests, and it is not clear whether there is any tendency to colonial nesting.

One of Australia's least-known birds of prey, the Square-tailed Kite (*Lophoictinia isura*) is rather similar to a Red Kite in general appearance, apart from the tail shape. Unlike that species, however, it does not appear to be a carrion-feeder at

Small Kites: 2
All these small kites are handsomely and distinctively plumaged. The Plumbeous Kite (2) and Mississippi Kite (3) are found in the New World, the African Swallow-tailed Kite (1) breeds in North African deserts, migrating to savannas in the non-breeding season, whilst the Square-tailed Kite (4) occurs across almost the entire Australian continent. *(Maps 33–36)*

all. Observations at a nest showed that the prey consisted almost entirely of fledglings of small birds, and it seems that during the breeding season at least it hunts by quartering woodland, plucking young birds from their nests while in flight. At other times of the year it forages also in open country, and is recorded as taking prey such as insects and reptiles from the ground.

BAT HAWK

Sunset at the Great Cave of Niah in Sarawak is the cue for an astounding spectacle as literally millions of nocturnal bats of many species and sizes pour out of its huge entrance, spreading over the forest like a black carpet unrolling in the sky. Mingling with them are giant diurnal fruit bats travelling the other way, and hordes of cave swiftlets dashing hither and thither. Presently, a different shape appears in the half-light, a large black shadow sweeping in and out of the cave mouth with great speed and agility on long, pointed wings. This is the best view likely to be had of a Bat Hawk (*Machaerhamphus alcinus*) unless one is discovered resting by day. Most of the activities of this strangest of raptors are compressed into the last half hour of daylight, when prey teems in colossal numbers and only time is in short supply.

To make efficient use of this vast food resource in the time available, a bird must not only be highly skilled at capturing aerial prey, but equally swift at processing it. Bat Hawks achieve this by anatomical modifications that enable them to catch bats and swallow them whole, without having to land. Basic needs are a large mouth, and a large crop and stomach. The latter is not unusual among birds of prey, but the structure of this bird's bill and gape certainly are. Long, as well as wide, the jaws are feathered for much of their length, and the horny part of the bill is relatively tiny, flattened from side to side, and strongly hooked. Extending far back below the eye, the gape is huge relative to the size of the head, and the general impression is rather like an enormous swift. Swifts, indeed, are nearly as important a prey as bats, and some have their wings rapidly plucked in flight before being swallowed.

Found thoughout the Old World tropics, the Bat Hawk is by no means confined to the vicinity of huge limestone caves like Niah. Anywhere that bats are abundant will do, and rivers, beaches and some urban areas may be frequented. In towns the bird may even pursue its prey into buildings, which probably seem to it little different from caves. During the day it sits motionless, usually in a shady tree. Apparently it also does some hunting at dawn, but there is less information about this, and probably this time of day is not so important to the bird as dusk.

Only at the start of the breeding season is the Bat Hawk at all likely to be seen flying in daylight, and nuptial displays near the nest site include spectacular aerobatics, with high-speed chases, grappling and rolling. Some weak, high-pitched whistles may be uttered in display, but for much of the time this is a silent bird. Twigs and branches broken off in flight are used to build the nest, which is unlined and usually sited high up in a tall tree. Occasionally nests are found in towns. One or two eggs are laid, and are incubated only by the female. She leaves the nest for a brief time at dusk, but whether this is to hunt for herself or to be fed by the male is unclear. Both parents bring food to the young, delivering it in a series of hasty visits only in the last twenty minutes before dark. Unfortunately, this makes observations of the bird's behaviour very difficult, but it would be interesting to discover when and how the young learn the unusual techniques they will have to use in dealing with their prey as adults. As far as can be told in dim light, it seems that a good part of the food brought to them, at least at first, consists of insects. The young fledge in about five to

Bat Hawk
The strange, crested Bat Hawk, with its unique, keeled upper mandible, is rarely seen as it spends most of the daylight hours perched in dense foliage, only becoming active at dawn and dusk when it sets out on its bat-hunting forays. (*Map 37*)

Slender-billed Kite
Smaller and greyer than the Snail Kite, and with a yellow, rather than red, eye, the Slender-billed Kite has the same food preference but a different hunting technique. It too preys on freshwater snails, but drops on to them from a perch rather than from in flight. *(Map 38)*

six weeks, and leave the vicinity of the nest soon afterwards.

Three geographical races occur in the Bat Hawk's extensive range, African birds in particular having much more extensively white underparts.

Snail Kite and Slender-billed Kite

Rarity and precarious status are often the price to be paid for specialized feeding habits, but the Snail Kite (*Rostrhamus sociabilis*) demonstrates that this need not always be so. It feeds entirely on freshwater snails of the genus *Pomacea*, but so abundant are these over much of the American tropics and subtropics that in places the Snail Kite is by far the most numerous bird of prey. It is ironic that in the USA the bird has long been called the Everglade Kite, as the Florida Everglades are very much a northern outpost, where the bird barely survives at the present time. The situation is very different in the marshes of the northern Argentinian Chaco. Here many hundreds may be seen almost anywhere, perched on posts or telegraph wires or flapping and gliding in leisurely flight low over the marshes. Concentrations almost as big may be seen on the Venezuelan Llanos or even along the coastal rice paddies of the Guianas. All the bird requires are the wet conditions in which the *Pomacea* snails abound.

Clearly the long slender hook with which the bill is furnished is the instrument used for extracting snails from their shells, but opinions are divided on the exact method employed. Basically the kite has to overcome two problems. The first is the operculum, a hard disc of shell material with which the shell entrance is sealed while the snail is retracted; the second is the columellar muscle with which the snail retracts itself, and by which it is anchored to the shell. One suggested method was that the kite waited patiently, holding the snail in one claw, until the snail began to emerge of its own accord, whereupon it was quickly impaled by the bill hook. This may sometimes happen, but careful observations have shown that usually the birds insert the hook between the operculum and columella, and then use it to cut through the columellar muscle. The snail's body can then be shaken free, and the shell falls to the ground. Piles of up to 200 shells can sometimes be found beneath regular feeding perches.

A bird so numerous can hardly avoid being gregarious, and Snail Kites roost and sometimes nest colonially. Courtship flights at the start of the breeding season are sometimes performed at a considerable height, and

Snail Kite
Where it is common in the American tropics, the Snail Kite outnumbers all other birds of prey, and is often recognized by its broad wings and rather ungainly flapping flight. Because of its very specialized diet of freshwater snails the bird is always to be found near expanses of open water or marshland, though its communal roost may be quite some distance away. *(Map 39)*

include short plunges and talon-grappling. A bleating cry accompanies these performances, and a cackle is uttered in response to disturbance, but this is generally not a noisy bird. The nest is an untidy but not very large structure of sticks, placed in marsh grasses or bushes only 3 feet (1m) to 16 feet (5m) above the water. Three or four eggs are laid, and these are incubated by both sexes for about 28 days. At 23 to 28 days the fledging period is short for a raptor of this size, perhaps reflecting the relative ease with which food can be obtained when the young leave the nest. Both parents care for the young, which have a distinctive cry. Little plumage variation is seen over the Snail Kite's extensive range, although geographical races based on measurements have been described.

Much scarcer than the preceding species, the Slender-billed Kite (*Rostrhamus hamatus*) has a more restricted distribution in northern South America. In general structure it is similar to the Snail Kite, though it is more thickset and shorter in the wing. A curious difference is that in this species the immature is similar to the adult, whereas that of the Snail Kite has a very distinct plumage, but as the two species have overlapping ranges it is to be expected that some difference in ecology exists between them. Diet is not the answer, since snails of the genus *Pomacea* are this bird's exclusive food also. Habitat differences appear to be the key, as this species is much more a bird of small pools and watercourses within forests or plantations. It is much more often solitary than the Snail Kite, although pairs or small parties are sometimes seen together. Diving displays by pairs or groups appear to be connected with courtship. Only one nest has so far been found, in Surinam. It was sited high up in a huge cotton tree growing in a coffee plantation.

STELLER'S SEA EAGLE

With its huge arched orange bill set against striking dark brown and white plumage, Steller's Sea Eagle (*Haliaeetus pelagicus*) is arguably the world's most impressive eagle, and very nearly the largest. Females weighing 20 pounds (9kg) have been recorded, though most birds are 4.5 to 6.5 pounds (2 to 3 kilogrammes) lighter than this. The genus to which this bird belongs has an extensive world distribution, and includes several other large eagles; however, they are not particularly closely related to other eagles, such as those in the genus *Aquila*, and if anything their nearest relatives are the Old World Vultures, and kites such as the Brahminy and Whistling kites (genus *Haliastur*). Unlike most other eagles, the sea eagles have the tarsus – the lower part of the leg – unfeathered, clearly as an adaptive response to their fish-catching lifestyle. Most are quite willing to scavenge as well as to catch fish, and their feet and talons are not especially powerful. Nevertheless, Steller's Sea Eagle is a bold and efficient predator when it chooses to be – its recorded prey including hares, young seals, sable, arctic fox and birds up to the size of Capercaillie (*Tetrao urogallus*) and geese. Stranded salmon are a major food resource at spawning time, but crabs, molluscs and carrion are also consumed at times. Young birds are particularly likely to take the latter, and are also recorded visiting slaughterhouses to feed on offal.

Steller's Sea Eagle breeds on the northern Pacific coast of the USSR and in North Korea, wintering mainly in Korea and northern Japan. Many wintering places are around rivers where salmon come to spawn. In such places the birds may be seen in considerable numbers, though they are solitary at other times of the year, and gatherings of these eagles on the sea ice off the northern Japanese island of Hokkaido are one of the world's great ornithological spectacles. An all-black form of Steller's Sea Eagle, recorded from Korea, may be a distinct race or only a colour phase, but it appears in any case to be very rare, and may even now be extinct.

With broad wings spanning up to 8 feet (over 2.4m) Steller's Sea Eagle is as impressive in flight as at rest, but it is more likely to be seen in the latter state as it spends relatively little time in the air. Probably this is because much of its prey is located by "still hunting", requiring only a brief pursuit flight to make a capture. Trees or rocks make suitable vantage points for the purpose, but when perched, as it often is, on gravel banks in rivers or on ice floes, it probably really is resting unless spawning salmon are nearby.

Deep barking notes repeated several times are the usual call, but a gull-like call is uttered during the soaring display flight. This is usually seen in March, shortly before the first egg is laid, and mating on the nest has been recorded about the same time. The nest itself is a huge stick structure up to 8 feet (2.4m) across and 12 feet (3.6m) deep. It is sited for preference in the top of a very tall tree, though sometimes on a cliff, and is re-used and refurbished year after year. Two eggs are laid, occasionally one or three, and the incubation period is about six weeks. "Cain and Abel" battles are not a feature of sea eagle breeding biology, so that two or three young are sometimes reared, although one is more usual. The young fledge after about ten weeks in the nest, but do not reach full adult plumage for four years, and may not be ready for breeding even then.

Relatively safe from persecution in the remote parts of its breeding range, Steller's Sea Eagle is potentially more at risk in its winter quarters, where pollution may also be a hazard in places. However, it appears still to be reasonably numerous at present. Individuals have wandered as far as China, and turn up fairly regularly on the Pribilof and Aleutian islands of Alaska.

Steller's Sea Eagle
Arguably the most magnificent of all birds of prey, Steller's Sea Eagle regularly takes prey up to the size of geese. The Korean form of the species lacks the white on the top of the shoulders, but retains the white tail.
(Map 40)

WHITE-TAILED SEA EAGLE

Once reasonably numerous on the coasts of the Scottish Highlands and Islands, the White-tailed Sea Eagle (*Haliaeetus albicilla*) has suffered fluctuating fortunes both in Britain and in the rest of Europe. In Scotland its demise as a breeding species took place during the late eighteenth and nineteenth centuries. This was the time of the "Clearances" when crofting communities in the Highlands were subjected to large-scale eviction to clear land for sheep farming and game preservation. Raptors – and especially this one, branded a lamb-killer – came under great pressure, to which was soon added the scourge of the collector as specimens began to acquire rarity value. More willing to feed on carrion than the Golden Eagle (*Aquila chrysaetos*) it was consequently much more vulnerable to poisoning. The last reported nesting took place in 1916 on the island of Skye, a former stronghold.

Unlike the Osprey, which passed through Scotland on migration even after its loss as a breeding bird, there seemed no natural way in which the White-tailed Sea Eagle could ever be re-established in Britain. It was not surprising therefore that some conservationists' thoughts should turn to reintroduction. The species has a number of features that make this technically feasible. It it trainable by falconry techniques (King James I of Scotland is said to have flown one) and hence amenable to "hacking back", or gradual acclimatization to the wild. Moreover, it regularly eats carrion as well as taking live prey, so birds can be easily provisioned while learning to fend for themselves. An additional crucial factor was a source of young birds. This was provided by the Norwegian population, currently Europe's largest. As pairs frequently fail to rear to fledging all the young that hatch, it was considered that taking young eaglets from the larger broods posed little threat to the Norwegian birds. A first attempt, by a private individual, was made at Glen Etive, Argyll, in 1959. An adult and two young were released, but the attempt failed, with one bird captured, one killed in a trap, and one lost without trace. Not until 1968 was another attempt made, this time on Fair Isle under the auspices of the Royal Society for the Protection of Birds. Two males and two females were released, but three disappeared, and one was last seen barely able to fly, and smothered with fulmar oil. It had evidently taken to attacking young fulmars on their nesting ledges, but the jets of stomach oil with which they defend themselves had proved ruinous to the eagle's plumage, probably fatally so.

Finally, in 1975, a long-term scheme was set up by the Nature Conservancy Council on the island of Rhum in the Inner Hebrides. Involving the regular importation of Norwegian birds over a period of years, it seems gradually to be bearing fruit. As it takes the young four or five years to reach breeding condition, and even then early attempts are likely to be failures, the project was clearly destined to take a long time. The first nesting by released birds took place in 1985, and since then six successful nestings have taken place, producing a total of eight young up to 1988, when six breeding attempts took place and two young were reared. As the birds grow more experienced, as well as more numerous, a secure population will eventually be established as long as the birds remain secure from persecution; egg collectors still remain a threat.

Norway's population remains substantial, and the eagle may return to Scotland, but elsewhere in Europe the picture is more worrying. Numbers actually increased for a time due to the Second World War, but this gain was rapidly cancelled out during the 1960s when pesticides began to take their toll. Scandinavia other than Norway was hard hit, and so was Continental Europe, where the main concentrations are now in Germany where an inland population exists by lakes and rivers. Eastwards, the range of the species extends right across the Asian USSR, and presumably a large population still exists there.

FISHING EAGLES AND COASTAL SCAVENGERS

Clear piercing calls echoing over the great lakes and waterways of Africa denote the presence of the African Fish Eagle (*Haliaeetus vocifer*). Rather a small species compared to other members of the genus, it is nevertheless abundant and conspicuous in many places, not least due to its frequent cries which have been described as "the voice of Africa". As an important indicator of the health of African waters, its biology has been the subject of intensive studies, and it is one of the few raptors whose daily routine has been quantitatively analysed, by a long series of dawn to dusk watches in Kenya. Roosting in trees, it calls at first light and moves to one of the fishing perches in its territory. It spends about 90 per cent of the day perched and about 10 per cent flying. Males fly more, and make more fishing sorties, than do females. Of its flying time, 36 per cent is spent soaring, partly in display, 9.5 per cent in territorial flights, 23.5 per cent moving from perch to perch and 31 per cent actively fishing. Fish are usually sighted from a perch, and seized

White-tailed Sea Eagle
Europe's largest eagle, the handsome White-tailed Sea Eagle is nowadays absent from many of its former haunts, due to extreme persecution from gamekeepers and stockmen during the eighteenth and nineteenth centuries. However, recent attempts to reintroduce the species into its former Scottish island haunts seem to be succeeding.
(*Map 41*)

after a short sally. Less often, and mainly in the case of males, the bird circles out across the water for a few minutes.

Although fish are the primary prey, waterbirds are also taken, including both adults and young of flamingoes; in fact the African Fish Eagle has been known to wipe out whole colonies of herons, spoonbills and cormorants. Immatures especially will take carrion, and sometimes turn up at lion kills or similar carcasses. This species is also strongly piratical, and will harass herons, storks, Ospreys or even other members of its own species to rob them of food. The fish it catches generally weigh 7 to 18 ounces (200 to 500 grammes) but some up to 6.5 (3kg) have been recorded. It can rise with a fish weighing up to 5.5 pounds (2.5kg) but anything larger has to be dragged along the water surface to the shore.

Near the Equator, display occurs all year round, though elsewhere it is mainly a feature of the early part of the breeding season. It chiefly consists of soaring flights by the pair of birds, with deep wing-beats and frequent bouts of calling. Trees are chosen for nesting, with some preference for thorny acacias or for euphorbias. Pairs have from one to

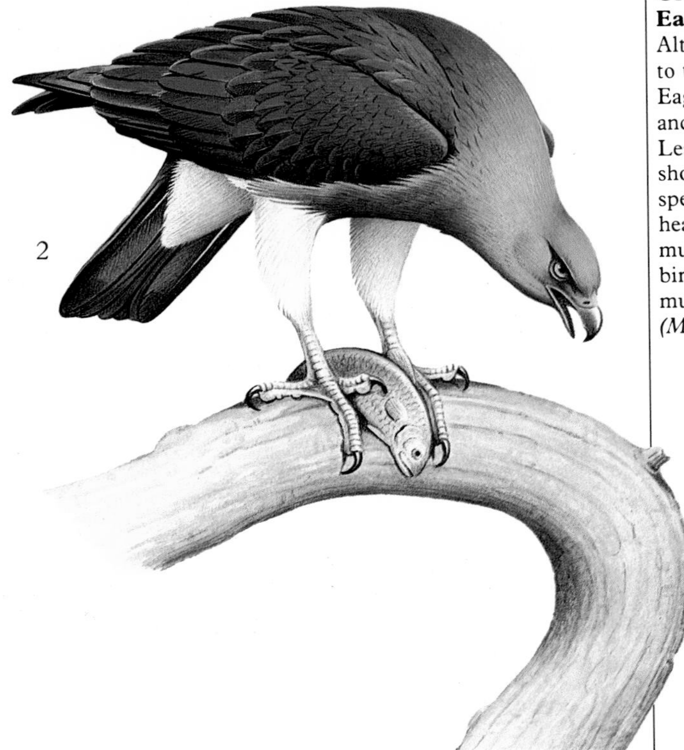

Lesser Fishing Eagle and Grey-headed Fishing Eagle
Although generally similar to the Grey-headed Fishing Eagle (1), the smaller size and virtual silence of the Lesser Fishing Eagle (2) should help identify the species. The larger Grey-headed Fishing Eagle is a much more conspicuous bird, with bare tarsi and much more vocal habits. *(Maps 42 and 43)*

four nests near the centre of their territory, though they find it difficult to keep more than two in good repair at any one time. They are made of sticks and papyrus fronds, lined with papyrus heads and sometimes weaver-birds' nests! Both sexes build, and both incubate the one to three eggs, which hatch after about six weeks. Although sibling fighting is not as severe as in some eagles, the first chick has often eliminated the other(s) by the tenth day. Although feathering is complete by seven weeks old, the young eagle has barely learned to feed itself by then, and does not make its first flight for a further three or four weeks. After fledging it remains in its parents' territory for up to two months. Young fish eagles are attacked if they venture into other eagles' territories, and they often band together in small parties and forage in untenanted areas.

A closely related species is the more plainly marked Madagascar Fish Eagle (*Haliaeetus madagascariensis*), whose habits are very similar to the foregoing species. Rather similar in colouring also is another smaller species, Pallas' Sea Eagle (*Haliaeetus leucoryphus*) of Central Asia, its range overlapping that of the White-tailed Sea Eagle.

Differing strikingly from preceding species in its all-white head, tail and underparts is the White-bellied Sea Eagle (*Haliaeetus leucogaster*) of southern Asian and Australasian coasts. It often hunts from a perch overlooking the water, and its diet includes a large proportion of sea snakes as well as fish. Young herons taken from colonies are also also frequent victims. The closely related Sandford's Sea Eagle (*Haliaeetus sandfordi*) of the Solomon Islands differs in possessing a brownish adult plumage which resembles that of the immature bird. It is less of a coastal species than most sea eagles, and occurs on forested mountains at altitudes up to 4000 feet (1220m). Phalangers and pigeons are apparently regular prey, rather than fish and carrion.

Smaller and plainer than most of the foregoing species, the two members of the genus *Ichthyophaga* are nevertheless even more highly adapted for fishing. Their talons are strongly curved, and the soles of their feet are furnished with spicules to aid in gripping fish. Consequently, their diet consists almost entirely of fish taken alive, without the carrion and stranded prey which supplements the menu of

Sea and Fish Eagles
All these Old World eagles are closely associated with aquatic environments, with fish forming the bulk of their diet, although they are not averse to taking other prey. The African Fish Eagle (1) is replaced by the Madagascar Fish Eagle (4) on that island, and in central Asia by Pallas's Sea Eagle (2). In Southeast Asia and Australasia it is replaced by the White-bellied Sea Eagle (3), and on the Solomon Islands by Sanford's Sea Eagle (5).
(Maps 44-48)

most *Haliaeetus* species. The two species are the Grey-headed Fishing Eagle (*Ichthyophaga ichthyaetus*) and the Lesser Fishing Eagle (*Ichthyophaga nana*). Inhabiting tropical Asia and its islands, these are birds of inland waters, often occurring within forested areas.

Bald Eagle

Despite its status as the emblem of the United States, the Bald Eagle (*Haliaeetus leucocephalus*) has fared no better than most birds of prey at the hands of man. Direct persecution by shooting and poisoning have been followed by the insidious effects of insecticides and other industrial pollutants, and despite recent improvements there is no room for complacency. Ironically the bird's main stronghold now is Alaska, where there was once a bounty system dedicated to its destruction, supposedly to protect salmon stocks. Even when it was afforded protection in 1940 Alaska was excluded, and bounty payments continued until 1951; during the 36 years the system had operated over 100,000 Bald Eagles had been shot. Recent estimates put the total Alaskan population at 10,000–15,000, while a mid-January count in 1979 gave a total of just 9824 for all the 48 contiguous states of the Union combined. Bald Eagles are abundant on the coast of British Columbia. Breeding populations also exist around the Great Lakes, and in eastern Canada, but totalling far fewer birds than in Alaska. Probably the second-ranking state in terms of Bald Eagle numbers is Florida; surprisingly, the eagles there migrate *north* in winter. Florida's Bald Eagles may also be the means of boosting Bald Eagle numbers elsewhere. A scheme started in 1985 utilizes the bird's natural capacity to lay a new clutch when the first one is lost early in incubation. Clutches taken in Florida are incubated and reared under controlled conditions to provide birds for restocking other areas; meanwhile, the Florida birds re-lay, and rear their second-clutch broods as normal.

Salmon stocks were never at risk from the Bald Eagle, in Alaska or anywhere else, for the numbers of prey control the number of predators, not the other way about. Nevertheless, great numbers of eagles are attracted to salmon spawning rivers, where they can feast on spent or stranded salmon – fish that are dead or doomed to die anyway. Along 10 miles (16km) of the Chilkat River as many as 3000–4000 have been counted in mid-November when spawning is at its height.

At other times, the Bald Eagle lives on a varied diet, much of it caught by active predation in addition to scavenging. Carrion taken in Alaska includes whale and seal meat as well as fish, while in Florida, opossums killed on the road are a useful food source. A good picture of the bird's lifestyle under relatively natural conditions was given by a detailed study during the 1970s of some fifty pairs on the island of Amchitka, part of the Aleutian chain. A small amount of interaction with man was provided by a garbage dump which was visited for carrion, particularly by young birds, but otherwise human interference was minimal. The eagles on the island obtained a large part of their food by hunting, and the team on Amchitka distinguished three main techniques. "Still hunting" from a cliff or pole overlooking the beach or tundra produced not only fish, but also rats, sea otter pups and wildfowl. Hunting while flying at a height was mainly employed to catch seabirds on the water, and often involved a spectacular stoop of up to 330 feet (100m). A third tactic made use of low-level flight, using the cover of wave troughs on the sea, or tundra hummocks inland, to achieve surprise. Auks at sea and ptarmigan or ducks on the tundra were often captured in this way, and two or more eagles sometimes joined forces to exploit the technique even more effectively. Birds are also sometimes taken in flight. In one such case the victim was a gull that had been mobbing the eagle with a group of others; suddenly the irritated raptor rolled over in flight and snatched the gull in its talons. Bald Eagles turn to piracy at times, often harassing Ospreys for fish, and sometimes snatching prey from the paws of sea otters as they float on their backs on the sea.

Benjamin Franklin opposed the choice of this species as symbol of the United States on the grounds that it was a scavenger and cowardly, and it is true that in most places humans can approach the bird's nest without qualms. However, this may simply be the result of shooting and

Bald Eagle
Regal and magnificent in bearing, the national symbol of the United States now survives in large numbers only in Alaska. Persecution, pollution and human intrusion have all played a part in its decline.
(Map 49)

persecution; the more undisturbed birds on Amchitka had no such inhibitions, and on several occasions attacked the observers fiercely, knocking them to the ground and inflicting lacerations. The nest itself is the usual gigantic pile of sticks typical of sea eagles, built usually in a tree, or on a rock stack where there are no trees. One to three eggs are laid, and incubated for some five weeks. The young fly at just over ten weeks old, but do not achieve the white head and tail of adulthood until four or five years of age.

Lappet-faced Vulture

Immense size, and brightly coloured bare skin on the head and neck, make the Lappet-faced Vulture (*Torgos tracheliotus*) one of the most impressive of all birds of prey, though hardly one of the most attractive. It epitomizes many features of the Old World Vultures, which, like their unrelated counterparts in the Americas, are primarily scavengers, seeking carcasses or garbage while soaring. An important difference, however, is that the Old World birds lack a highly developed sense of smell, and consequently are entirely reliant on vision to find their food. This restricts the range of habitats they are able to exploit, as a clear and extensive field of view is essential for locating food by sight alone. They are therefore birds of open country, be it plains, savannas or mountains, and they have never been able to colonize rainforest in the way that the New World Vultures have.

Largest of the African vultures, the Lappet-faced is second only to the European Black Vulture in size among the Old World birds of prey, with a wing-span approaching 9 feet (2.7m) and a weight of up to 15 pounds (6.8kg). Smaller vultures move aside when it comes to a carcass, and with sideways blows of its heavy, powerful bill it is often the only one capable of gaining entry to a recently dead large animal unless it has previously been opened up by mammalian predators. Its strong bill also enables it to cope with pieces of tough skin and bone discarded by others, so it may be the last at the feast as well as the first. Bare skin on the head and neck is particularly extensive in this species, perhaps because it may need to excavate very deeply when dealing with fresh corpses. The Lappet-faced is often accompanied by the White-headed Vulture (*Trigonoceps occipitalis*), which is nearly as big, but the Lappet-faced is a more aggressive species and is prepared to charge with lowered head and half-spread wings at any other bird that does not give way.

Inhabiting mainly arid or semi-desert areas and some wooded grasslands, it is usually seen singly, though in some sub-desert areas it may be seen in groups of up to forty or fifty. Where griffons (see below) are the commonest large vultures, it probably depends on these to a considerable extent for the initial location of food. It roosts in trees, sometimes in pairs, and by day may spend long periods perched near a carcass but not feeding. There is evidence that it may kill some small or weak mammals for itself, and it has an unusually powerful grip for a vulture. Locusts and termites may also be taken where abundant, and the birds often raid flamingo colonies for adults, young and eggs.

Breeding habits of the Lappet-faced Vulture have been well studied. The species is a solitary nester in East Africa, with nests spaced from 0.5 miles (0.8km) to 4 miles (6.4km) apart. However, in Chad it may reach much greater densities: several nests in one tree have been recorded, and the birds sometimes share a tree with nesting White-backed Vultures. Situated typically at the top of a thorny tree, the nests may measure up to 10 feet (3m) across and 3 feet (1m) thick, and consist of a flat platform of sticks with a shallow depression in the centre lined with dry grass. Both male and female take part in building and refurbishing the nest, which may be used for many years. A single egg is normally laid, and this is incubated by both parents for a period of about seven weeks.

On hatching, the young vulture weighs about 7 ounces (200g). It is clad in thick down, and even at this stage the bill looks noticeably heavy. Until it is three weeks old, one or other adult is with the chick most of the time, either brooding it or sheltering it from the sun. The tips of the primary feathers begin to appear at about a month old, and the young vulture is capable of flying at about seventeen weeks, although it does not usually do so until eighteen or nineteen weeks. Even then it remains near the nest and dependent on its parents for a further one or two months.

Lappet-faced Vulture
By far the largest tropical African vulture, the immense and powerful Lappet-faced Vulture easily drives other scavengers away from a carcass. It is normally only met with in very small parties, and is solitary outside the breeding season. (*Map 50*)

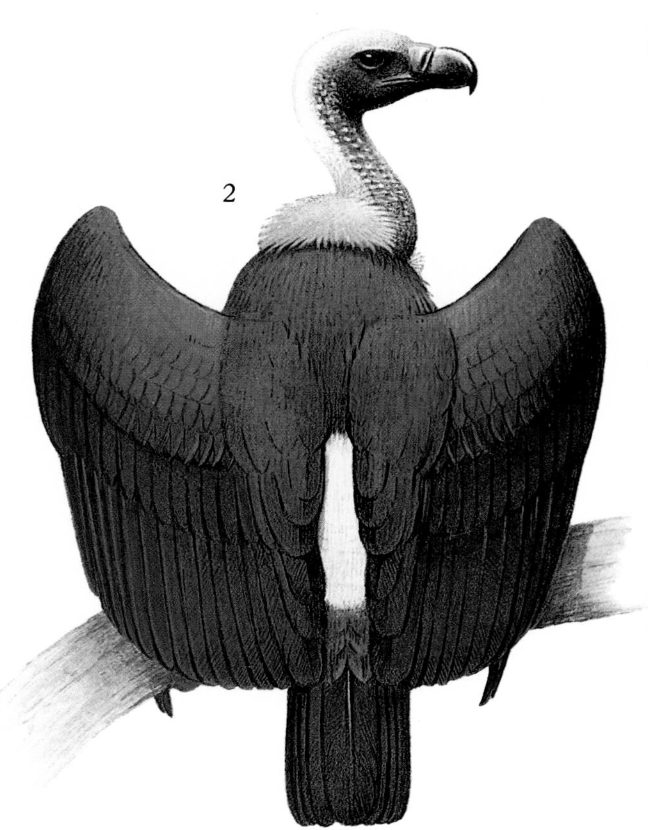

Griffon Vulture and African White-backed Vulture
Only ever likely to be confused with Rüppell's Griffon, the African White-backed Vulture (2) is identified by its white back-patch, pale underwing-coverts, dark bill and uniformly pale brown plumage. The Griffon Vulture (1) is the only large pale vulture occurring in its range, and is therefore easy to recognize.
(Maps 51 and 52)

GRIFFONS OF EUROPE, ASIA AND AFRICA

"Griffon" is commonly used as a general term for Old World Vultures of the genus *Gyps*: however, without additional qualification the name applies specifically to the Griffon Vulture (*Gyps fulvus*) of Eurasia. All griffons are of medium to large size, heavy-billed (though less so than the Lappet-faced Vulture), and have the head and neck covered with a thin fluffy layer of down rather than being completely bare. A ruff of long feathers surrounds the base of the neck. Most of the species have the unusual feature of a tail consisting of fourteen feathers, two more than in the majority of birds. Sociable in habits, these vultures nest in colonies on cliffs or in trees.

As the only member of the group occurring in Europe, the Griffon Vulture has been particularly well studied, and it typifies the genus in many respects. Like all vultures it depends on conditions that provide plentiful rising air currents to permit the long spells of soaring flight during which it seeks its food. For the Griffon, these are largely provided by updraughts in mountainous areas, but it forages also in some arid or desert areas, where thermals meet the same need. Spain and the Balkans are its main strongholds in Europe, and it has shown a considerable decrease during the past century – almost certainly connected with more prosperous farming conditions which have reduced the supplies of dead animals on which it depends. Poisoned bait, usually intended for other animals, has also taken its toll. In Asia the species' range extends through the Altai Iran, the Hindu Kush and parts of the Himalayas, and in most of these areas its population is much healthier. A few Griffons also breed in North Africa.

Food is located by sight, either directly or by watching other vultures, and up to a hundred may gather at a carcass. Surprisingly timid, they may take some time to venture right up to the dead animal, but once there they specialize particularly on the soft internal tissues, their very long and flexible necks and sharp-edged bills aiding penetration. There is little evidence that they ever attack animals that are fit and well, though they may at times hasten the end of sick or injured creatures.

High circling flights and other aerial displays by members of a pair around the nesting cliffs mark the onset of breeding, usually about the middle of February in southern Europe. Colonies average about fifteen to twenty pairs, but may include as many as a hundred in favoured areas. Nests are made of sticks and grass, and are not particularly large, generally not more than 3 feet (1m) across. A single egg is laid and incubated for seven to eight weeks, by both parents, changing over twice a day. The fledging period is about sixteen weeks. Fed by the parents for a time after leaving the nest, the young vulture itself becomes capable of breeding at four or five years old.

Griffons breeding in Asia also include the Indian White-backed Vulture (*Gyps bengalensis*), the Indian Griffon (*Gyps indicus*) and the Himalayan Griffon (*Gyps himalayensis*). The Indian White-backed is locally common in parts of India and Southeast Asia, and prefers relatively wet habitats. It will enter towns and villages, and thus can take advantage of garbage, slaughterhouse refuse and the like. Its nesting colonies are situated in villages or along rivers or

Old World Vultures: 1
More sociable than other Old World Vultures, all these birds have relatively long, slender necks and bills, ideally suited to reaching inside carcasses. The southern African Cape Vulture (5) has a Himalayan counterpart, the Himalayan Griffon (4); Rüppell's Griffon (3) is found across central Africa, whilst the Indian Griffon (2) and the Indian White-backed Vulture (1) have almost identical ranges across India and Southeast Asia.
(Maps 53-57)

canals. Although normally entirely a carrion-feeder, there is a curious record of one attacking a moribund calf which raised enough strength to grasp the vulture and kill it before dying itself. The Indian Griffon has a northern race inhabiting the Himalayan foothills and other mountainous country, and a southern race inhabiting the plains of India and Southeast Asia. As the name suggests, the Himalayan Griffon is a bird of very high mountain ranges. A large and aggressive species, it dominates all others except the Black Vulture at a carcass. Like the preceding species, its diet includes a good deal of human flesh, as well as that of yaks.

Common in East African plains and savannas, the African White-backed Vulture (*Gyps africanus*) is the main participant at many a feast provided by the large mammals of that continent. Its main competitor in many areas is Ruppell's Griffon (*Gyps rueppellii*), only slightly smaller in size but showing a preference for drier areas and even deserts. Southern Africa is the home of the Cape Vulture (*Gyps coprotheres*). Like the Griffon of Europe it has felt the adverse effect of modern farming practices, with domestic animals in South Africa now routinely buried when they die. Attacks by this species on living animals, especially sheep, appear to be well authenticated, and may result from this man-made shortage of carrion.

The Lammergeier or Bearded Vulture

More predatory and active in its feeding habits than most vultures, the Lammergeier (*Gypaetus barbatus*) is as distinctive in appearance as it is in its habits. Indeed its relationship to the other Old World Vultures has sometimes been questioned, though it shows many anatomical similarities to the Egyptian Vulture, which also has interesting feeding behaviour.

With its long wedge-shaped tail, long narrow wings and striking black "beard" contrasting with the white face, the Lammergeier is a handsome and impressive bird, quite lacking the repellent aspect of many vultures. Strangely, the glowing orange colour of its underparts is imparted by oxides from the ledges and caves where it roosts. These are apparently deliberately rubbed on by the bird, and it is possible that this behaviour is related to the functioning of the oil gland whose secretion aids feather conditioning.

Though now a threatened species in Europe, the Lammergeier still maintains good populations in the Middle East, Central Asia and highland areas of eastern and southern Africa. Strychnine in bait has been the main cause of its decline in Europe, where now only some seventy to ninety pairs remain, chiefly in the Pyrenees and Greece. Throughout its range it is a bird of mountains, spending much of its time on the wing, soaring and gliding with a grace and agility unmatched by any other vulture. When descending, the long tapering wings are swept back, giving the bird the appearance of a gigantic falcon.

Easily intimidated at a carcass by Griffons or Black Vultures, the Lammergeier is nevertheless more capable of raptorial behaviour than most vultures. It is the only one that regularly carries food in its talons, and although this is usually picked up dead, there are records of live prey such as monitor lizards being seized in this way. Repeated accounts mention the bird trying to force large animals such as goats, chamois and even people over precipices, and there may well be substance in some of these reports. Certainly it has been recorded feeding on all these, and more, whether or not it was instrumental in their demise. Perhaps better known is its habit of dropping bones to break them. These are carried in the feet to a height of up to 200 feet (60m) above a favoured rock slab which the bird approaches downwind, turning rapidly into the wind as the bone is released in order to follow it down. Several attempts may be needed before the bone breaks, but when it does so the Lammergeier is well adapted to extract the marrow with its gouge-like tongue. Other items of food such as pelican eggs and tortoises are recorded as being treated in the same way.

Lammergeiers have a large territory, 7 to 10 miles (11 to 16 kilometres) in diameter, within which are one or two regular breeding sites. Breeding activity is heralded by spectacular aerial displays by both members of a pair. Undulating flights with swoops and dives of several hundred feet (up to 200 metres) are common, or the birds may zoom past the nesting ledge, twisting and rolling in flight. Talon-grappling between male and female has also

Lammergeier
Unique habits are matched by an equally distinctive appearance in this species – the tuft of dark throat-feathers providing the bird with its alternative name of Bearded Vulture. In flight the diamond-shaped tail and long wings create an unmistakable silhouette.
(Map 58)

Egyptian Vulture
Renowned as one of the very few tool-using birds known to science, the Egyptian Vulture is quite easy to identify by its creamy-white plumage and long lanceolate neck-feathers.
(Map 59)

been recorded, sometimes with the birds cartwheeling through the air together. In all these features they resemble eagles more than vultures. Nests are sited on ledges, or in crevices or caves on cliffs. They are huge piles of branches up to 8 feet (2.4m) across and 3 feet (1m) deep, with a thick lining of wool, dung, rags or other refuse. Bones, horns, hooves and other feeding debris is scattered around, and the whole vicinity is spattered with droppings, in messy contrast to the bird's majestic appearance. One or two eggs are laid, rarely three, and these are incubated for some eight weeks, mainly by the female. Both parents bring food for the young, either in the feet or bill, or in the crop, in which case feeding is by regurgitation. Even quite small chicks can swallow pieces of bone up to 8 inches (20cm) long. Commonly only one young survives to fledge at an age of about fifteen weeks. Dependent still for some time after its first flight, the young Lammergeier will not reach breeding age until at least five years old.

EGYPTIAN VULTURE AND HOODED VULTURE

Small vultures, with slim bills, the Egyptian Vulture (*Neophron percnopterus*) and Hooded Vulture (*Necrosyrtes monachus*) are able to eat scraps or pick at meat through openings in carcasses too small for their larger cousins. Both occur in Africa, although the Egyptian Vulture is also found in southern Europe, the Middle East, southwestern and central Asia, and in the Himalayas and India. In the northern part of its range the species is migratory, with most of the European birds migrating as far south as the southern borders of the Sahara. Open country with short grassland or even more arid terrain is the bird's preferred habitat, and it is seen only rarely in high rainfall areas with dense woodland.

Primarily a scavenger, rarely killing prey for itself, the Egyptian Vulture is nevertheless recorded as taking flamingo chicks. At carcasses with other vultures, it is usually the last to feed, even yielding to the Hooded Vulture which also feeds on scraps. Other food items recorded include termites, grasshoppers, dung-beetles, small crustaceans and snails. However, it seems to have developed a liking for eggs, and at flamingo and White Pelican colonies it picks up eggs and smashes them on to rocks in order to feed on the spilt contents. However, this bird has developed an even more remarkable technique for dealing with Ostrich eggs. Having selected a suitable stone, it grasps it in its bill and walks to the Ostrich's nest. Then, standing over the

Hooded Vulture
The contrast between the bare skin of the crown and hind-neck, and that of the face and throat, gives rise to this species' name. The Hooded is the smallest of the African vultures, and is therefore usually the last to feed at a carcass. It is, however, becoming more associated with man, and is often a useful and unconcerned scavenger around settlements.
(*Map 60*)

egg, it hurls the stone downward on to the shell until it shatters, and the vulture gets its reward. Recorded in South Africa as long ago as 1836, this behaviour has only recently been observed in Tanzania, and constitutes one of the rare instances of tool-using by animals other than man.

Usually a solitary breeder, requiring rocky cliffs or mountains from which it seldom wanders during the breeding season, the Egyptian Vulture builds its nest on a crag or in a small cave. Very occasionally, one may nest on a building in a town. In display, one or both birds may perform dives and swoops, then, coming together, the pair may roll and present talons. One to three eggs, but usually two, are laid, and they are incubated, at least during daylight hours, by both sexes. Although evidence is sparse, it is most probable that both adults tend the young.

Being the southerly counterpart of the Egyptian Vulture, the Hooded Vulture is found throughout Africa south of the Sahara, in habitats ranging from desert to forest, where it plays a similar but apparently more sedentary role. Over most of west and northeast Africa it is a common scavenger, especially at rubbish dumps in towns. However, it is more widespread in savannas and grasslands where it is less dependent on man, whilst further south in Kenya and Tanzania it ceases to be a town scavenger altogether and becomes much more closely associated with pastoralists at cattle kraals.

In the breeding season there is little obvious nuptial display, although a pair may soar and dive together. Although primarily a solitary nester, in areas of high abundance it may give the impression of semi-colonialism. The nest of sticks is usually built in a tall tree, at heights of 23 to 130 feet (7 to 40 metres) and is lined with green leaves, grasses and other debris, which is added to throughout the season. The single egg is incubated by both sexes, with the female taking the major part, feeding on food regurgitated by her mate on to the edge of the nest.

Four Distinctive Old World Vultures

Bizarre feeding habits are not the only features that distinguish the Palm-nut Vulture (*Gypohierax angolensis*) from its relatives. Several features of plumage and structure recall the sea eagles, and the species has been regarded by some authorities as a link between this group and the Old World Vultures. Although it preys on crabs, molluscs and fish, its favourite diet consists of the husks of Oil Palm (*Elaeis guineensis*) nuts (hence its name), and of Raffia (*Raphia vinifera*) fruit. Its purely African distribution therefore coincides very closely with that of these two trees, in coastal mangroves, tropical forest and well-wooded savanna. Although most often seen perched, it flies with rapid wing-beats and can soar well. Courtship flight, high over the breeding area, consists of soaring, interspersed with mock dives, and may occasionally include somersaulting. Both sexes build the stick nest, which measures about 3 feet (1m) across by 1.5 feet (0.5m) deep and is often decorated with Oil Palm racemes. The nest is always sited in a large tree, usually in a main fork at a height of 30 to 210 feet (9 to 64 metres). Since nest construction can take up to six weeks, the nest is repaired annually and is used for as long as it lasts. The single egg, which is white with heavy chocolate-brown, paler brown, and lilac markings, is apparently incubated by the female alone, and incubation and fledging combined appear to last about five months.

Throughout India and the Himalayas up to 6500 feet (about 2000m), and in Burma, Thailand, the Malay Peninsula and South Vietnam, the extremely large Indian Black Vulture (*Sarcogyps calvus*) is to be found all the year round. It is much less gregarious than other vultures, and often only one or two individuals will be present at a carcass where large numbers of other vulture species may be competing. In common with other large vultures, much of the day is spent soaring on thermals, with wings held above the horizontal in a wide "V". The bird is quick to spot and descend to a carcass, even a relatively small one, and is known to glean corpses from the edges of grass fires. In the breeding season the pair performs spectacular aerial displays, twisting and diving over the nesting area and calling noisily. If a suitable tree is not available, the nest of sticks and leafy branches may be found in a bush, at a height as low as 3 feet (1m), although a tree-nest will be sited at any height up to 115 feet (35m). New nests are remarkably small structures, some 2 feet (0.6m) across by perhaps a foot (0.3m) deep; however, additional material is added annually, resulting in final dimensions of 7 feet (2m) by 5 feet (1.5m), often with an unsavoury lining of foliage mixed with skin, fur and feathers. Although not a colonial nester, the bird will occasionally use a tree containing the nest of some other vulture species. The duties of incubation and feeding of the chick are shared by both parents.

Although having a range extending from Spain, eastwards in a broad band across southern Europe, then from Afghanistan and Baluchistan, across Turkestan, Tibet and northeast Mongolia, north to 64°N in the Urals, the Himalayas and on to Assam and China, the huge European Black Vulture (*Aegypius monachus*) is nowhere numerous; indeed, it is considered by some authorities to have a population as low as 200 pairs in Europe. Usually solitary, or in small groups, the bird prefers mountainous terrain with nearby low-lying plains for hunting. When at a carcass it is dominant over all other vultures, even Griffons, and often its mere presence is enough to deter other prospective feeders.

In display, a pair may circle close together high above the nest, performing rolls with talons interlocked and then falling in a cartwheeling descent. Both sexes annually add sticks to the already huge nest, built high on top of a tree, but incubation of the single egg is carried out mainly by the female. Tending the chick, however, is a shared responsibility, and the whole nesting cycle may last as long as eight months.

Also scarce, yet strikingly beautiful, the White-headed Vulture (*Trigonoceps occipitalis*) is a normally solitary bird of open semi-desert and bushveld savanna. It is found in tropical Africa south of the Sahara. At carcasses it gives way

Old World Vultures: 2
These vultures have their generally dull plumage set off by brighter colours elsewhere. The Indian Black Vulture (1) has pinkish neck-lappets; the European Black (2) has bluish skin on the head and neck, and a bluish-purple cere; the White-headed (3) has pinkish-white head- and neck-skin, and a black-tipped pink bill, whilst the Palm-nut Vulture (4) shows orange-flesh facial skin, and a grey cere. (*Maps 61-64*)

to larger vultures, and feeds mainly by picking up dropped scraps. No obvious forms of display are known, although a pair may soar close together, suggesting mutual display. The birds breed in solitary pairs, building a grass- and hair-lined nest of sticks up to 7 feet (2m) across. It is sited some 26 feet (8m) above the ground on top of a thorny tree, usually an acacia, although in western Africa baobabs are frequently used. The single egg is believed to be incubated by the female alone, but few details are known of the fledging of the chick.

Introducing the Serpent Eagles

Relationships of the birds included in the genus *Spilornis* are a notorious headache in bird classification. Distributed from India across Southeast Asia and on to the East Indies, they still require considerable study before their precise relationships can be established, or even before the correct number of species can be finally agreed upon. Three are recognized here, following recent research work. As their names suggest, the Philippine Serpent Eagle (*Spilornis holospilus*) is confined to the Philippine Islands, whilst the Celebes Serpent Eagle (*Spilornis rufipectus*) is restricted to the islands of Sulawesi (Celebes) and Sulu.

Philippine Serpent Eagles seem to prefer open country with scattered trees, along river valleys, forested clearings and cultivated land. Little else is known about the species, despite its being fairly common, but due to its general similarity to the Celebes Serpent Eagle it is assumed to differ little from it.

Turning to the Celebes species, this is more likely to be found inhabiting forests, particularly forest edges, and grassy woodlands, where it sits patiently for hours on a tree-perch, watching for the small snakes, lizards and small rodents on which it preys. It is often seen in the company of the Woolly-necked Stork (*Ciconia episcopus*), which also hunts snakes; but whether this is coincidence or there is some advantage to one or other individual has yet to be demonstrated. Also, the species is often seen on the wing, frequently giving screaming calls. This may be part of its courtship display, but with no information currently available on the species' breeding biology this can only be speculation. However, it is generally assumed to be similar to that of the Crested Serpent Eagle.

Distributed from India, across a large part of Southeast Asia, to southeast China, Taiwan (Formosa), and the Ryukyu Islands, the Malaysian and Indonesian regions south to Bali, and east to Borneo and Palawan, the widespread Crested Serpent Eagle (*Spilornis cheela*) has many well-marked mainland and insular forms, and is extremely variable, particularly in size. Indeed, some of these very distinct forms have occasionally been considered separate species. Throughout its range it is normally resident, although in India it is possibly subject to some local migration or wanderings.

It is found at forest edges, along wooded streams, and around villages and cultivation. In the Himalayas it can be found in mountain forest, normally up to 10,000 feet (3050m). It is usually seen singly or in pairs, and often likes to perch for long periods on some vantage point from which it can scan the ground below for prey on which to pounce. It takes mainly snakes, frogs, lizards, rats and mice, and occasionally injured birds or crabs. When soaring, Crested Serpent Eagles are often conspicuous, and frequently draw attention to themselves by their distinctive calls.

In the breeding season a pair will soar above the breeding area, often calling noisily and performing aerobatic displays which may include stoops, rolls and dives with half-closed wings, or sometimes with wings vibrating rapidly. The nest, built 20 to 80 feet (6 to 25 metres) up in a tree, consists of sticks and twigs, and is sometimes lined with green leaves. A single egg is laid, and is incubated by the female alone for about thirty-five days. The young bird fledges in approximately sixty days, and appears to be dependent on its parents for some time after leaving the nest.

Serpent Eagles: 1
Although very similar in appearance to the Crested Serpent Eagle (3–5) which varies considerably across its extensive range, the Philippine Serpent Eagle (2) does not overlap that species' range and should therefore be readily identified when seen. Rufous breast plumage and a dark head help to distinguish the Celebes Serpent Eagle (1) from its close relatives.
(Maps 65–67)

BATELEUR

As African as the zebra, the flight silhouette of the Bateleur (*Terathopius ecaudatus*) is as memorable in its way as the thunder of the great herds. In fine weather the adult, with its exceptionally long, pointed wings, and feet protruding slightly beyond the very short tail, is commonly to be seen on the wing, and may fly continually for most of the day. It has a majestic sailing flight, gliding steadily, sometimes with the wing-tips swept back, and since it lacks a long tail periodically canting from side to side in order to steer. This habit gives rise to the use of the French name "Bateleur", a term applied to a tight-rope walker, rocking slightly from side to side while using a long balancing-pole. Even when perched, this colourful species cannot be confused with any other bird of prey: its stubby appearance and apparent lack of tail give it a distinctive silhouette, while the loose feathers on the back of the head produce a ruffed effect.

Widely distributed throughout Africa south of the Sahara, down to the Transvaal, the Bateleur is found in savannas, woodlands and semi-desert thornbush. It is not normally found in forested and very mountainous terrain, although it does breed up to at least 8000 feet (2440m) and occasionally as high as 15,000 feet (4570m) in parts of Ethiopia. In many areas it is apparently sedentary, especially near breeding sites, but it is known to be nomadic at times, and may possibly be a regular migrant within the tropics. In western Africa there is some evidence of north-to-south movements in response to wet and dry seasons.

The Bateleur is a versatile and powerful predator, taking a wide variety of prey including birds up to the size of guineafowl, mammals as large as dik-dik, and even reptiles up to the size of a monitor lizard. It is not averse to taking grasshoppers and termites on the ground, and roads are often patrolled for carrion from road kills. Sometimes piratical attacks are made on other birds, usually on large carrion-eaters such as vultures.

In the breeding season, the Bateleur performs spectacular chasing courtship flights. The male may dive down at the flying female who, rolling on to her back, presents her talons as he shoots past. Courtship display may also include the male flying with loosely-dangling legs, and in addition to the characteristic loud "*kow-ah*" call, the wings may be flapped to produce a loud "*whup-whup-whup*" noise. Very rarely, a bird may execute 360° lateral rolls, accompanied by this same wing-noise. Pairs frequent the same breeding areas for many years, and the nest, a solid structure of sticks with a deep central cup lined with green leaves, is used in successive years, and either built or repaired by both sexes. It is most commonly situated in a large tree, 15 to 65 feet (4.5 to 20 metres) above the ground, and usually within the leaf canopy so that it is shaded for most of the day. Invariably a single unspotted chalky-white egg is laid, and this is incubated mainly by the female, although the male may occasionally take some part. The incubation period is the longest of any African eagle, lasting at least 52 days, and once hatched, the young bird, which fledges after 95 to 115 days, is tended by both sexes. Breeding can occur at almost any time of the year, and most if not all pairs do not breed every year. This trait, coupled with the fact that full maturity is not attained until five or six years of age, would seem to indicate that the bird is very long-lived.

Whilst not at present one of the most endangered of the world's birds of prey, the Bateleur is, nevertheless, potentially vulnerable. It is extremely nervous of human presence near the nest, and such disturbance almost always results in desertion. In complete contrast to this, the bird's almost unbelievable tameness in captivity, coupled with its unusual and handsome appearance, obviously make it an attractive pet. Such pressures, combined with increased human intrusion into the species' habitat, could easily result in a rapid and possibly disastrous decline in numbers.

Bateleur
The Bateleur plays an important role in the folklore of many peoples, and is frequently associated with death or warfare. Some African tribes believe that the bird never lands, while the Mashona believe that it carries away the spirit of someone recently departed – usually a powerful figure such as a tribal elder or chief.
(*Map 68*)

Short-toed Eagle
Europe's only snake eagle, the Short-toed Eagle's almost totally white underside, contrasting with the darker upperside, plus its frequent bouts of hovering when hunting, should ensure its correct identification anywhere. Communal feeding is frequently seen, and a pair will often share the prey captured by one individual.
(*Map 69*)

SNAKE EAGLES OF EUROPE AND AFRICA

Europe's only snake eagle is the Short-toed Eagle (*Circaetus gallicus*) which has three well-marked geographical forms. Northernmost is the race breeding from southern Europe and North Africa east to China, migrating to northern tropical Africa in winter. It inhabits open stony or thinly-wooded hillsides, sub-desert steppes and desert fringes. The other two forms are found respectively in western and west-central Africa and in northeastern to southern Africa, where they occupy a range of habitats from sub-desert and dry grassland to open woodlands.

Finding snakes requires specialized foraging techniques and the Short-toed Eagle is most often seen hunting while soaring, or hovering on slowly-winnowing wings. It usually patrols at heights of 100 to 300 feet (30 to 90 metres) and on spotting a snake it drops, often in stages, with talons extended, finally plunging to grasp its prey. Large snakes are killed on the ground, where they are caught, dismembered, and eaten on the spot. Smaller snakes are carried into the air and swallowed whole, after they have been crushed by being passed through the talons. Short toes, after which this eagle is named, permit a more powerful grip on the slippery prey.

The large, round, ummarked white egg is laid in a rather small nest of sticks. It is incubated by the female alone for 45 to 50 days, and fledging of the single young takes a further 70 to 90 days.

Resident throughout woodlands and more arid thornbush of Africa south of the Sahara, south to Cape Province, the Brown Snake Eagle (*Circaetus cinereus*) is a rather large and

African Snake Eagles
A rather lethargic species, spending much of its time perched, the Brown Snake Eagle (1) has heavily-scaled legs and thickly-padded breast feathers as protection against snake bites. Unique in the genus, the Southern Banded Snake Eagle (2) has a distinctively barred underside and a triple-barred tail, whilst the Smaller Banded Snake Eagle (3) has a single broad, white tail-band, and an almost uniformly coloured underside.
(*Maps 70–72*)

powerful snake eagle. It differs in habits and in most of its habitat preferences from the Short-toed Eagle, but where their ranges do overlap, the former hunts in wooded areas and the latter in more open country. It is rather more lethargic than the Short-toed Eagle, and is usually seen perched in a tree for long periods, intently scanning the ground. Hunting is mainly from such a perch, and prey, which is generally larger than that taken by the Short-toed Eagle, consists mainly of snakes, both venomous and non-venomous, and includes cobras as well as puff-adders, boomslangs, blind snakes and black mambas.

The male's display attracts attention from far away, as he soars high, calling loudly and raucously. The single white egg is laid in a rather small nest. It is incubated by the female alone, and takes about 45 days to hatch. Fledging, which is unusually long, lasts about 105 days.

Restricted to the coastal woodlands of eastern Africa, from southern Somalia and northern Kenya south to Natal, the Southern Banded Snake Eagle (*Circaetus fasciolatus*) is a small, rather thickset snake eagle unlikely to be confused with any other, except for the similarly-sized Smaller Banded Snake Eagle. It is a little-known and somewhat secretive raptor of heavy woodland and forests. It is probably migratory from southern to northern parts of its range in winter as it is relatively numerous in northern coastal Kenya between July and October. Breeding habits are also something of a mystery, but it is known that the egg is white or greenish-white, with a few reddish streaks.

Although more widespread in Africa than the preceeding species, the Smaller Banded Snake Eagle (*Circaetus cinerascens*) is nevertheless somewhat uncommon over most of its range. It is found from Sierra Leone east to western

Ethiopia, and from eastern Kenya south to the Zambezi Valley and northern Botswana. It prefers well-wooded moist savannas, forest edges and riverine districts. It commonly takes snakes from trees, as well as from the ground, and these are mainly smaller species, although one bird has been seen with a large venomous cobra. The bird also takes some lizards and frogs. Again, little is known about this species' breeding biology, although the egg is reported to be white and unmarked, with a rough texture.

Island and Forest Serpent Eagles

The little-studied and poorly-known Nicobar Serpent Eagle (*Spilornis klossi*) is endemic to Great Nicobar Island, the largest and most southerly island in the Nicobar Group in the Bay of Bengal. It is smaller than the smallest race of the Crested Serpent Eagle which, however, it resembles in some respects, and is certainly the smallest raptor to be honoured with the name eagle! Details of the species' nesting and breeding habits are unknown, but prey items recorded include lizards, rats, a small bird and an Emerald Dove.

Although regarded by some authorities as a race of the wide-ranging Crested Serpent Eagle (*Spilornis cheela*), the Andaman Serpent Eagle (*Spilornis elgini*) is here considered as a distinct species. It is known to inhabit inland forest clearings and tree-scattered hillsides, but details of its breeding behaviour and nest are as yet undiscovered, although they are probably similar to those of the Crested Serpent Eagle. A race of the latter also occurs in the Andaman Islands, but frequents coastal areas rather than forests.

Occurring in western and west-central Africa south to Gabon, the Congo Serpent Eagle (*Dryotriorchis spectabilis*) is a little-known species inhabiting dense primary forest, where it apparently frequents the understory or the lower branches of the taller trees. It is a specialized forest-adapted snake eagle, with large eyes which enable it to hunt in poor light for snakes, lizards (especially chameleons) and amphibians, and possibly also small mammals. Distinctly different in proportions from serpent eagles of the genera *Spilornis* and *Circaetus*, it has very short wings and a long tail. It has been described as harrier-like in habits, which is rather surprising for a short-winged forest species. Nothing is known about its nuptial displays or breeding habits. However, it is quite vocal and is reported to give a cat-like miaowing, and a low, nasal "*cow-cow-cow*", which is repeated at intervals for long periods, often attracting observers' attention. This is thought to be an advertisement call associated with mating behaviour as it is used only during the period June to November which is believed to be the breeding season. Information on the bird's nesting habits is, however, still completely lacking.

Restricted to the island of Madagascar, and then almost certainly only to the northerly parts of the humid forests in the east, up to about 2000 feet (610m), the Madagascar Serpent Eagle (*Eutriorchis astur*) is another very rare species. Most of our current knowledge of the bird comes from museum specimens, but it has been recorded eating a large chameleon, and presumably takes other prey such as snakes and lizards and possibly also small mammals. Despite several intensive searches, the species had, until very recently, not been seen since the 1930s, although there were unconfirmed reports of its presence in the Marojejy Reserve in the 1960s and 1970s. However, a recently-confirmed sighting of a single bird in 1988 is heartening news.

Serpent Eagles: 2
The erectile head-ruff of the Andaman Serpent Eagle (4) separates it from all except the Andaman form of the Crested Serpent Eagle. The large eye, chestnut collar, and short-winged, long-tailed appearance make the Congo Serpent Eagle (1) equally distinctive. No other Malagasy bird looks like the grey-plumaged Madagascar Serpent Eagle (3), whilst the Nicobar Serpent Eagle (2) is the only Serpent Eagle occurring there.
(*Maps 73-76*)

African Harrier Hawk
Even narrow tree-bark cracks and crevices offer little protection to lizards when a Harrier Hawk is probing for food with its unique 'double-jointed' legs. Its unusual hunting technique, overall grey colour, broad white tail-band, and yellow legs and face make this species quite unmistakable.
(Map 77)

HARRIER HAWKS AND CRANE HAWK

An unusual and specialized raptor of distinctive appearance, the African Harrier Hawk (*Polyboroides typus*) occurs in Africa south of the Sahara, in various forested and woodland habitats, especially along river valleys, forest edges and moderately dense mixed cultivation. Apparently sedentary in most of its range, it is, nevertheless, a wet-season migrant from the northern tropics to the Sahel area.

Besides having a noticeably small and slender head, the bird is remarkable in having double-jointed "knees" (intertarsal joints), which allow the lower part of the leg to bend both forwards and backwards. This feature enables the bird to probe into awkward holes and crevices in trees, its preferred method of hunting for prey, and it obtains almost all of its food by using this slow, systematic searching technique. It can often be observed clambering up tree trunks with flapping wings, as it searches for the nestlings of hole-nesting species such as barbets, starlings and woodpeckers, as well as for small mammals and reptiles. In West Africa, where Oil Palms are often abundant, it visits these to feed on the husks of the palm fruits, as well as locating animal prey amongst the palm frond debris. Colonies of weaver birds are regularly raided, the bird hanging upside-down from the nests, or from branches, as it reaches into the nests to take the eggs or nestlings. Attacks on heronries have also been recorded.

In the breeding season the male performs undulating flights, and on his upward climb the wing-beats are exaggerated, with the wings almost touching below the body. When both birds are involved, the male dives down at the soaring female and she rolls, extending her legs up towards his, and they briefly touch talons. The nest, built of thin sticks with a copious lining of green leaves, is sited either in the tree canopy or in a rock-crevice at the base of a tree or bush. One to two (occasionally three) eggs are laid, with both sexes incubating, although the female takes the major part. Hatching is thought to occur in about thirty-five days.

Madagascar Harrier Hawk and American Crane Hawk
Black flight-feathers, pale grey plumage, yellow soft parts, and very long legs make the Madagascar Harrier Hawk (2) a very distinctive bird. Equally distinctive, despite considerable racial variation, is the similar-looking, and somewhat lanky, Crane Hawk (1) of Central and South America.
(Maps 78 and 79)

During the fledging period, which is believed to last about fifty days, feeding of the young is shared by both parents, the female taking an increasing share of the work-load as time passes.

Playing much the same role on the island of Madagascar as does the preceding species on the African mainland, the morphologically and ecologically similar Madagascar Harrier Hawk (*Polyboroides radiatus*) is, nevertheless, considerably smaller. It occurs on Madagascar in all wooded areas from sea level up to 5000 feet (1524m) but avoids dense forest. It regularly frequents banana plantations where it hunts for a particular species of lizard, and it is not uncommon in mangrove swamps. It systematically searches holes and crevices when climbing trunks of trees, in much the same agile manner as its relative in mainland Africa. It is also recorded as taking small mammals, frogs, occasionally carrion, and locusts when swarming.

In the American tropics, the Crane Hawk (*Geranospiza caerulescens*) occupies the same ecological niche as the Harrier hawks of the African region, to which it also bears a striking resemblance. Possessing the same reversible leg-joints, its hunting and feeding methods follow very much the same pattern, again indicating its ecological role, but whether these ecological counterparts are examples of a close relationship, or of convergence, is uncertain. The species shows a preference for the vicinity of water, so long as there is cover nearby, and is often found in woodland interspersed with small streams and pools, or in forested swamps. It feeds on lizards, tree-frogs, snakes, large insects, and birds' eggs and nestlings. Its breeding habits are believed to be similar to those of its African relatives.

Occurring in tropical lowlands from Mexico to eastern Bolivia, northern Argentina and Paraguay, the Crane Hawk exhibits considerable geographical variation, and although two or three species were formerly recognized, these are currently considered as one species represented by some five or six races.

Hen Harrier

Drifting buoyantly across open country, the Hen Harrier (*Circus cyaneus*) can be appreciated by observers over a large part of the Northern Hemisphere. Migrating south in autumn, the birds of Europe and Asia move as far as the Mediterranean basin, the Middle East, northern India, Burma and China, while those of North America travel to Central America and the northern Antilles.

Hen Harriers are found in a wide variety of habitats including moorland, young conifer plantations, coastal and inland marshes, sand-dunes, and open grassy areas. Like all harriers they fly quite low, normally less than 10 feet (3m) above the ground. Their flight is extremely graceful, and the birds often glide for considerable distances on half-raised wings, followed by a few leisurely wing-beats. In this way a hunting bird systematically searches to and fro, then suddenly pounces with outstretched talons, on to its prey. Occasionally, to achieve the same end, the bird will make a swift pirouette or half-turn in flight, with tail fanned, followed by a stall and then a sudden drop. This slow flight not only gives the bird more chance of seeing its prey, but also enables it to exploit its highly-developed hearing, which is a feature of all harriers. Prey consists mainly of small songbirds and their fledglings, voles, young hares and rabbits, frogs, small reptiles, and some insects. Though the bird is typically a solitary feeder throughout most of the year, a number of individuals may sometimes congregate at a locally-abundant food source such as a high build-up of field voles. The bird usually roosts singly, on the ground, in moist grassy or rushy areas, on flattened grasses or small mounds, but communual winter roosts are not uncommon. Typically, these consist of ten or so individuals, although larger roosts, holding as many as fifty birds, have been recorded. In larger roosts the birds fly in shortly before dusk, and disperse again soon after daybreak to their individual hunting areas.

During his often spectacular display flight, now widely known as "skydancing", the male Hen Harrier may climb steeply to a height of about 100 feet (30m), follow this with a side-roll, or even a somersault, and finish with a steep dive which is only checked just above the ground. This sequence may be repeated several times. In the early days of display the female watches her mate from a perch, either in a tree or on the ground; he may even try to attract her while she is hunting. Later, as she becomes more interested, the pair engage in mutual soaring and diving, and although her performance is less spectacular than his, following a smoother, more undulating path, it can sometimes involve her rolling over, and presenting talons. During this time, and in the vicinity of the nest, this normally silent species indulges in considerable vocalization, especially when food is being passed between mates.

The nest, composed of small sticks and a variety of reeds and grasses, is usually in a slight hollow in the ground, protected by surrounding vegetation and varying in diameter from about 15 inches (38cm) in dry situations, to up to 3 feet (1m) by several inches deep, in wet locations. Construction is carried out mainly by the female, although both sexes gather suitable material, employing both feet and bill to carry it from relatively short distances away. Clutch size varies from four eggs to six, occasionally up to eight, and may, at least in part, be governed by prey availability. Incubation, which is by the female alone, fed by the male at the nest, commences with the second or third egg and lasts for about thirty-five days. The staggered egg-laying, with intervals of two days or more between eggs, results in a considerable size difference between the youngest and oldest chicks. The young are fed by the female, on prey dropped by the male and caught by the female in mid-air. Fledging occurs after some thirty-seven days, but pre-fledging mortality is relatively high.

Generally, Hen Harriers form a monogamous pair-bond, especially where nesting pairs are clearly isolated from others. On the other hand, bigamy and polygamy are very common in populations where nests are sited as close as 150 feet (46m) apart. Strangely, this behaviour has been proved to be detrimental to the overall population, with the successful fledging rate dropping as the incidence of polygamy increases.

Hen Harrier
Although quite easily mistaken, at a distance, for a gull, the male Hen Harrier's beautiful grey plumage and white rump are unmistakable when viewed clearly. The brown female is much less easy to identify, but typical harrier habits, plus the locality and habitat, should aid identification of both sexes.
(*Map 80*)

Spotted, Marsh, and African Marsh Harriers
Although their females are difficult to distinguish, the males of the Spotted Harrier (1), Marsh Harrier (2) and African Marsh Harrier (3) should present no real identification difficulties, due to their very distinctive plumages. All hunt in typical harrier fashion, although this simply increases the problem of female identification where the species' ranges overlap. (*Maps 81-83*)

Black Harrier
Easily distinguished from other harriers by its dark colour, white rump and very distinctly barred tail, the Black Harrier can also be identified on the wing by its pied appearance.
(Map 84)

HARRIERS – THE SLOW-FLYING SPECIALISTS

As elegant in plumage as it is graceful in flight, the Spotted Harrier (*Circus assimilis*) occurs throughout most of Australia, occasionally wandering south into Tasmania. Northwards, it is also found in the Celebes, Lesser Sunda Islands and Timor. Mainly a bird of open grasslands and lightly-timbered plains in the lower rainfall areas and tropical northern parts, it hunts in typical harrier fashion, beating and gliding low, with wings held in a wide "V". It feeds on small animals such as young rabbits, birds and reptiles, but also takes large insects such as grasshoppers. In display the male may climb to a great height, from which he usually descends in slow spirals or side-slips, occasionally plummeting down with half-closed wings. The species is unique among the harriers in that it prefers to build its flat, bulky platform nest in a low tree rather than on the ground. Two to four eggs, but most commonly three, are laid, and are almost certainly incubated by the female alone. Precise details concerning the species' breeding cycle are sadly lacking, and although incubation and fledging together are said to last about 100 days, this unusually long period certainly requires verification.

Smaller, much slimmer, and generally paler brown than the European Marsh Harrier, the African Marsh Harrier (*Circus ranivorus*) is resident locally in marshy areas of northern Kenya, Uganda, eastern Zaire and Angola, and south to Cape Province. It mainly frequents marshes and reedbeds, and neighbouring grassland and farmland. Hunting follows the typical harrier pattern, with the bird repeatedly traversing low over the same ground, and hovering briefly before plunging with raised wings and extended feet on to its prey. Small mammals, adult birds and fledglings, lizards, frogs and insects form the bulk of its diet, although it is not averse to taking fish. In nuptial display the male may soar alone and perform short undulating dives, rising again and repeating the pattern. When joined by the female, he soars to a great height, and then dives down at her, while she, rolling on to her back, presents her claws. Typically, the nest is formed of reeds and dead vegetation, and is sited in a reedbed. Other details concerning the species' breeding habits are scant, although it is known that the three to six eggs are incubated for 35 days, with the young fledging in a further 36 to 40 days. It is believed that the male plays a greater part in the rearing of the chicks than do the males of more dimorphic harriers.

Breeding from Western Europe east to central Asia and Japan, and wintering mainly in Africa and southern Asia, the Marsh Harrier (*Circus aeruginosus*) seems to prefer reedbeds, swamps, marshes, and flood plains for hunting and nesting. In Australasia the bird is known as the Swamp Harrier, and is sometimes considered a distinct species. It takes a variety of prey, ranging from small mammals, especially small rodents, and birds, including nestlings and eggs, to frogs, snakes and fish, and even some carrion.

In the breeding season the male may perform a high circling flight, occasionally flying with quick, stiff, jerky wing-beats, and calling at irregular intervals. He may also dive down at the female, who wards him off with her claws. The nest, built mainly by the female, is usually placed in a dense reedbed, and she alone incubates the clutch of three to eight eggs, for some 31 to 38 days. During incubation, and the 55 to 60 days' fledging period, the male brings in food, and calling the female off the nest, performs an aerial food-pass – throwing the food to the female, who catches it in mid-air.

Endemic to southern Africa, the little-known Black Harrier (*Circus maurus*) is mainly a bird of dry country, although it may hunt along the fringes of wet areas. In the southwestern Cape and Natal it is also found in mountainous areas, where it is known to hunt over snow-covered ground. It is usually seen singly, quartering the ground in typical harrier fashion, and its prey consists of birds, small rodents, amphibians and insects. Further study of this uncommon species is required, since virtually nothing appears to be known about its breeding habits.

SOUTH AMERICAN AND EURASIAN HARRIERS

Closely related to the Hen Harrier of the Northern Hemisphere, the Cinereous Harrier (*Circus cinereus*) is found in western and southern South America, from Colombia south to Tierra del Fuego, and eastwards through Paraguay to southeastern Brazil, Uruguay and the Falkland Islands. The species seems fairly undemanding in its choice of habitat, for it can be found in a variety of open grasslands and marshes, from Chilean lowlands up to levels of about 13,000 feet (4000m) in Ecuador. Prey, in the form of small vertebrates, is much the same as in other harriers, and is taken using the same typical low-flying, systematic, quartering method. The three or four white eggs, laid in a relatively small ground-nest of rushes and grasses, are incubated almost exclusively by the female, for about thirty days.

Wintering mainly in Africa south of the Sahara, in India, and sporadically in the Middle East, the Pallid Harrier (*Circus macrourus*) breeds in steppes and grassland plains, from sea level up to about 16,500 feet (5030m) from far eastern Europe across to central Asia. Unusually for a harrier, roosting is always on dry ground, and during migration the species often roosts communally, in quite large numbers, among tall grasses. Hunting, involving tireless quartering of the ground for prey such as small mammals and birds, reptiles and insects, is much as in other harriers. Nuptial displays also follow the usual harrier pattern, with the male soaring, diving and rising again, then diving down at the female, who reacts with a partial roll and the presentation of talons. However, in contrast to most other harriers, display and pairing take place during the northward migration, so that most birds arrive at their breeding grounds already paired. The ground-nest, usually on a slight rise in tall herbage, may be just a scrape, or an untidy accumulation of various materials. It normally contains four or five eggs, which are incubated solely by the female for about thirty days, the young fledging in about a further forty days.

A summer visitor to Europe and central Asia, from wintering quarters in Africa and India, Montagu's Harrier (*Circus pygargus*) prefers heaths, young forestry plantations, rough pasture and crops, but may overlap with the Marsh Harrier in reedbeds and marshes, and with the Hen Harrier on moorland. It catches ground-living birds and their young, shrews, voles, frogs, small lizards and snakes, and large insects. In nuptial display the male performs undulating dives and upward swoops, similar to the Hen Harrier. In the nest, sited in cover on the ground, the female incubates the four or five eggs for about thirty days, and the young leave in about a further forty days, although they may still continue to use the nest as a nocturnal roost for a while.

The breeding area of the very distinctive Pied Harrier (*Circus melanoleucus*) extends from eastern Siberia south to Mongolia, North Korea and northern Burma, while its winter quarters are farther south, in India, Sri Lanka and Burma, where it shows a distinct preference for rice paddies. It hunts over open steppes and low-lying damp areas, taking small prey including some insects, in much the same way as Montagu's Harrier, which it appears to replace in the Far East. Display is much like that of other similarly-sized harriers, and occasionally, as in the Pallid Harrier,

South American and Eurasian Harriers
Resembling the Chimango Caracara, the Cinereous Harrier (2) can best be distinguished by the lack of a white rump and wing-patches. The Pallid Harrier (1) is paler than Montagu's Harrier (3), and also lacks that species' black wing-bar, although identification of the females is more difficult. The striking black and white Pied Harrier (4) is quite unmistakable, while the handsome tri-coloured Long-winged Harrier (5) is one of the most distinctive of all harriers.
(Maps 85–89)

pairs are formed before they arrive at the breeding grounds. The nest is most often sited in cover, on boggy ground, and the female incubates the four or five eggs for about thirty days, with the young fledging after about forty days.

A bird of lower altitudes of South America, the Long-winged Harrier (*Circus buffoni*) ranges from Colombia, Trinidad and the Guianas, south to Argentina, and west to eastern Bolivia and parts of eastern Chile. It frequents streams, lagoons, marshy areas or pampas, where it takes small birds, mammals, frogs and reptiles, hunting them in typical harrier fashion. It is known to lay three unmarked, pale bluish-white eggs in a ground-nest, sited among rushes. There is confusion over the various plumages, further complicated by the existence of a black phase in both sexes.

GOSHAWK

One of the largest and possibly most impressive species of its genus, the Goshawk (*Accipiter gentilis*) is distributed right around the Northern Hemisphere, roughly between latitudes 35°N and 65°N, and is represented across this huge range by some nine geographical forms. It is mainly a bird of the trees, being equally at home in both deciduous and coniferous woodland. The species is a partial migrant, some northern areas being vacated every winter, probably as a response to reduced food availability rather than climatic conditions. It is prized by the falconer, for although difficult to train, it is superb when flying "from the fist". On the other hand, it is unjustly maligned by game preservers, for it takes far more vermin than game species.

Although they winter alone, most Goshawks pair for life, and at the start of the breeding season the female returns to the previous year's nesting area where she attracts her mate by screaming persistently. The pair then indulge in aerial display above the nesting area, performing various soaring, diving and swooping manoeuvres, interspersed with periods of level flight with slow, harrier-like wing-beats; the whole being accompanied by much mutual calling.

The nest may be an old one, in which case it is chosen by the female, but if a new one is to be built, the choice appears to be the male's, and he builds it entirely unaided. The female does, however, take some part in the refurbishment of an old nest. The nest is a bulky, flattish, untidy structure of dead twigs, sometimes lined with bark or green conifer-sprigs. It is usually sited in a tree-fork, at a height of between 30 and 65 feet (9 and 20 metres). During nest-building, and the early incubation period, the pair, upon waking, invariably indulge in a period of song, which seems to be almost unique since the majority of birds of prey are totally silent during the early morning. At this time there is also considerable prey-offering to the female by the male, usually in mid-air, accompanied by much loud calling and screaming.

The clutch is usually of three (although it can be of one to five) rough-shelled, unmarked pale blue or off-white eggs. They are laid at three-day intervals, and the 36 to 38 day incubation period, in which the male takes a small part, commences soon after the laying of the first egg. However, experiments have shown that during this early period the incubation temperatures are not high enough to start embryonic development, and the result is an almost simultaneous hatching of the chicks. Up until that time the male does virtually all the hunting for both himself and his mate; however, with the growth of the chicks the female seems to suddenly regain her hunting instinct, and commences to capture prey both for herself and for the chicks. Indeed, a female has been seen to leave the nest and kill a bird which she had obviously seen while brooding. The species is extremely aggressive during the 80 to 90 days that eggs and young are in the nest, and many individuals have been known to strike humans just walking through the nesting wood. Goshawks have no hesitation in attacking anyone foolish enough to attempt to climb up to the nest itself.

Utterly fearless and determined in pursuit of its prey, the Goshawk is capable of amazing aerial agility and, over short distances, astonishing bursts of speed. It will even resort to scrambling along branches or through tangled undergrowth in its relentless desire to make a kill. The species takes prey up to the size of grouse (family Tetraonidae) – to which it is particularly partial – or a young hare, and the kill is effected by a two-footed, vice-like grip. This awsome killing ability is further enhanced by the bird's almost blood-red

Goshawk
Great size, colour pattern and, at close quarters, the red eye easily identify the Goshawk. Its long-tailed, short-winged structure is ideally suited to high-speed manouevring within woodland, which is the species' preferred habitat. (*Map 90*)

eye, which it holds wide and virtually unblinking throughout. The bird is not averse to taking nestling songbirds, returning time and again until it has emptied the nest; it has also been observed wading in shallow water, attempting to catch ducklings, although these last two occurrences are unusual, and are assumed to be the result of food shortage at the time when the male was feeding both the female and her recently hatched young. Usually, the prey is plucked and devoured on the ground, more rarely in a tree, or even an old nest. Often, larger prey items are not consumed in their entirety; after plucking, in the case of a mammal, the stomach is usually removed and rejected, although the other internal organs are eaten. There is some evidence, though records are scarce, that Goshawks occasionally store partially-eated food, and return to it later. This is possibly because, since the species takes a higher proportion of mammalian prey than most other members of the genus, the kill is sometimes simply too big to be swallowed and digested in one meal.

Hawks of Africa and the Far East

Similar in general appearance to the European Goshawk, Henst's Goshawk (*Accipiter henstii*) is, however, very difficult to study since like other forest goshawks, it nearly always remains within cover. Moreover, it is restricted to the more humid and forested parts of Madagascar, from sea level up to 6000 feet (1830m), and is rather uncommon, and thought to be declining. It is rarely seen hunting in the open as it catches most of its prey, consisting of birds and small mammals, within the tree-cover. At the beginning of the breeding season, the pair soar high above the forest in display flights, calling frequently. The only nest so far described was a bulky affair of sticks, lined with dead twigs, sited about 40 feet (12m) up in a tree, and overhanging a small stream in gallery forest. It contained two white eggs in early November, so it is assumed that the species breeds during the dry season, that is, between September and March.

Although distributed throughout all the well-forested areas of Africa south of the Sahara, and up to 10,000 feet (3050m) in the east, the Black Sparrowhawk (*Accipiter melanoleucus*) is nevertheless somewhat uncommon. In its favoured habitat the species is generally silent and unobtrusive, which allows this specialized bird-eater to successfully capture its prey using swift, agile, manoeuvres and chases. Despite taking many medium-sized species, up to the size of the Olive Pigeon (*Columba arquatrix*), the bird seems not to take game-birds, which it obviously could do by darting out from forest-edge cover. On the other hand, it is an amazingly daring poultry thief, returning daily to the same enclosure, and totally ignoring human presence unless positively deterred with the gun!

The species appears not to perform any spectacular aerial displays, and only occasionally soars high above the forest. Nests, built in tall trees at heights between 26 and 130 feet (8 and 40 metres) above ground, are made of sticks, with a copious lining of green leaves. The two to three eggs are incubated mainly by the female, probably for about thirty days, and the young take a further thirty-five or so days to fledge.

Occurring on several islands to the west, north and east of New Guinea, such as the Moluccas, Solomon Islands and New Britain, and doubtless other adjoining islands, the rare Meyer's Goshawk (*Accipiter meyerianus*) is a large, powerful species, which is infrequently observed and usually seen only in flight. The recent record of a bird at about 4600 feet (1400m) in the Kraekte Mountains of New Guinea, indicates that the species' distribution is still imperfectly known. Courtship or display flights, if any, are also not known, and the species' nesting habits have still not been described. Little else is known about the species, but examination of a dead specimen showed it to have consumed a large bird, which may have been a domestic fowl, and possibly indicates a preference for birds as prey. Also, a female taken in the Solomon Islands had enlarged gonads at the end of September, which may indicate the time of breeding.

Like the preceding species, Bürger's Sparrowhawk (*Accipiter buergersi*) is a rare and poorly-known *Accipiter*. It frequents lower mountain forests in eastern New Guinea, between 1600 and 5600 feet (490 and 1700 metres). Displays and nesting habits are unknown, and prey is assumed to be birds.

Hawks of Africa and the Far East
On Madagascar, Henst's Goshawk (2) acts very much like the Goshawk of Europe, being generally similar in size and appearance. In Africa, the Black Sparrowhawk (3) is most easily recognized by its large size, and by the dark upperside contrasting with the white underside. Throughout its range, normal adults of Meyer's Goshawk (1) are distinct from any other hawk: however, on New Guinea, black phase birds could be mistaken for Bürger's Sparrowhawk (4).
(*Maps 91-94*)

Japanese Sparrowhawk and Besra
Long considered a single species, the Japanese Sparrowhawk (1) and the Besra (2) are now recognized as distinct and separate species. The Japanese Sparrowhawk can be distinguished by its lack of a black throat-streak, its paler overall colouring, and its four dark tail-bars.
(Maps 95 and 96)

ASIAN AND ISLAND-DWELLING HAWKS

In many respects very like the Besra, the Japanese Sparrowhawk (*Accipiter gularis*) breeds in the eastern USSR, Japan and China, and winters south through Japan, China and Southeast Asia to the Greater and Lesser Sunda Islands, occasionally as far south as Timor. In winter it is found in all types of open and partially-cleared country, including scrub, mangrove and forest. In its breeding haunts it acts very much like other small sparrowhawks, frequenting woodlands and forests where it takes mainly small or medium-sized birds, for example thrushes; it has, however, also been observed chasing larger birds, such as Green Pigeons (*Treron sieboldii*). The nest, which may be as high as 40 feet (12m) up in a tree, is small, constructed of sticks with a lining of bark and green leaves, and usually contains a clutch of three eggs.

The commonest resident sparrowhawk of the forests of southern Asia, India and parts of Indonesia is the Besra (*Accipiter virgatus*). It is found at altitudes up to 10,000 feet (3050m) in dense mountain forests, westwards from western China to the Himalayas, and from India south to the Andaman Islands, as well as in Borneo, the Philippines, Java and Sumatra.

Northern populations are partly migratory, moving down in winter to the plains of northern India, Indo-China, Hainan, and southern China. The species always hunts in dense woodland, taking a variety of small birds, large insects, and even lizards, which it pursues with surprising speed and boldness. Display takes the form of mutual chases, accompanied by much soaring and calling. Usually, two to four eggs are laid in the stick nest, which has a lining of greenery. Generally it is sited in a tree, on top of an old crow or pigeon nest, or even, perhaps, on a squirrel drey.

Found mainly in the drier parts of the island of Madagascar, up to about 3300 feet (1000m) the uncommon Madagascar Sparrowhawk (*Accipiter madagascariensis*) might almost be considered a half-size version of Henst's Goshawk (*Accipiter henstii*). However, in appearance it is extremely similar to the European Sparrowhawk (*Accipiter nisus*), with general habits and lifestyle somewhat similar. Birds occasionally observed soaring over the breeding area are assumed to be indulging in display flights. The rather flat nest of sticks with a lining of finer twigs is built in a tree, sometimes well away from the trunk, and an average clutch appears to consist of three eggs.

Males of the Celebes Sparrowhawk (*Accipiter nanus*) and Vinous-breasted Sparrowhawk (*Accipiter rhodogaster*) are virtually impossible to tell apart, which causes considerable problems on Sulawesi (Celebes), east of Borneo in Indonesia, where both species occur: on the other hand, females are easily distinguished since those of the Vinous-breasted Sparrowhawk are much larger.

The Celebes Sparrowhawk is a rather rare species, occurring in the mountain forests of Sulawesi, mainly around 3000 to 6500 feet (900 to 2000 metres) where it hunts birds almost exlusively, although it is also known to take grasshoppers, and occasionally even poultry chicks. Nothing is known about the bird's display and breeding behaviour, but a flattish stick-nest, found in a small tree in August, is assumed to belong to this species. Unfortunately,

Island-dwelling Accipiters: 1

The diminutive Madagascar Sparrowhawk (3) looks like a half-size Madagascar Goshawk. Adult males of the Celebes Sparrowhawk (1) are apparently inseparable from those of the Vinous-breasted Sparrowhawk (5), whose female, however, is much larger. Both the Moluccan Sparrowhawk (2) and New Britain Sparrowhawk (4) have chestnut collars, but as they occur on different islands, identification is not a problem.
(*Maps 97-100*)

Cooper's Hawk
Intermediate in size between the Sharp-shinned Hawk and the Goshawk, Cooper's Hawk is the equal of both in the boldness of its hunting methods. Its choice of prey – mainly birds such as flickers and thrushes – reflects the male's size, though the larger female bird will take prey as big as grouse.
(Map 101)

the only evidence of eggs was a single white one, found beneath the nest and presumed to have been dropped by a predator.

Found on the neighbouring islands of Muna, Buton, Peling, and Sula, as well as on Sulawesi, the Vinous-breasted Sparrowhawk inhabits forest, forest edges, mangroves, and groves of Tamarind trees near villages from sea level to over 2000 feet (610m). As the species is extremely similar to the preceding one, it is speculated that its habits are also somewhat similar.

The Moluccan Sparrowhawk (*Accipiter erythrauchen*) is found on the islands of Batjan, Halmahera, Morotai, Obi, Ambon, Ceram and Buru a little farther east. The species has a similar appearance to the Celebes Sparrowhawk, and is to be found from sea level to 4600 feet (1400m). Little else is known about the species, but it is presumed to behave rather like other small sparrowhawks.

Closely related to the preceding Moluccan Sparrowhawk, the New Britain Sparrowhawk (*Accipiter brachyurus*) is endemic to the island of New Britain, east of New Guinea,

Sharp-shinned Hawk
Care should be taken not to confuse the Sharp-shinned Hawk with Cooper's Hawk where the species' ranges overlap. Most easy to distinguish are the differently-sized male Sharp-shinned and female Cooper's.
(*Map 102*)

where it frequents forest edges and partially-cleared areas from around sea level up to at least 3000 feet (900m). It is another little-known species, whose lifestyle and nesting habits are yet to be described.

COOPER'S HAWK AND SHARP-SHINNED HAWK

An exclusively North American species, and in every way a typical *Accipiter*, Cooper's Hawk (*Accipiter cooperii*) ranges from southern Canada, down through the United States as far as northwestern Mexico. However, the species is a partial migrant, and in winter has been recorded as far south as Costa Rica. There is even a single record from Colombia of a Manitoba-ringed bird! The species is always closely associated with woodland, and usually breaks cover only when hunting. The bird takes a variety of prey, including some lizards, amphibians and large insects, but its main prey are birds such as flickers (*Colaptes*), meadow-larks (family Icteridae), thrushes (*Turdus*) and starlings (*Sturnus*), as well as mammals as large as squirrels (*Tamiasciurus*) and chipmunks (*Tamias*). Additionally, since the female is considerably larger than the male, she is able to deal with prey up to the size of Ruffed Grouse (*Bonasa umbellus*). The fairly high incidence of open-country birds in its diet demonstrates that the bird is quite willing to hunt away from woodland. Capture of prey usually takes the form of patient observation from an inconspicuous perch, followed by a sudden swift dash which takes the prey completely by surprise.

Breeding commences with courtship flights, performed by either or both birds, usually above the nest site but not infrequently over open country. The nest, always at least 33 feet (10m) up in a tree, most commonly a conifer, is built almost exclusively by the male, and is constructed of twigs, grasped by the feet whilst in flight, and broken off by the bird's weight and momentum. Following some early morning "duetting" between the pair, and provided the weather is good, the male spends the entire morning nest-building, approaching and departing in low-level flight, with near-vertical ascents and descents to and from the nest. Much of the afternoon is spent in hunting for food for both himself and his mate. Both before and during incubation the cup is lined with bark, and the four or five eggs hatch after about thirty-six days. The young take from 30 to 34 days to fledge, and become independent at about eight weeks.

Another exclusively American species, the Sharp-shinned Hawk (*Accipiter striatus*) is distributed from the tree-limit of North America, down to South Carolina and Alabama, and Nicaragua; it is absent from Panama and Costa Rica, but reappears in the Andes of Venezuela down to eastern Bolivia, northern Argentina, across Paraguay and southern Brazil, and down to Uruguay. Birds breeding in northern North America winter in the central United States south to Costa Rica.

With such an enormous range the bird is found in a variety of habitats, and at widely differing elevations, but it is always a bird of forested country and exhibits a marked preference for conifers. Like many small *Accipiters*, the species' main diet consists of small birds, although it will also take small mammals as well as lizards and insects, and the larger female is capable of dealing with rather bigger prey than her mate. Prey is captured using the usual sudden surprise dash from cover.

Surprisingly, there seems to be little recorded information about display in this species, but it is assumed to be rather like that of other similarly-sized members of the genus. Although deciduous trees are sometimes selected, the nest is most often sited in a conifer, at the point where a number of horizontal limbs meet the trunk. It is a relatively large structure, built of twigs, and with a lining of bark. Both sexes share in the incubation of the four to five eggs, which hatch almost simultaneously after 35 days. The young fledge after a further 24 days, the smaller males being the first to quit the nest. The young are dependent on the parents for a time after fledging, and are probably fully independent after about 18 to 20 days.

GOSHAWKS OF THE TROPICS

The most common medium-sized sparrowhawk in forests and well-wooded areas of Africa south of the Sahara is the African Goshawk (*Accipiter tachiro*). However, the bird is so variable that some authorities have split it into several species. Having a general preference for fairly dense cover, in which it tends to skulk, the bird probably gives the impression of being less common than it really is. It is fond of flying along hedgerows or tree-lines, and then suddenly bursting through or over the cover to take its prey totally by surprise. It preys on birds, mammals, and occasionally lizards, frogs and insects, taking a fair number of its victims on the ground. In breeding display, either or both birds will circle slowly, high above the tree-tops, and intersperse this with glides and wing-flapping, accompanied by much calling; occasionally, the display will culminate in a high-speed dive into the tree-tops. Although an old nest may be re-used, most nests are built anew each year, by both birds, between 23 and 65 feet (7 and 20 metres) high in a densely-foliaged tree. It is small, made of sticks with a lining of leaves and finer twigs, and usually contains two or three eggs, which are incubated by the female alone. They hatch at two- to four-day intervals, after about thirty days, and fledging occurs after a further thirty or so days.

Virtually nothing is known about the habits and life-history of Gray's Goshawk (*Accipiter henicogrammus*), which is resident in the Moluccas, on the islands of Batjan, Halmahera and Morotai. Generally considered as the Moluccan replacement for the Australian Goshawk (*Accipiter fasciatus*), the species seems to be similarly associated with woodland. Also, examination of a dead bird revealed that it had recently eaten a juvenile Scrub Hen (*Megapodius freycinet*), so medium-sized birds presumably form part of the species' diet.

The Grey-throated Goshawk (*Accipiter griseogularis*) is another species which is restricted to the Moluccas, and about which very little is known. It is represented on the islands by three fairly distinct races, which do not seem to interbreed. The species' principal habitat appears to be woodland, and recorded prey include lizards and rats.

Found on the Solomon Islands, the Santa Cruz Islands and the island of Feni, the Pied Goshawk (*Accipiter albogularis*) is another species about which virtually nothing is known concerning life-history and breeding habits. It is thought, at least by some authorities, to form a superspecies with the Black-mantled Accipiter (*Accipiter melanochlamys*), the New Caledonia Sparrowhawk (*Accipiter haplochrous*) and the Fiji Goshawk (*Accipiter rufitorques*). If so, it presumably follows a similar lifestyle, inhabiting woodland and preying, in typical *Accipiter* style, on birds, small mammals and reptiles. The nest has never been found, but is probably built of sticks and concealed high in a well-leafed tree.

Tropical Goshawks
Although superficially similar, the African Goshawk (1) and Grey-throated Goshawk (3) cannot be confused, as the former is African whilst the latter is confined to the Moluccas, where the round-winged, rather weak-footed Gray's Goshawk (2) is also found. The usual form of the Pied Goshawk (4) is not uncommonly replaced by an equally distinctive, and uniformly coloured, slate-grey dark phase.
(*Maps 103-106*)

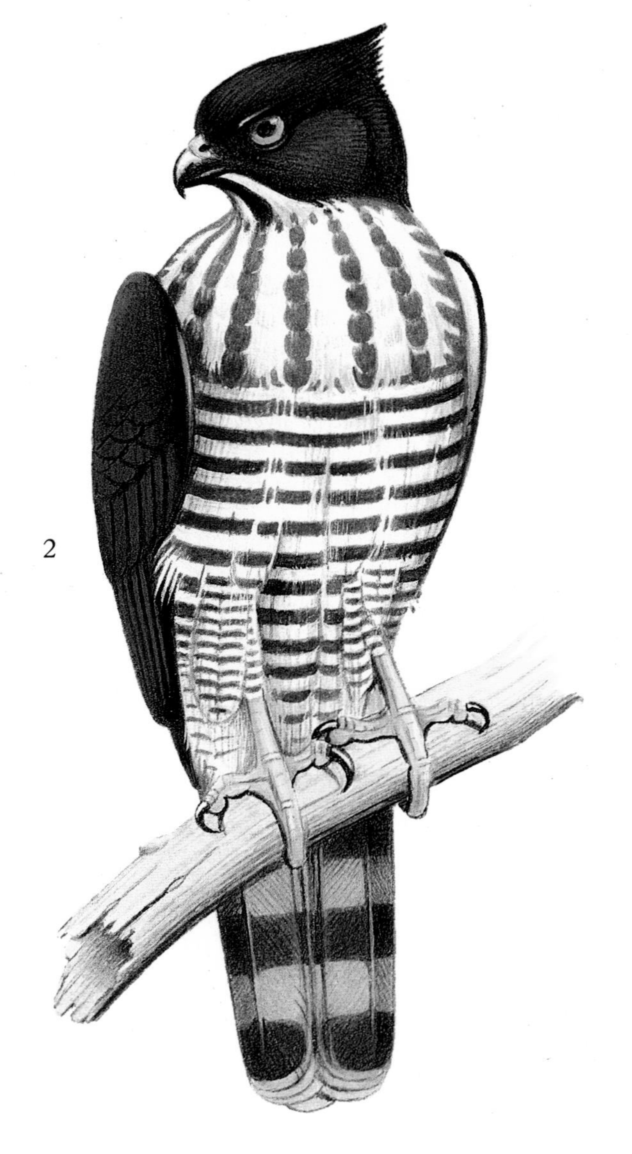

Crested Goshawk and Celebes Crested Goshawk
Considered in some quarters to form a superspecies, or even to be conspecific, the Crested Goshawk (1) and Celebes Crested Goshawk (2) are both small, stockily-built goshawks with powerful legs, short middle toes, and distinctive, crested plumage. (*Maps 107 and 108*)

Hawks of the Far East and South Seas

Found at all altitudes from sea level up to at least 6500 feet (nearly 2000m) in suitable tropical forests, the Crested Goshawk (*Accipiter trivirgatus*) is distributed through south India and Sri Lanka; from south of the Hamalayas east as far as Taiwan and the Philippines; and south to Indonesia. Although somewhat secretive, the species is certainly not shy, and often permits close human approach when perched overlooking some clearing or track, watching for prey. It feeds mainly on birds, but also takes lizards and small mammals, and has even been seen catching bats in Borneo. The leaf-lined stick nest is built high in a tree, and the two or three eggs are generally thought to take less than seventy days from laying to fledging.

A little-known species occurring on Sulawesi and some off-lying islands, the Celebes Crested Goshawk (*Accipiter griseiceps*) is essentially a species of forests, sometimes even of mangroves, and has been known to occasionally wander into areas of cultivation. It feeds on small birds and mammals, as well as lizards and large insects. Nothing else seems to be known of this robust little *Accipiter's* life-history or breeding cycle, although a single stick nest, similar to that of a Goshawk (*Accipiter gentilis*), has been found built in a fork of a small tree.

A species with a very similar distribution to that of the preceding species, the Spot-tailed Accipiter (*Accipiter trinotatus*) is also extremely poorly known. Throughout its range it is a bird of virgin forest and mangroves, with a tendency to remain in deep cover; it is therefore difficult to observe and study. Usually its presence is detected by its voice, which is unlike that of any other *Accipiter* on the islands, and is described as a "*hee*" note, given, with pauses, four to six times. The bird is also reputed to give a cat-like "*miaow*". Although it is known to prey on small lizards and snakes, as well as birds, bats, frogs, snails and grasshoppers, its long leg bones and short toes are thought to be adaptations for reptile-hunting.

Apparently restricted to the mountains of New Britain,

Island-dwelling Accipiters: 2

Deriving its name from its distinctively-marked tail, the Spot-tailed Accipiter (2) has long legs and short toes, adapted for ground feeding. In its native forests, the black, slate-grey and white patterned New Caledonia Sparrowhawk (5) is a ferocious bird-predator. The Blue and Grey Sparrowhawk (1) of New Britain has obvious bluish-black upperparts, and faintly-barred whitish underparts. The black and chestnut plumage of the handsome Black-mantled Accipiter (3) is very distinctive, as is the normal black-breasted phase of the Imitator Sparrowhawk (4), but in its white-breasted and black phases, confusion with the Pied Goshawk may arise.

(*Maps 108-112*)

Sparrowhawk
Over much of its range, this is the only Accipiter of its size – a dashing, agile and versatile hunter of birds, small mammals, lizards and large insects. In this species the degree of sexual dimorphism is striking both in size and in colour.
(Map 113)

the Blue and Grey Sparrowhawk (*Accipiter luteoschistaceus*) is yet another *Accipiter* about which almost nothing at all is known. Presumably feeding methods are much as in other similar members of the genus, but breeding habits must remain purely speculative.

An uncommon mountain forest bird, found only in New Guinea, the very distinctive Black-mantled Accipiter (*Accipiter melanochlamys*) lives at altitudes from 5000 to 11,500 feet (1520 to 3500 metres). The difficult terrain that the species has chosen as its habitat makes observation and study extremely difficult, and as a result, virtually nothing is known about any aspect of its lifestyle. It is known, however, to hunt in forests and occasionally through cultivated areas, in much the same way as many other members of the genus.

The jungle-covered islands of Choiseul and Ysabel in the Solomon Islands are the home of the distinctive Imitator Sparrowhawk (*Accipiter imitator*), which seems to have no really close relatives. Apart from its typical form, the species has both a white-breasted phase and a black phase, which are almost indistinguishable, in the field, from similar forms of the Pied Goshawk (*Accipiter albogularis*). This, combined with the almost impenetrable nature of the bird's habitat, makes field studies of the species virtually impossible, resulting in there being no information available concerning the bird's breeding and life-history.

As its name suggests, the New Caledonia Sparrowhawk (*Accipiter haplochrous*) is endemic to the island of New Caledonia, where it inhabits dense forests. It is known to be a ferocious and determined predator on birds. One individual is recorded as having pursued a domestic fowl into a kitchen, while another was observed attempting to capture a parrot of almost its own size. Other recorded prey include lizards and grasshoppers. Unfortunately, this appears to be the current extent of our knowledge of the species.

Sparrowhawk and Levant Sparrowhawk

Widespread throughout almost the entire Old World, north of the tropics up to the Arctic Circle, and from the Canaries across to western China and southern Kamchatka, the Sparrowhawk (*Accipiter nisus*) is closely associated with all types of woodland, and even with open country with scattered clumps of trees. Birds from the north of the range migrate south for the winter into Africa, sometimes as far as the Equator, and into India and Burma.

Levant Sparrowhawk
The grey rather than rufous cheeks, red eye, and more heavily-barred underparts should help to separate the Levant Sparrowhawk from the Sparrowhawk, which, in their area of overlap, it replaces at lower altitudes. It can be distinguished from the Shikra of tropical Asia and Southern Africa by the greater number of dark inner-tail bars.
(Map 114)

The species may appear less common than it really is, for it spends much of its time perched in cover, and is therefore easily overlooked. When hunting prey, which is mostly birds, but with some small mammals and occasional insects and lizards, the bird employs the usual *Accipiter* method of an unobtrusive approach, with a sudden change of speed and direction to totally surprise its victim. All prey is killed by crushing in the feet, and due to her greater size the female is able to take larger prey than her mate. The species is capable of extremely high-speed short-distance flight, with amazingly agile manoeuvrings, and so determined is it in the chase, that it has been known to crash into buildings, and even to break windows, sometimes resulting in its own demise.

Single birds are occasionally seen lazily wheeling and soaring high in the sky, and this seems to be just sheer enjoyment; in display, however, both birds soar and swoop over the breeding area, with shallow undulations and steep dives. The somewhat untidy stick nest, built by both birds, is usually sited between 20 and 50 feet (6 and 15 metres) up, near the trunk of a tree, a conifer being selected whenever possible. Since the four or five eggs are laid at two-day intervals (or longer), and incubation, by the female alone, only commences with the second or third egg, it takes between 39 and 42 days for the last egg to hatch. The female goes through her moult during this period. The staggered hatching results in some size differences between the chicks, and they fledge after 24 to 30 days, the smaller, thinner-tarsused males departing first. The fledglings remain in the vicinity, dependent on their parents, for about a further four weeks.

With a much smaller breeding range than the previous species, the Levant Sparrowhawk (*Accipiter brevipes*) seems not to interact with that species, despite the fact that much of its range overlaps with that of the Sparrowhawk. Levant Sparrowhawks breed east from the Balkans across to Astrakhan, and south to Asia Minor, migrating in winter to Iran, Syria, Palestine and Egypt, and some individuals have been known to reach the Sudan and Tanzania.

Although easily confused with the Sparrowhawk, the species' hunting and breeding habits are somewhat different. Found mostly along wooded river valleys, it tends to hunt low over the ground, with a sudden dash from cover; or, a pair may beat along the clear edge of wooded land. The species preys mainly on small birds and ground mammals, with the occasional bat; adults also take a few insects, but immature birds take large numbers.

Display seems not to have been recorded in this species, but if it occurs, would presumably be similar to that of its close relatives. The nest, invariably in a deciduous tree, is sited some 16 to 33 feet (5 to 10 metres) up, and is a small, loosely-knit structure, with a lining of green leaves. The female alone incubates the three to five eggs for 30 to 35 days, and the young are assumed to fledge after 40 to 45 days. The young remain in the vicinity for about a further fifteen days, and once independent they set off on their southerly migration.

ISLAND HAWKS OF THE INDO-PACIFIC REGION

Occurring on all the large to medium-sized islands (possibly including Rotuma) in the Fiji group, the Fiji Goshawk (*Accipiter rufitorques*) is the only endemic *Accipiter* there, and is unlikely to be confused with the only other two endemic hawks, namely the Peregrine Falcon and the Marsh Harrier. It is widespread throughout a variety of habitats, from dense forest to urban parks, where it may be seen preying on small birds, lizards and large insects. The loosely-constructed nest, built of sticks, with some greenery, but without any lining, is placed up to 80 feet (24m) high in a tree, and may contain up to three eggs. Other aspects of the bird's breeding behaviour, and display (if any), have still to be studied.

The striking New Guinea Grey-headed Goshawk (*Accipiter poliocephalus*), endemic to New Guinea, its western satellite islands, and some eastern satellites (Fergusson and Misima), occurs from near sea level up to 3300 feet (1000m). It frequents forest, secondary growth, gallery forests and forest edges, where it is reasonably common. It is inconspicuous, and is usually seen singly, perched or in flight, near forest edges, where prey items include large insects and small reptiles. The species is not reported to soar like many other *Accipiters*, and breeding and nesting habits are still not known.

Slightly larger than the preceding species, but otherwise very similar, the New Britain Grey-headed Goshawk (*Accipiter princeps*) may possibly be simply a race of the former. Endemic to the island of New Britain, the bird is known only from mountain forests between 2500 and 4750 feet (750 and 1450 metres). It is apparently very uncommon, and details of its feeding and breeding habits must, at least for the present, remain purely speculative.

Breeding across central, eastern and southern China, in Korea, and on Taiwan, the Grey Frog Hawk (*Accipiter soloensis*) is a very small *Accipiter*, which winters mainly south to Burma, Thailand, the Philippines, northern Sulawesi, the Greater Sunda islands, Moluccas, and occasionally to the western Papuan Islands. Some northern birds may, however, winter in southern China and Hainan. As its name suggests, the bird has a preference for frogs, which it stoops on, either from a perch or while on the wing. This habit means it does not need to employ the speed and stealth normally associated with sparrowhawks, and the bird will also take lizards and large insects. The species is found, at lower altitudes, in open woodlands near swampy ground or rice paddies, and being a sociable species, once arrived at the breeding areas, males can be seen, often in small groups, repeatedly pursuing females. In display, the male performs vigorous undulating climbs and spectacular steep dives, and although pairs are very obvious at this time, often calling and soaring together, they are much less in evidence once nesting has begun. Each year, a new nest is built, and being a loose and flimsy structure of twigs, with a lining of green leaves, and occasionally bark, it is constructed remarkably quickly. It is built in a tree, usually between 20 and 40 feet (6 to 12 metres) up; sometimes as high as 65 feet (20m). The female alone incubates the three or four eggs for rather less than thirty days, and the young fledge in about the same time.

Being the only *Accipiter* on the Nicobar Islands, the Nicobar Shikra (*Accipiter butleri*) cannot be confused with any other species there. It is very similar to the Shikra (*Accipiter badius*), with which several authors have merged it. Although not rare, the species is somewhat shy and

Island-dwelling Accipiters: 3
A common small sparrowhawk of the Far East, the Grey Frog Hawk (1) can be identified by its rufous-washed underparts, as well as by its liking for frogs. The very similar New Britain Grey-headed Goshawk (4) and New Guinea Grey-headed Goshawk (5) may prove to be conspecific. With the Peregrine and Marsh Harrier the only other hawks on Fiji, there is no difficulty in identifying the Fiji Goshawk (3), the most easterly Polynesian *Accipiter*. The Nicobar Shikra (2) is the only small sparrowhawk in the area, and is impossible to confuse with any other species.
(*Maps 115-119*)

retiring, and its habit of frequenting the tops of tall trees (from which it often calls) makes it difficult to observe. Its prey appears to consist mainly of lizards, and it is thought to breed twice a year, nesting 50 to 65 feet (15 to 20 metres) up in a tree. The tree-top calling referred to above is believed to be part of the breeding display.

TINY SPARROWHAWK

The smallest member of the genus *Accipiter* is the aptly-named Tiny Sparrowhawk (*Accipiter superciliosus*), found in tropical and sub-tropical areas of Central and South America. Its range extends from southeastern Nicaragua to Ecuador and eastern Peru; east to the Guianas and Brazil; and south to Paraguay and northern Argentina. The bird inhabits scrubby forest-edges, thickets and woodland clearings, usually not flying much above 33 feet (10m) above the ground. Little else seems to have been learned about its life-history, but a clutch of three eggs has been collected, in Brazil, from a nest in a tall tree.

FRANCE'S SPARROWHAWK

A small species, occurring on Madagascar and the Comoro Islands, France's Sparrowhawk (*Accipiter francesii*) is found mostly in forests and woodlands, and also in savannas up to 6500 feet (2000m); it is, however, not so common in the drier southwest of Madagascar. Unusually for a species in this genus, prey, consisting of reptiles (especially chameleons), large insects and a few birds, is mostly taken on the ground. Also, it is much more prone to perching in the open, and is remarkably tolerant and confiding of human approach. Another odd feature of the species' lifestyle is that pairs are often seen together, even in the non-breeding season. The large nest, made of sticks, is sited 33 to 50 feet (10 to 15 metres) up, usually in a forest tree, but occasionally in an isolated situation. The normal clutch would seem to be three or four eggs, apparently incubated solely by the female. Display, and other details of the species' life-history, have not been observed.

HAWKS OF CENTRAL AND SOUTH AMERICA

A rare species of humid or wet forests, with a very restricted South American range, the American Collared Sparrowhawk (*Accipiter collaris*) is known from only a few localities in Colombia and Ecuador, with one record each

Tiny Sparrowhawk
Very aptly named, the Tiny Sparrowhawk of South America is identifiable not only by its small size, but also by its finely-barred underside.
(*Map 120*)

American and African Sparrowhawks
Probably the Tiny Sparrowhawk's subtropical representative, the American Collared Sparrowhawk (1) differs in being more heavily barred, and having a white collar. The robust Grey-bellied Goshawk (5) differs from the following two species by lacking the rufous thighs. The Bicoloured Sparrowhawk (3) and Gundlach's Hawk (4) seem to form a superspecies with Cooper's Hawk; however, this may never be proven, since Gundlach's Hawk is extremely rare, and possibly even extinct. Unusually for an *Accipiter*, France's Sparrowhawk (2) takes a great deal of its prey on the ground.
(*Maps 121-125*)

Shikra
Most easily identified by the regular chestnut underside barring and the almost uniformly grey tail, the Shikra is nevertheless one of the more difficult birds of prey to identify in many parts of its extensive range across tropical Asia and southern Africa.
(Map 126)

from Venezuela and Peru. Its breeding and feeding habits are, as yet, unknown.

A rather secretive species which has suffered from deforestation and persecution, Gundlach's Hawk (*Accipiter gundlachi*) is endemic to Cuba and superficially resembles Cooper's Hawk (*Accipiter cooperii*) of North America. It frequents forest edges, swamps, wooded coasts and mountains below 2600 feet (800m). Little else is known about the species, although the eggs are said to be unspotted.

With a South American range extending from southern Mexico, south in the Andes to Tierra del Fuego and in the east to Paraguay and northern Argentina, the Bicoloured Sparrowhawk (*Accipiter bicolor*) is mainly found in forested areas up to 6500 feet (2000m), most commonly in second-growth deciduous forest. The species seems to prefer broken woodland with clearings and open forest edges where it can most easily hunt small to medium-sized birds, either from a favoured perch or by agile and rapid pursuit. The nest is a well-built structure, of both green and dry sticks, and also other materials, placed fairly high in a tree near a clearing, or at the forest edge. In Chile, the bird lays four eggs, which the female incubates for about twenty-one days; it is assumed, however, that fewer eggs are laid in the tropics. Throughout its extensive range it exhibits a good deal of geographical variation, and some of its currently-recognized five races have sometimes been regarded as separate species.

Apparently rare throughout its entire range, the Grey-bellied Goshawk (*Accipiter poliogaster*) is found in lowland forest areas of South America, including Surinam, the Guianas, Venezuela, Colombia, Ecuador, Peru, Brazil, Paraguay and Argentina. It has been found in humid lowland forest, riparian forest edges, and in patches of dense woodland. In Colombia it has only been recorded during the austral winter, suggesting that it is a migrant from the south. So strikingly different is the immature plumage, bearing a remarkable resemblance to the adult Ornate Hawk Eagle (*Spizaetus ornatus*), that until recently it was considered a separate species (*Accipiter pectoralis*). There appears to be little else known about the habits of this stockily-built goshawk.

SHIKRA

A fairly common and widespread bird of the savannas, wooded grasslands and cultivated areas of tropical Asia, and Africa south of the Sahara, the Shikra (*Accipiter badius*) has

African Sparrowhawks
The small-headed Ovampo Sparrowhawk (1), is probably often overlooked due to its superficial resemblance to the Gabar Goshawk. The Rufous-breasted Sparrowhawk (2) is a fast-flying and aggressive bird-hunter of eastern and southern Africa. The smallest African sparrowhawk, the African Little Sparrowhawk (3) has a rather plump appearance, and is often surprisingly tame, as is the Red-thighed Sparrowhawk (4), which some authorities treat as a race of the former. A typical forest *Accipiter*, the Chestnut-bellied Sparrowhawk (5) is difficult to observe, due to its shy and skulking habits.
(*Maps 127-131*)

both migratory and non-migratory populations. West African birds move south to breed in the dry season (October to March), and return north in the rains (April to September); similarly, the northern Asian populations travel to India and Malaya for the winter. The species takes a variety of birds, from sparrow-size up to doves or quail, as well as small mammals, lizards, frogs, locusts, dragonflies, and winged termites. It prefers to hunt by dashing out rapidly from cover, and takes most of its prey from the ground, although it is not averse to catching some on the wing. In nuptial display, the male flies over the tree-tops, with fluttering wings, occasionally rising and falling, and sometimes being joined by his mate, at which time the pair indulge in noisy and spectacular aerobatics. The often small and somewhat flimsy nest is made of rather thin sticks, with a sparse lining of green leaves, and is sited at any height from 16 to 65 feet (5 to 20 metres), well out on a side-branch. Current observations suggest it is built solely by the female, who incubates the two to four eggs, for 30 to 35 days, also totally unaided. Unfortunately, there is no information on the development of the chicks, but fledging seems to take longer than thirty days.

SPARROWHAWKS OF AFRICA

Superficially resembling the more common Gabar Goshawk (*Melierax gabar*), the rather rare Ovampo Sparrowhawk (*Accipiter ovampis*) is found in Africa from Ghana east to Ethiopia, and south to eastern Transvaal and Namibia. Possibly it is merely a migrant to western Africa, since breeding has only been confirmed in the species' southern African range. Its habitat is semi-arid broad-leaved savanna and thornbush veld, and the bird avoids forest and very dry areas. An apparently shy and retiring species, it seems to prefer to remain within dense cover, where it hunts mainly birds up to the size of the smaller doves, as well as some insects and small mammals, which are usually taken on the

Variable Goshawk: 1 Ranging from Tasmania in the south, through western and northern Australia to various islands to the north and west, the Variable Goshawk has a bewildering number of colour and size forms, some of which may be distinct species. In its typical all-white form, it is unmistakable as it lurks in cover, watching for prey which it hunts in more or less typical *Accipiter* fashion. (*Map 132*)

ground. Display appears not to have been described in detail, but is thought to include calling from the tops of tall trees. The nest is usually built in a dense tree, and is a small platform of sticks, sometimes with a lining of bark. It is known that the usual clutch is two or three eggs, but no other breeding details have been recorded.

Closely related to the European Sparrowhawk (*Accipiter nisus*), the Rufous-breasted Sparrowhawk (*Accipiter rufiventris*) is found in eastern and southern Africa, from Ethiopia south to the Cape, normally inhabiting both deciduous and evergreen forests and plantations (up to 12,000 feet (3660m) in Ethiopia). Prey, which ranges from passerines to small domestic fowl, with a few small mammals and sometimes termites, is captured with a quick dash from a perch, and taken either in flight or on the ground. An alternative method is for the bird to fly swiftly behind covering vegetation and then shoot over the top in a surprise attack, often capturing a bird on the other side off-guard. Outside the breeding season the species is generally shy and unobtrusive, and even when breeding the birds do not appear to perform any spectacular aerial displays, although the pair may circle high over the nesting area, calling frequently. The nest, often built in a fir, is small, constructed of sticks, and may be as high as 50 feet (15m) above the ground. It is jealously guarded by both birds, and human intruders may be attacked vehemently. The incubation period of the two to four eggs is unknown, but fledging of the chicks, which appear to hatch over a few days, is known to take about twenty-five days.

The smallest African *Accipiter*, the African Little

Variable Goshawk: 2
The name of this bird is a masterly understatement. A bewildering variation in size and plumage is the hallmark of the species right across its wide geographical range. The forms illustrated here are a grey race (1), the white form of the Australian race (2), and a vinous-chested race (3), but many other variants occur – mostly isolated on small islands in Southeast Asia.
(Map 133)

Sparrowhawk (*Accipiter minullus*) is instantly recognized, throughout its eastern and southern African range, due to its very small size. It occurs from sea level up to 6500 feet (2000m), in habitats ranging from forest to thornbush. Although somewhat shy, once located, the bird is usually tame and confiding, and will tolerate close approach. When hunting, the bird is extremely swift, and capable of surprising agility. Its prey consists of small birds, insects, and some small mammals and reptiles. Increased early morning calling, and carrying of nest material on fluttering wings, appears to be the extent of courtship display. The female gathers most of the nest material, but the small nest, often placed as high as 80 feet (24m) in a tall tree, is built by both birds. It is poorly-constructed, and much material falls to the ground. The small cup is not lined until the 30- to 32-day incubation period of the two to three eggs commences. This task is mainly the duty of the female, although the male does play his part. Fledging takes a further 25 to 26 days, and the young are dependent on the parents for at least a week after quitting the nest.

Very similar to the preceding species, the Red-thighed Sparrowhawk (*Accipiter erythropus*) is a retiring and little-known species, inhabiting dense West African forests, from the Gambia to Cameroon, the Congo and western Uganda, and southward to Angola. The bird mainly hunts small birds and some large insects, much as the preceding species. What little else is known about the bird makes it inseparable from the previous species, and more research is needed to substantiate the bird's status.

Another little-known species, the Chestnut-bellied Sparrowhawk (*Accipiter castanilius*) is resident in the dense forests of West Africa, from Nigeria and Cameroon eastward to eastern Congo. It is a secretive species, keeping to dense cover except when it briefly enters forest clearings to hunt small birds, lizards, and mammals, and it is a fearless thief of domestic poultry. No other details have been recorded.

VARIABLE GOSHAWK

Inhabiting Australia, New Guinea and a number of adjacent islands, the appropriately-named Variable Goshawk (*Accipiter novaehollandiae*) exhibits great racial variation in both size and colour, and some twenty races are currently recognized. In Papua New Guinea four colour phases are

Australian Goshawk
Strong underside barring is usually sufficient to separate this species from the otherwise similar Variable Goshawk, while in flight the underside generally appears paler and less heavily barred than that of the Australian Collared Sparrowhawk.
(Map 134)

found – normal-phase adults having the upperparts, including the crown and sides of the head, brownish-grey, and the underparts rufous to reddish-brown, with or without paler barring. A pure-white phase, found only on the mainland, is similar to birds found in northern Australia, although the latter are slightly larger. Adults of the two rare dark phases are either entirely dark leaden-grey, or dark grey above and chestnut below.

Ranging west to the Moluccas and Sumbawa (Indonesia) and east to the Solomon Islands, in general the paler forms are found in the more western parts of the range while the darkest forms occur in the Solomons. The more vinous-chested forms, for example *rubianae, rufoschistaceus,* and *bouganvillei,* are found on islands such as New Georgia, Rendovo, Choiseul and Bougainville. These races have unbarred, plain rufous-chestnut or vinous underparts, and have often been referred to as the Vinous-chested Goshawk.

In Australia the Variable Goshawk has a pure-white phase known as the White Goshawk, which predominates in the southeast, and again becomes more common in the Kimberley region of the northwest. In Tasmania, the breeding population consists entirely of white-phase birds. The Australian subspecies *A. n. novaehollandiae* breeds in forest, including the mangrove fringe, in the north, but is mainly found in forested areas adjacent to the coast in the east and southeast. In different areas, the proportion of white to grey birds varies, with grey-plumaged individuals generally predominating in the more interior parts of the range. However, birds of either phase may interbreed, although intermediate-plumaged birds are rare. Grey birds are generally more numerous in heavily-forested regions, especially in the northeast, while white birds are found in more lightly-wooded areas. It has often been remarked that the White Goshawk bears a remarkable similarity to a white cockatoo, both perched and in flight. It often occurs in areas where flocks of Sulphur-crested Cockatoos (*Cacatua galerita*) are quite common, so the disguise of white plumage probably enables it to escape detection more easily when hunting. This species is more powerful and thickset than the Australian Goshawk (*Accipiter fasciatus*).

Variable Goshawks can be found singly or in pairs in Australia, and particularly favour tree-lined watercourses. On occasions, birds may be seen soaring and circling high over the terrain, and they can be readily identified in flight by their characteristic broad wings, rounded, fanned tail, and very pale underparts and underwings. The species is a bold hunter, flying directly in pursuit of its prey, striking at incredible speed, and taking unwary birds by surprise, often in ambush. Grey Goshawks attack their victims both in the air and on the ground, usually preying on small birds, mammals, snakes and other reptiles, and also taking some large insects. The female, being a little larger than the male,

Doria's Goshawk, Red Goshawk and Collared Sparrowhawk
Doria's Goshawk (1) is found only in New Guinea, and is unlike any other indigenous species there; the Red Goshawk (2) and Australian Collared Sparrowhawk (3) have similar ranges, but their plumages are totally different.
(Maps 135–137)

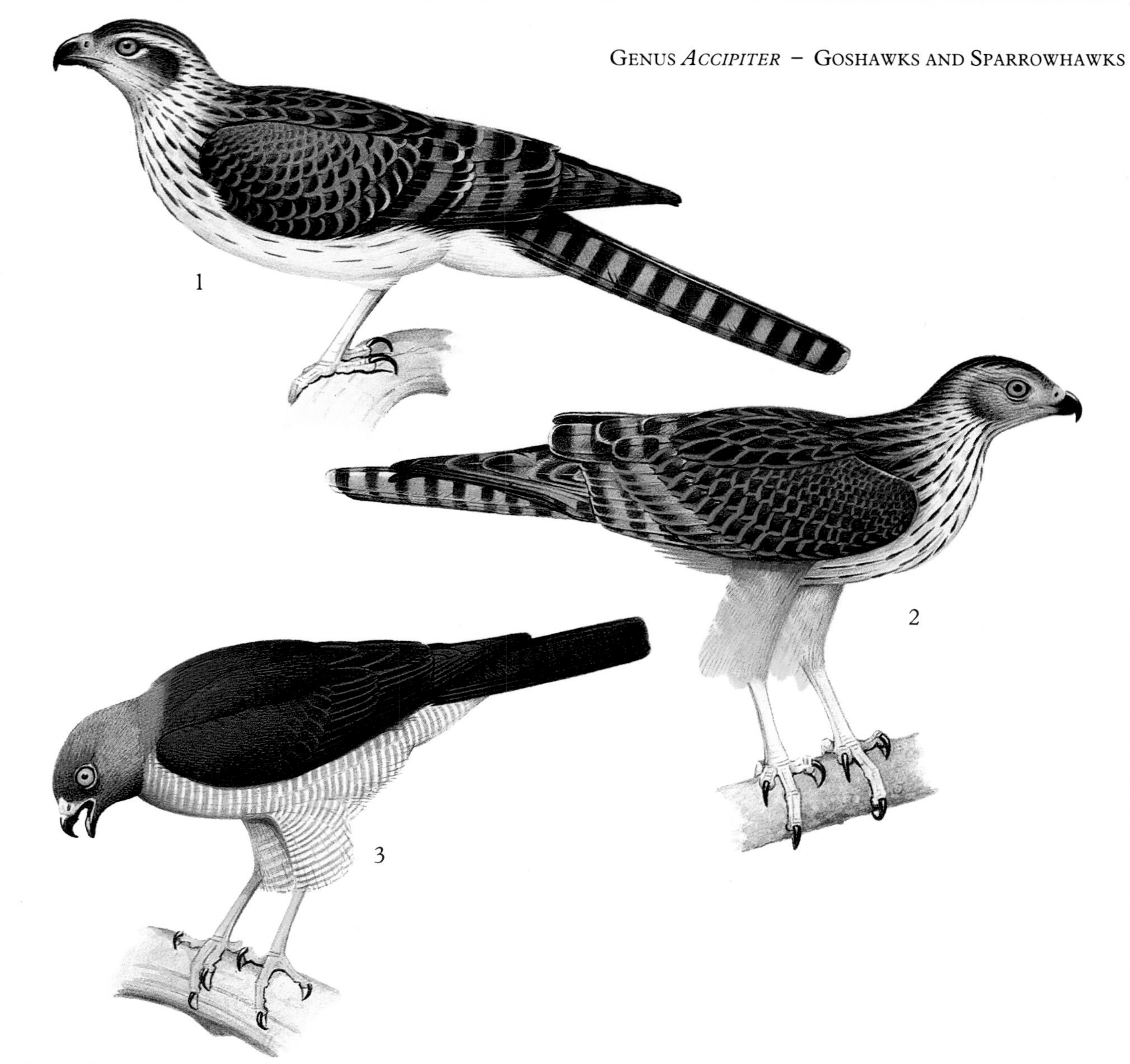

is able to take larger prey, such as currawongs and parrots. In the breeding season, paired birds indulge in display flights which include swooping, circling on downcurved wings, and flying in close proximity. The substantial nest is placed high in a tree, usually from 30 to 100 feet (9 to 30 metres) above the ground. It is constructed mainly of sticks, lined with twigs and leaves, and is built by both sexes. The female generally incubates the two to four whitish eggs, and after hatching she closely guards the young while the male hunts and brings prey to the nest for both her and the young. The fledging period is not recorded, although it is probably similar to that of other medium-sized hawks.

THE GOSHAWKS OF AUSTRALIA

A typically large, fierce and aggressive *Accipiter*, the Australian Goshawk (*Accipiter fasciatus*) is common throughout Australia and Tasmania, and is also found in New Guinea and Indonesia and on nearby islands. In Australia it inhabits various types of open savanna woodland, but avoids the denser forests. Island populations seem to prefer even more open terrain; they are associated with woodland clearings, and occasionally hunt over open hillsides. Prey, which includes various birds and their young, mammals such as young rabbits, snakes, lizards, frogs and large insects, are usually taken on the ground, but the hawk will also take birds on the wing. When hunting, the Australian Goshawk is stealthy and silent, moving through dense cover in short flights. This skulking behaviour makes it difficult to observe, and also makes it appear less common than it really is.

Details of the species' display appear not to have been recorded. The nest, sited 80 feet (24m) or more up in a large tree, and made of sticks with a lining of green leaves, is built by both birds. The two to four eggs are incubated mainly by the female, with the male taking a minor part. Incubation lasts for about thirty days, and fledging may take in excess of fifty days.

Restricted to the New Guinea mainland, Doria's Hawk (*Megatriorchis doriae*) is widely but thinly distributed in the forest interior, from sea level up to 4600 feet (1400m), and sometimes even higher. It is an inconspicuous, medium-sized hawk which due to its somewhat secretive habits is not often observed. Although it does not soar, it is occasionally seen flying at the forest edge or over the tree-tops, and is known to prey on smaller birds, up to the size of the Lesser Bird of Paradise (*Paradisaea minor*). The bird often perches quietly for long periods on the same branch, and may call from time to time. The usual call is described as a

Long-tailed Hawk
A long, white-spotted tail and white-rumped dark plumage are all that distinguish this rather secretive and little-known species.
(Map 138)

distinctive, long drawn-out, descending hissing whistle. The species' nesting and breeding habits remain unknown.

A rare breeding bird of the forests and woodlands of north and northeastern Australia, the Red Goshawk (*Erythrotriorchis radiatus*) is found in tropical open woodland, rainforest edges, and dense riverine vegetation. It is a large, powerful and rapacious hawk, with an extremely rapid flight, and is capable of killing large birds such as ducks and cockatoos; other prey items include small herons, lizards and nestlings of other birds. Being very thinly distributed throughout its range, the species is probably the rarest Australian bird of prey, and is seldom seen. The large stick nest is apparently constructed by the female alone. It is sited high in a tree, and normally contains one or two eggs. Other details of the bird's life-history are still, as yet, unknown.

Widely distributed in Australia and Tasmania, and on New Guinea and a few neighbouring islands, the Collared Sparrowhawk (*Accipiter cirrhocephalus*) is a bird of woodland and scrub, and even tree-scattered desert areas and wooded gorges where pools attract small birds. It preys principally on small to medium-sized birds, hunted in woodland or open country, and being an active, bold and fierce hawk, it is capable of taking quite large prey compared to its own small size. Being a difficult species to observe, details of display and mating have not yet been recorded. The platform nest of small twigs, with a lining of green leaves, is most often sited at a height of 23 feet (7m) or more, most often in a eucalyptus tree. Where tall trees are available, the nest is usually inaccessible. It is presumed that the two to four eggs are incubated by the female unaided, and incubation and fledging periods have yet to be confirmed.

AFRICAN FOREST AND SAVANNA HAWKS

A rather skulking and little-known species, confined to the Upper and Lower Guinea forest of western and central Africa, the Long-tailed Hawk (*Urotriorchis macrourus*) looks very like an *Accipiter* except for its enormously long tail, which exceeds the total length of its head and body. It lives mainly in dense tall canopy, where it is difficult to observe, but very occasionally individuals may be seen flying across clearings and roads. Prey items include arboreal mammals such as squirrels, rodents and forest birds, and it has also been reported taking poultry from around African villages. The species' breeding habits and nest have not been described.

Inhabiting the arid bushlands and drier woodlands of Africa, from Senegal to Sudan, south to Angola, north-eastern Natal and eastern Transvaal, as well as south-western Morocco and Saudi Arabia, the Dark Chanting Goshawk (*Melierax metabates*) spends most of the daylight hours perched on tree-tops, tall termite mounds or telegraph poles. From such natural and man-made vantage-points it

African Goshawks and Lizard Buzzard
All confined to Africa, the very similar Dark (1), Pale (2) and Southern (3) Chanting Goshawks more or less replace each other, with some overlap, in suitable habitat, whilst the Gabar Goshawk (4) co-exists with them all as it specializes in bird prey, rather than in catching terrestrial vertebrates and insects. In the same way, the largely reptilian diet of the Lizard Buzzard (5) seems to allow it to exist without conflict alongside all the other species depicted here.
(Maps 139–142)

Grasshopper Buzzard
As its name implies, the Grasshopper Buzzard is largely an insect-feeder. It is especially partial to grasshoppers, and can catch its prey either on the wing or on the ground. It is a frequent and often numerous attendant at bush-fires, capitalizing on the fleeing insects and small mammals. (*Map 143*)

watches intently for its prey below, which consists mainly of lizards. Most prey is caught in a quick swoop to the ground. At other times, the bird will also walk about on the ground, when due to its long tail and legs it gives the impression of a miniature Secretary Bird. It is also capable of running quite fast. Prey items consist mainly of lizards, small snakes, small ground mammals and large insects, and the occasional game-bird or dove. This bird can be confused only with the Pale Chanting Goshawk, and where the two overlap it is normally distinguished by its generally darker grey colour, brighter red legs and cere, and barred rather than pure-white uppertail-coverts.

Early in the breeding season the male perches conspicuously on top of a tree and "chants" repeatedly. The call is a clear melodious whistling "*wheeeo-whew-whew-whew*", or "*wheee-pee-pee-pee*". He may also soar over the breeding area, either alone or with the female. Both sexes build the nest, usually in a thorny acacia. One to two pale bluish eggs are laid, and are incubated by the female, but usually only one young survives. The incubation and fledging periods are apparently not known.

Closely resembling the preceding species in both habits and plumage, the Pale Chanting Goshawk (*Melierax musicus*) is, however, associated with more arid, less wooded country. Its range in Africa is discontinuous, with two widely separated areas of distribution; one in the northeast, extending from Somalia, Ethiopia and northeastern Kenya, south to Tanzania, and the other ranging across southern and southwestern Africa. Prey is almost invariably caught on the ground following a short, quick swoop from a perch, and is then carried back to the perch to be dealt with. The bird catches mainly lizards, but will also take small mammals, birds and large insects.

A much smaller bird than the chanting goshawks, with a relatively longer tail and shorter legs, the Gabar Goshawk (*Melierax gabar*) is widespread in savanna and bush country throughout Africa south of the Sahara. In appearance and habits it resembles a small *Accipiter*, and preys largely on small birds, which it catches in flight. The species is dimorphic, one form being grey with white barring below, and the other mostly black.

The stiff plumage and relatively long legs of the Lizard

The *Butastur* Buzzards of Asia
The bright chestnut wings and tail of the Rufous-winged Buzzard (1) make it impossible to confuse with any other species within its range. At close range, the white eye of the White-eyed Buzzard (2), combined with the pale wing-patch, black-streaked white chin and throat, are equally diagnostic. The grey head, black-streaked white chin and throat, yellow eye and cere, and broadly-barred tail help to distinguish the Grey-faced Buzzard from its relatives in their small area of overlap in Southeast Asia (3). *(Maps 144–146)*

Buzzard (*Kaupifalco monogrammicus*) are probably adaptations for catching prey in the tall grass of its preferred habitat, namely the denser kinds of savanna and thornbush of Africa south of the Sahara. Commonly seen perched on some favourite vantage-point, such as a bare branch, the bird will make a swift plunge to the ground to seize its prey, which includes snakes, lizards, small mammals and birds, and larger insects. It has also been accused of taking domestic poultry, but this has yet to be proved conclusively. Although some prey is eaten on the ground, most is dealt with back at the perch. Other birds generally pay little heed to this hawk, and do not mob it.

THE GRASSHOPPER BUZZARD AND ITS RELATIVES

The four species of *Butastur* buzzard replace each other geographically, except for a small area of overlap in Southeast Asia. All are of similar size and plumage.

An ecologically specialized hawk of open savanna and grassland, feeding entirely on insects caught either on the ground or in flight, the Grasshopper Buzzard (*Butastur rufipennis*) is found in Africa from Senegal east to Somalia, and south to Kenya and northern Tanzania. It is frequently seen feeding on grasshoppers and other insects fleeing from grass fires. It often perches on low bare branches for long periods, and is then often quite tame and easy to approach. The flight is buoyant, easy, and rather harrier-like, but with longer glides and fewer flaps.

The species is a regular migrant, moving into the drier parts of its range to breed during the wet season, then returning south to woodlands in the dry season. There, the birds tend to be nomadic in some areas, with large numbers appearing in certain localities in one year, but none the next. The Grasshopper Buzzard is gregarious on its southward migration and also in its dry season range, sometimes occurring in small parties or large flocks of fifty to a hundred or more, particularly near grass fires or termite swarms. Its breeding habits are poorly known. The nest is most often built in a low tree, but is occasionally found as high as 40 feet (12m). The nest, constructed of sticks, is

South American Forest Hawks: 1
Despite its considerable geographical variation, the striking black and white appearance of the White Hawk (1) can hardly be confused with any other species. The rather uniform colouration and single broad white tail-band of the Plumbeous Hawk (2) make it an equally distinctive species, while the white underparts, neck and head, and contrasting black back and face-mask will quickly identify the aptly-named Black-faced Hawk (3).
(Maps 147–149)

solid, deep, and lined with leaves, in which one to three rufous-marked, bluish-white eggs are laid. Details of incubation and fledging periods are unknown.

Permanently resident in Lower Burma, Thailand, southeast Borneo and Indonesia, the Rufous-winged Buzzard (*Butastur liventer*) is found in open and thinly-forested country, often near rivers and lakes, as well as in cultivated areas, especially rice paddies. It often likes to perch for long periods on a post, or the bare branch of a tree, occasionally dropping to the ground for prey, which includes frogs, lizards, freshwater crabs and insects.

The distinctive white eye of the White-eyed Buzzard (*Butastur teesa*) makes it instantly identifiable throughout its range, which extends from northwestern India, south to Kerala, and east to Assam and Burma. It is similar in habits to the preceding species and is found in dry, open country, thin woodland, and also in areas of cultivation. Most of the bird's hunting is carried out from a perch, with a drop to the ground to catch some large insect or lizard, although it may occasionally resort to walking purposefully across the ground in search of prey. In some areas it is quite tame and confiding, taking little notice of the observer.

Breeding farther north than other members of the genus, the Grey-faced Buzzard (*Butastur indicus*) spends the summer months in Manchuria, northern China and Japan (Hondo), but migrates south to winter in Indo-China, Indonesia, and less commonly in Burma, Malaya and the western Papuan Islands. On its southerly migration, the species tends to be gregarious, moving in small, loose flocks, but the spring migration is much less concentrated, with birds arriving at their breeding areas over a longer period. While the bird selects paddy fields or open country with scattered trees for its winter quarters, in its breeding grounds it prefers wooded country with clearings for hunting. Habits are similar to the preceding species, and prey includes small snakes, lizards, frogs, small mammals, and insects. At the beginning of the breeding season, single birds or pairs soar over the breeding areas, calling noisily, and this appears to be the extent of the species' breeding display. The nest, constructed of sticks and lined with leaves and bark, is built in a tree, and more greenery may be added throughout the incubation period. The two to three eggs are incubated solely by the female, and fledging appears to take about thirty-five days.

FOREST HAWKS OF SOUTH AMERICA

The unmistakable White Hawk (*Leucopternis albicollis*) is a large, strikingly white hawk, distributed from southern Mexico and Central America, south to southern Amazonia and the Matto Grosso. It is instantly recognizable in flight, and is frequently to be seen wheeling low over humid forest, either singly or in pairs or even threes, its very broad wings and relatively short, broad tail producing a distinctive silhouette. At other times it is lethargic and easily

Black-chested Buzzard Eagle
A broad-winged, wedge-tailed flight silhouette combined with subtly elegant plumage colour and pattern are the distinguishing features of this beautiful but not very well known species from the mountains and dry upland regions of South America.
(Map 150)

approached, especially when perching for long periods on a dead tree or some other vantage-point, scanning the ground for reptiles such as lizards and snakes, which are its main prey. It is a bird of mixed forest, frequenting forest edges and clearings, and preferring swampy or well-watered areas. The few nests that have been discovered have been sited up to 80 feet (24m) high in large trees. All were built of twigs, with a lining of dead and green leaves, and contained one or two eggs. At present, no further details of the species' breeding habits are known.

The uncommon, rather small and stocky Plumbeous Hawk (*Leucopternis plumbea*) has a fairly restricted range in the humid and wet forest of eastern Panama, western Colombia and Ecuador, and extreme northwestern Peru. It does not soar and is generally found at low to moderate heights inside the forest. The species' restricted distribution, and particular habitat requirements, mean that virtually nothing is known about its breeding habits or lifestyle.

Resembling a miniature version of the White Hawk, the Black-faced Hawk (*Leucopternis melanops*) is found north of the Amazon River, in parts of Brazil, the Guianas, southern Venezuela and eastern Colombia and Ecuador, up to 3300 feet (1000m). Unlike the White Hawk, however, it rarely soars, apparently preferring to remain within dense cover, including mangroves, and only visiting clearings, forest edges or river banks to hunt. Prey is believed to consist mainly of small reptiles, and more rarely, birds. Very little else is known of the species' life-history or breeding activities.

BLACK-CHESTED BUZZARD EAGLE

The wide-ranging Black-chested Buzzard Eagle (*Geranoaetus melanoleucos*) is a large, impressive South American bird of prey found from the Merida Andes of Venezuela, south through Colombia and the main Andes range to Tierra del Fuego, and locally to southern Brazil in the east. It is a bird of open and rugged country, or thinly-wooded areas, where the climate is relatively dry. Although single birds, or pairs, may often be seen soaring effortlessly for long periods high over the countryside, the species is somewhat ponderous, and often extremely reluctant to leave its perch. Prey items include small mammals, especially cavies and rabbits, snakes and sometimes small or incapacitated birds. It is also known to visit carrion, and a group of birds seen shuffling around in sand-dunes near Lima were assumed to be

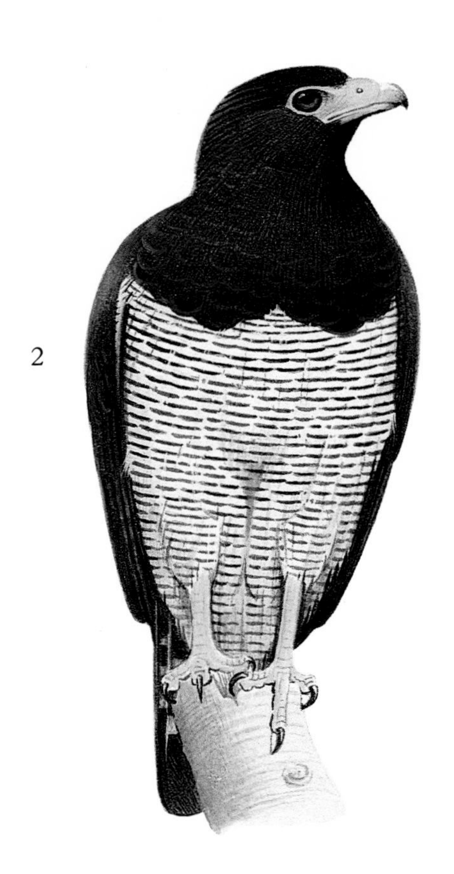

Slate-coloured Hawk and Barred Hawk
The Slate-coloured Hawk (1) of the swamps and backwaters of northern South America is distinguished by its red legs, grey-black plumage and single white tail-bar. Its close relative the Barred Hawk (2), an inhabitant of wet sub-tropical mountain forest from Costa Rica to Ecuador, is the largest and perhaps the most impressive of the *Leucopternis* hawks. *(Maps 151 and 152)*

searching for insects. Prey is usually eaten on the ground where it is killed, only rarely being carried up into trees.

In a recent report, a trio of birds, floating on the wind along a ridge, were seen to make repeated rolls as they approached the observer, and on one occasion two birds grappled with one foot. It is unclear, however, if this was part of a courtship display, or a family group. Typically, the nest is built on a ledge, often incredibly high on the side of a deep canyon, or more rarely, when cliffs are unavailable, in a tree. It is a large structure of sticks and dead branches, and may be used consecutively for many years. Normally two eggs, white with spots and blotches of chestnut or brown, are laid, but clutches of one and three have been recorded. Details of incubation and fledging periods are unknown.

MORE SOUTH AMERICAN FOREST HAWKS

With a South American distribution extending from Amazonia outwards through Venezuela, eastern Colombia, Ecuador, Peru, Bolivia and Brazil, the stockily-built Slate-coloured Hawk (*Leucopternis schistacea*) is a medium-sized hawk of flooded backwaters, swamps and forested streams. Typically found along the borders of watercourses, perching quietly in the open, it periodically drops down on to its prey, which is generally thought to include frogs and snakes. Although it is usually reported to be unsuspicious and easily observed, very little seems to have been published on the species' habits or breeding behaviour.

The largest and possibly most handsome member of the genus *Leucopternis*, the Barred Hawk (*Leucopternis princeps*) has a patchy distribution extending from Costa Rica south to northern Ecuador, in wet sub-tropical mountain forest. The statement that the species is rare may simply be due to the difficulty of human access to its preferred haunts, for up to three birds can often be seen gliding, soaring and diving above the tree-tops, while giving noisy calls, described as a loud "*wheeyoor*", followed by a rapid series of "*weep*" or "*yip*" notes. The bird is a static hunter, perching for long periods on an exposed limb, watching out for reptiles such as snakes, and probably also lizards. Other details, including the species' breeding and nesting habits, remain to be described.

Very little seems to be known about the feeding and breeding activities of the White-browed Hawk (*Leucopternis kuhli*), one of the smaller species of the genus *Leucopternis*. It is found in forested areas south of the Amazon, from the Para region down to eastern Peru and Brazil.

Living mainly in lowland forest and wooded regions of eastern and southern Brazil, the White-necked Hawk (*Leucopternis lacernulata*) is evidently rare and very localized. Very little is known or published about the species' habits, and its nest and breeding cycle remain undescribed. However, prey is known to include large spiders, grasshoppers, beetles and ants. The species must be at risk from habitat loss, at least in the south of its range, since the only recent records in that region are from areas of dense forest in the Serra do Mar, Paraná.

The Semiplumbeous Hawk (*Leucopternis semiplumbea*) is another small, chunky hawk with short, rounded wings, and like several others of the genus it rarely (or never) soars. It

South American Forest Hawks: 2
These closely-allied Central and South American hawks are most easily distinguished by their tail-patterns. Of the two white-headed species, the White-necked Hawk (2) has a narrow black terminal band, whilst the Mantled Hawk (5) has the terminal half white. The White-browed Hawk (1) and Semiplumbeous Hawk (4) both have narrow white subterminal bands, but the white eyebrow of the former, and the reddish-orange cere and legs of the latter, will separate the two. Finally, the white tail of the Grey-backed Hawk (3) has a broad subterminal black band.
(*Maps 153-157*)

Common Black Hawk
This large black hawk, with a single white bar across its white-tipped tail, is most often found in low-lying coastal savanna country in the southern USA and northern South America where it preys on amphibians and other aquatic creatures.
(Map 158)

occurs almost exclusively in the wetter and more heavily forested regions of South America, from Honduras, Nicaragua and Costa Rica, down through Panama and parts of western Colombia to northwestern Ecuador. In some areas it is the commonest hawk of primary forest, and is frequently seen flying or gliding across clearings. It is found singly or in pairs, and is often seen in trees, perched at varying heights. The distinctive call is a whistling "*ooee ooee ooee ooee*", which is given frequently during the day, advertising the presence of the bird which would otherwise remain unnoticed. Prey items include lizards and snakes. It nests deep inside the forest, and has been recorded building a nest at about 80 feet (24m) from the ground, in a medium-sized tree.

The Grey-backed Hawk (*Leucopternis occidentalis*) has a restricted range in western Ecuador and northwestern Peru, where the species is known to have declined seriously due to forest destruction. In many respects it is similar to the White Hawk (*L. albicollis*), and presumably has similar preferences, although its habits remain largely undescribed.

An inhabitant of primary forest of southeastern Brazil, eastern Paraguay and northern Argentina, the Mantled Hawk (*Leucopternis polionota*) is reported to have become extremely scarce. Very little is known about its habits or nesting activities, and the immature plumage has never been described. Prey items are known to include birds and small snakes.

CRAB-EATERS AND MANGROVE HAWKS

The four species comprising the genus *Buteogallus*, described below, are all very similar in both lifestyle and appearance, and are restricted to Central and South America.

The broad-winged, short-tailed Common Black Hawk (*Buteogallus anthracinus*) ranges from the southern USA and Mexico, down through Panama as far as northwestern Peru, and is also found on some of the off-shore Caribbean islands. The species is most commonly found in coastal lowlands of mixed savanna with areas of water and grassland. It also occurs along wooded rivers and stream banks in the interior, but seldom, if ever, in dense woodland. Hunting is generally carried out with the bird concealed on a low perch, from which it drops down on to its prey, consisting mainly of crabs, frogs, reptiles and fish. Large insects such as

Crab-eating Hawks and Great Black Hawk
The handsome broad-winged, short-tailed Rufous Crab Hawk (1) of northern South America is an inhabitant of low-lying, swampy areas, where it feeds exclusively on crabs. Another mangrove-dwelling, crab-eating bird, the Mangrove Black Hawk (2) of Central and South America will also take stranded fish. The Great Black Hawk (3), though having a similar range, inhabits a wider habitat range than the previous two species, tends to fly higher, and is less selective in its choice of food.
(Maps 158–160)

grasshoppers, and occasionally small mammals, are also taken, while small birds rarely figure in its diet. Where they are common, land crabs and sea crabs are the bird's favourite food. To handle its difficult prey the hawk stands over the crab, securing its claws and legs with one foot at either side of the crab's body. The bird then rips off the carapace by hooking its bill under the front edge and pulling sharply backwards.

The species does little soaring, except in the breeding season when the birds also become more vocal, giving a series of high-pitched whistles and sometimes also a harsh "*ka-a-a-ah*". Nests are placed in trees from 16 to 100 feet (5 to 30 metres) above ground, and are built of sticks with a lining of twigs and some green leaves. Generally a single greyish-white egg is laid. Other details of the breeding cycle are unrecorded.

The Rufous Crab Hawk (*Buteogallus aequinoctialis*) is a buzzard-like hawk with broad wings and a short tail. It is a coastal and mangrove species found from southeastern Brazil north to Venezuela and Panama. As its name suggests, this hawk specializes in catching crabs, which it hunts from a low branch overhanging a muddy creek. When suitable prey is spotted, the bird drops down and seizes the crab in its claws, returning to dry land or a convenient perch where the carapace is torn off and the soft parts eaten. In certain favoured spots the remains of large numbers of crabs may sometimes be found littering the ground. The bird also forages on mud-flats, or may occasionally swoop down on crabs from low flight. In Surinam the species apparently confines itself to just two species of crab, identified as *Ulcides cordatus* and *Callinectes bocourti*. In the breeding season a pair have been observed to stoop repeatedly at each other in the air while calling. The nest of twigs with a lining of green leaves is placed in a tree, and usually contains a single whitish or yellowish egg with reddish-brown or lilac-grey spots.

Having much the same lifestyle as the Common Black Hawk, but being entirely confined to the mangrove zone of the Pacific coast, from southern Mexico to northwestern Peru, the Mangrove Black Hawk (*Buteogallus subtilis*) is said to also frequent sand-bars and mud-flats, where it stalks around looking for crabs and dead or stranded fish. Little else seems to be known about the bird, and some authorities regard it as simply a race of *B. anthracinus*.

Ranging through Mexico and Guatemala to Costa Rica,

Savanna Hawk
The predominantly rufous-coloured Savanna Hawk has a distinctive upright posture when perched, and in flight has the appearance of a rather long-winged buzzard. At times it may be confused with the Fishing Buzzard, although the latter has a white head.
(Map 161)

the Great Black Hawk (*Buteogallus urubitinga*) is a rather sluggish hawk, very like, but somewhat larger than, the Common Black Hawk (*Buteogallus anthracinus*). It is most often found alone, and often perches on the highest tree-tops. It soars well, and in the breeding season has been observed circling high in the air, calling noisily with a loud, whistling scream. It is fairly common and widespread, and is usually found at the edges of forest or in the vicinity of forested or wooded rivers or pools, as well as in mangroves and along the sea coast.

SAVANNA HAWK AND FISHING BUZZARD

A large, handsome species with very long, broad wings and a short tail, the aptly-named Savanna Hawk (*Heterospizias meridionalis*) is a sluggish, long-legged hawk, adapted to living in open country with a few scattered trees, and often with some marshes or ponds. The species is found from eastern Panama to tropical South America, west to Ecuador, eastern Peru and Bolivia, and south to central Argentina. When the bird is alarmed or excited the long feathers on the nape may be raised, producing a semi-crested appearance. It is a rather inactive and clumsy bird, usually seen perched in a rather upright posture on a fence post or low branch. Occasionally it may be seen walking about on the ground, and it is able to move quite rapidly when aroused. Low perches are used as look-outs for prey, which is usually captured on the ground, though occasionally the bird may stoop on prey from flight. Prey items include small snakes, fish, lizards, frogs and toads, small mammals and various large insects. Sometimes, groups of up to several dozen birds are attracted to grass fires, or will follow agricultural implements such as ploughs, in search of disturbed insects, lizards and small rodents.

At the beginning of the breeding season, two or more birds may be seen soaring high in the sky, and calling with a high-pitched "*kree-ee-ee-er*". The nest is often placed in an

Fishing Buzzard
A rather specialized and easily-identified neotropical species, the Fishing Buzzard is closely associated with wet locations. The soles of its feet are armed with thorny spicules, much as in the Osprey, as an aid to grasping the fish that comprise its main prey.
(*Map 162*)

isolated tree: it is constructed of branches and twigs, and normally contains a clutch of one or two bluish-white eggs. Other information on incubation and fledging periods is lacking.

The Fishing Buzzard (*Busarellus nigricollis*) is, as its name implies, a specialized neotropical species adapted for fishing. The undersides of its toes are covered with small prickly spines, which enable it to grasp and catch fish. This "fishing hawk" is usually seen perched on a tree or bush near water, especially where there is floating vegetation. Normally, the bird will swoop down with hardly a wing-beat, and snatch a fish from near the surface without even wetting its plumage. At other times it fishes by dropping feet-first into emergent or aquatic vegetation, or rather awkwardly into shallow water near the banks, often becoming saturated. On such occasions it must spend quite a long time drying out its non-waterproof plumage. Its prey consists almost exclusively of fish, and in Guiana it includes the armoured fish *Hoplosternum*. It is also known to prey on lizards, snails and small rodents, and some aquatic insects, but all these items are presumably only taken when fishing is poor. The species is found from southern Mexico and Central America south to the Guianas, Brazil, Peru, Venezuela and Colombia, and also in Paraguay and north-central Argentina.

Usually unsuspicious and frequently quite common in some parts of its extensive range, the bird may often be seen cruising low over swampy or marshy areas, although it also soars well. The call is a guttural croak or a reedy whistled scream "*wheeeeeah*", first rising then falling. Typically, the nest is a large structure of sticks, sometimes decorated with green foliage. It is sited some 40 to 50 feet (12 to 15 metres) up in a mangrove or other tree, at the edge of a swamp, or sometimes in a plantation. One greyish-white, brown-blotched egg appears to be the norm, although this and other details of the species' breeding habits require further study.

COMMON BUZZARD

Most evident when soaring majestically and effortlessly over hillsides and valleys, with wings raised in a shallow "V", occasionally giving a loud, plaintive mewing call, the Common Buzzard (*Buteo buteo*) lives mainly along the margins of woodland, preferring to hunt in open country, typically where small areas of woodland alternate with open, undulating terrain, meadows, heaths or marshland. It has an extensive Old World range, breeding from the Azores and Cape Verde Islands through Europe and Central Asia to the Soviet Far East and Japan. The more northerly breeding populations of eastern Europe and Siberia migrate south in the autumn, and while a few winter in southern Europe, northern Africa and Saudi Arabia, the majority undertake a spectacular journey to eastern and southern Africa. Other northern populations over-winter in India, Burma, Malaysia, Indo-China and southern China. Since the species is essentially a soaring one, its migration is highly concentrated, in order to avoid long flights over large expanses of water such as the Mediterranean. In the eastern Mediterranean, large numbers pass through the Bosporus between mid-September and mid-October, while farther south, in Israel, tens of thousands of birds that regularly winter in Africa, pass through Eilat in both spring and autumn, together with impressive numbers of other raptors such as Steppe Eagles (*Aquila rapax*) and Black Kites (*Milvus migrans*).

Though the Common Buzzard has survived persecution rather better than some raptors – for example, the Red Kite (*Milvus milvus*) – it has nevertheless declined dramatically over the years, and in Britain that decline has been well documented in old churchwardens' accounts since these officials were empowered to pay a bounty on species branded as vermin. The system began in the sixteenth century and reached its peak, boosted by Acts of Parliament, in the late seventeenth and eighteenth centuries. Its cessation came about in part due to the near disappearance of buzzards and kites from Britain, and partly because the enclosure of land for agriculture increasingly passed such tasks of "control" into the hands of the estate game-keepers.

Buzzards hunt mainly from a perch, usually a branch or convenient telegraph pole, gliding down when prey is seen and quickly seizing it in the talons. At other times they may glide low over rugged hillsides, or even hover, rather kestrel-like, in search of prey. From time to time a Buzzard may also wander about somewhat awkwardly on the ground, seeking smaller prey-items. The bulk of its prey consists of small rodents, including various mice and voles, and other small mammals such as rabbits, but birds, reptiles, amphibians, large insects and earthworms are also taken. Carrion appears to play an important part in the bird's diet during the winter months.

At the beginning of the breeding season the Common Buzzard performs conspicuous aerial displays above its breeding haunts. On fine days, single birds or pairs are often seen soaring or slowly circling high up, calling repeatedly. One or both birds may perform spectacular dives followed by steep upward ascents, before dramatically stooping again, with wings folded close to the body. Both sexes help with the building of the nest, or with the renovation of one from a previous year. The nest is usually placed in a tree, normally at a height of 16 to 80 feet (5 to 24 metres), but sometimes, in relatively treeless areas, the birds may nest on rocky crags or ledges. The nest itself is constructed of sticks, or heather and roots, and lined with smaller branches or twigs with green leaves. In Central Europe egg-laying starts in mid-March, and a month later in the more northern areas of Europe. Two to four eggs are laid at intervals of two to three days, and are incubated by both sexes for about thirty-five days. In the early days after hatching, the male brings in all the food while the female broods the young or remains at the nest to guard them. After eight to twelve days, both sexes take part in bringing prey to the young, although the female tears it into pieces and feeds it to the young until they are strong enough to do this for themselves. There is much variation in the size of the young, and if prey is difficult to find, one or more chicks may die of starvation. The chicks remain in the nest for some 50 to 55 days and become independent between six and eight weeks later.

Common Buzzard
Easily identified on the wing by its broad, round-winged appearance, the Common Buzzard is a rather lethargic flyer, more often seen soaring and wheeling than in level flight. Formerly much persecuted in Britain by the game-keeping fraternity, the species is now afforded legal protection as it has been proved to take far more small mammal and invertebrate prey than ground birds, and will even take carrion.
(*Map 163*)

Broad-winged Hawk and Swainson's Hawk
Although they breed on opposite sides of the northern USA, the Broad-winged Hawk (1) in the east, and Swainson's Hawk (2) in the west, on migration the two species arrive simultaneously in vast numbers over Central America, where they contribute to the most spectacular autumn passage in the entire Western Hemisphere.
(*Maps 164 and 165*)

SOME OF THE BUZZARD'S NEW WORLD RELATIVES

A summer visitor to eastern North America, and with resident populations in the Caribbean, from Cuba to Tobago in the West Indies, the Broad-winged Hawk (*Buteo platypterus*) is a stocky, medium-sized *Buteo* with a preference for broad-leaved and mixed woodlands. The autumn migrations of this species are often spectacular, and in mid-September, from famous vantage-points like Hawk Mountain in Pennsylvania, many thousands may be observed passing south to their wintering quarters, which extend from southern Florida and southern Mexico to Bolivia and northern Brazil. When hunting, the bird typically perches low, watching for prey such as mice, frogs, small snakes and insects.

A breeding bird of the Great Plains and more arid areas in western North America, and wintering mainly on the pampas of Argentina, Swainson's Hawk (*Buteo swainsoni*) has slightly longer, narrower and more pointed wings than other *Buteos*. It is most often seen soaring high over open plains or prairie, on slightly upturned wings. When not on the wing it often perches for long periods on fence posts, banks or boulders, watching for prey, which consists mainly of large insects (predominantly grasshoppers and crickets) but also includes small rodents, reptiles and amphibians, and occasionally bats and birds.

Swainson's Hawk is a gregarious species for much of the year outside the breeding season, and this is most strikingly evident during the annual migrations. Although initially spread across a broad front as they move south from the USA in the autumn (fall), the birds are progressively concentrated into a narrow flyway as they approach the Central American isthmus. Here, thousands may be seen soaring over mountain ranges in Costa Rica and Panama. The same thing happens during the return journey in spring, although the routes differ somewhat from those of the southward flight. Recently, a small population consisting mainly of immature birds has taken to wintering in Florida where the birds inhabit freshly ploughed fields. Migrants in Argentina used to follow locust swarms, but as these have become less common the hawks too have become less concentrated geographically. However, it appears that on their journey to their winter quarters they rarely eat or drink, whereas moving northwards in the spring the birds travel at a more leisurely pace and do take some food *en route*.

American Buzzards: 1
These New World buzzards can be distinguished as follows: the Rufous-thighed Hawk (1) has a black back and rufous thighs; Ridgway's Hawk (2) is more or less reddish-rufous, with a grey tail; the Short-tailed Hawk (4) is single-coloured, blackish-brown, with a relatively short tail; the nearly white tail of the White-tailed Hawk (3) is characteristic, whilst the white tail with a single black band, generally grey plumage, and reddish back and shoulders, should all help to identify the Red-backed Buzzard (5).
(Maps 166–170)

Grey Hawk and Galapagos Hawk
An overall greyish appearance, with white-banded tail and whitish-barred underparts, are diagnostic of the Grey Hawk (1). The generally dark brownish-black Galopagos Hawk (2) is the only hawk on the Galapagos Islands. The male is noticeably smaller than the female in this species.
(Maps 171 and 172)

A little-known inhabitant of humid forests, forest edges and broken forest on steep hillsides, the Rufous-thighed Hawk (*Buteo leucorrhous*) occurs from northern Venezuela and Colombia south through the mountains to northern Argentina, southeastern Brazil and Paraguay. Although single birds may occasionally be seen soaring low over the forest, this is about the extent of our current knowledge of the species.

Endemic to Hispaniola and its small satellite islands, Ridgway's Hawk (*Buteo ridgwayi*) is found in lowland woods and fairly open country. It is a little-studied species, but is known to prey on small rodents, lizards and birds. The few nests that have been discovered have been in trees, between 26 and 50 feet (8 and 15 metres) above the ground.

A rather active hawk which soars well, and often to great heights, the Short-tailed Hawk (*Buteo brachyurus*) has a typical broad-winged, short-tailed, *Buteo* shape. It is found locally in southern Florida, and from central Mexico south to northern Argentina, Paraguay, and southeastern Brazil. While in Florida it is a bird of mangrove and cypress swamps, less often found in pines and open country; in Central America it is mostly found in open and partially-wooded country in lowlands and foothills.

Found in suitable open and thinly-forested country from southern Texas south to Central America, and from northern and eastern South America south to northern Patagonia, the White-tailed Hawk (*Buteo albicaudatus*) is a large, handsome and robust species which, in southern Texas, prefers open coastal grasslands and semi-arid inland brush areas. It often perches conspicuously on top of telephone poles, bushes or even on the ground. It also soars well, and in favourable winds is able to hover, sometimes with barely perceptible wing-beats, while hunting for prey, such as rabbits, rats, snakes, lizards, frogs and insects, and occasionally ground-living birds.

Ranging from the Andes of Colombia, down western South America to Tierra del Fuego and the Falkland Islands, the Red-backed Buzzard (*Buteo polyosoma*) is a large, broad-winged *Buteo* of open country which may also be seen soaring over mountain slopes, usually near or above the tree line. Like the White-tailed Hawk (*Buteo albicaudatus*) it hovers characteristically, and regularly perches both on rock ledges and on the ground.

The smaller Grey Hawk (*Buteo nitidus*) is found in forest borders and lightly-wooded areas, often in the vicinity of water. It ranges from the southwestern USA, south to western Peru, central Argentina and southeastern Brazil, and is also found in Trinidad. Swift and agile in flight compared with most members of its genus, the Grey Hawk specializes in capturing fast-moving lizards. Birds, snakes, mammals and large insects are also taken as prey.

The Galapagos Hawk (*Buteo galapagoensis*) is endemic to, and the only hawk on, the Galapagos Islands. It is quite fearless of man, although it has been extirpated from some of the islands. The total population is in the order of about 130 pairs. Unusually in raptors cooperative polyandry is a notable feature of the species' breeding biology.

Harris's Hawk and Roadside Hawk
With chestnut shoulders and thighs and black-tipped white tail, the Harris's Hawk (1) is handsome and easy to recognize. Another New World species, the Roadside Hawk (2), although having a variety of plumage types, is readily identifiable by its barred tail and chestnut wing-patch.
(Maps 175 and 176)

BUZZARDS OF AMERICA AND AFRICA

Although Gurney's Buzzard (*Buteo poecilochrous*) is generally larger than the very similar Red-backed Buzzard (*Buteo polyosoma*), where the two species overlap some individuals are often difficult to distinguish. However, Gurney's Buzzard occurs farther north, in the higher levels of the Andes, from southern Colombia to northern Chile and northwestern Argentina. The species seems to occur mainly in wooded valleys, and is said to breed on rocky cliffs. Nothing else appears to be known about the bird, except for the claim that it occasionally calls persistently for up to five minutes.

Sometimes confused with the Turkey Vulture (*Cathartes aura*), which it perhaps mimics, the Zone-tailed hawk (*Buteo albonotatus*) has long wings of uniform width and a rather long tail. Its range extends from the southwestern USA to Central America, and locally in northern South America south to Peru, Bolivia and Paraguay. The bulky, leaf-decorated stick nest is built between 26 and 100 feet (8 to 30 metres) up in a tree, and usually contains two eggs.

The Hawaiian Hawk (*Buteo solitarius*) is endemic to the island of Hawaii, where it is reported to be fairly common. It is a small dimorphic *Buteo* which is found singly or in pairs, and is often seen soaring over forests or more open country.

The Red-tailed Buzzard (*Buteo ventralis*) is found from the Patagonian forests of southern Chile and Argentina,

Buzzards of Africa and the Far East
The only buzzard found on the island, the very common Madgascar Buzzard (2) is impossible to confuse with any other bird, whilst on the African mainland, the African Mountain Buzzard (1) looks like a smaller and darker mountain forest version of the Common Buzzard. The pale-headed Upland Buzzard (3) of dry upland steppes of the Far East is considered by some to be conspecific with the Long-legged Buzzard.
(*Maps 182-184*)

south to the Strait of Magellan. Much still needs to be discovered about the species' lifestyle, but it appears to be an inhabitant of wooded country. The only two nests so far discovered were both in trees, at heights of more than 115 feet (35m) above the ground.

The Ferruginous Hawk (*Buteo regalis*) lives in dry, open country in southwestern Canada and the west-central USA, wintering in the southern part of its range and south to northern Mexico. It often hovers when hunting, capturing species such as ground squirrels, prairie dogs and rabbits, as well as some ground-dwelling birds and some snakes and large insects. There is growing evidence that the species is becoming scarce and is in need of legal protection.

Closely related to the widespread Common Buzzard, the African Mountain Buzzard (*Buteo oreophilus*) has an interrupted African range extending south from south-eastern Ethiopia to northern Tanzania, then reappearing in southern Africa from Cape province eastwards to the north-eastern Transvaal. In the north of its range it is a strictly montane species, resident in forests at altitudes up to about 13,000 feet (4000m), but in the south it is found at much lower levels, in forests or plantations, mainly of pines, and is not at all a species of high mountains. The bird spends much of its time soaring above the tree-tops like other members of the genus, or perched on a branch, and feeds on small mammals, reptiles, amphibians and insects.

The Madagascar Buzzard (*Buteo brachypterus*) is the only buzzard found on its home island, and is the commonest bird of prey on that island with the possible exception of the Black Kite (*Milvus migrans*). It is similar in many respects to the preceding species, living at levels up to 6500 feet (2000m) in both wooded and open country, and it may often be observed soaring high, in typical buzzard-like fashion. All prey is taken on the ground, the bird either dropping on to it from flight, or from an observation perch. The range of prey includes frogs, reptiles and small ground-based mammals, as well as insects and occasionally carrion. The nest is placed either on a crag or, when in a tree, between 33 and 66 feet (10 and 20 metres) above the ground. The two eggs appear to be incubated solely by the female.

A very large buzzard found in steppes or open plains, mountains and deserts of central and eastern Asia, the Upland Buzzard (*Buteo hemilasius*) is a partial migrant. It winters in the southern parts of its nesting range in Kazakhstan and the Soviet Far East, while more northerly birds migrate to winter in northern India, Burma, central China and Korea.

American Buzzards: 2
Despite having both light and dark phases, the Hawaiian Hawk (1) is easily identified in its native Hawaii. Some individuals of Gurney's Buzzard (2) are difficult to distinguish from the Red-backed Buzzard, which seems to prefer higher altitudes. The Red-tailed Buzzard (3) and Ferruginous Hawk (4) are both large and robust, with fairly distinctive plumages, particularly the tails. The white-barred tail of the otherwise black-plumaged Zone-tailed Hawk (5) makes it quite unmistakable.
(Maps 177–181)

Red-tailed Hawk
The rufous or chestnut-coloured tail of the powerfully built Red-tailed Hawk is its best distinguishing feature. The bird's habit of soaring frequently, and its distinctive loud voice, also help to make it a relatively easy bird to identify.
(Map 185)

RED-TAILED HAWK AND RED-SHOULDERED HAWK

The commonest *Buteo* in North America is the Red-tailed Hawk (*Buteo jamaicensis*), which is distributed throughout well-timbered areas of Alaska and Canada, down through the USA to western Panama, and also in the West Indies. Throughout this range the species breeds in a wide variety of habitats, from forests and woods with adjacent cleared areas to prairies and more arid desert areas; it is absent, however, from tundra, and rare in extensive unbroken forest. In the more northern parts of its range it is migratory, wintering south from the southern USA to Central America.

Hunting is carried out either from a suitable perch, which is often very high, so that the bird dives down 200 feet (60m) or more on to its prey, or from the wing, when the bird glides and circles low over a hillside before finally swooping down on to its victim. The bird takes mammals from the size of meadow mice up to chipmunks and rabbits, as well as various snakes, lizards and many ground-living birds, but being an opportunistic feeder, almost anything is likely to succumb to it, including insects and creatures too heavy for it to carry. It is a powerful and aggressive hawk, vigorously defending its nest or winter territory and often harassing other birds of prey, including eagles; it is also known to attack human intruders at the nest. The species has a variety

Red-shouldered Hawk
The reddish colouring on the shoulders and breast, combined with the three, pure-white, equal-width tail-bars, are diagnostic field characteristics of this species.
(Map 186)

of calls, depending on the situation, ranging from short, duck-like noises to a distinctive, harsh, descending "*keeeeeeer*".

At the beginning of the breeding season the pairs engage in much soaring, accompanied by loud calling. The male may indulge in mock stoops, with the female rolling over and presenting talons in mid-air. He may also perform a series of shallow dives, and may either pull out from a dive and return to high soaring, or finalize it by settling on a perch, at which times mating often occurs. A large nest of twigs, lined with finer material, is built by both sexes. It is usually sited in a tall tree, although occasionally it is built on a rock ledge, while in desert regions it may be placed in a tall cactus. Nests are often refurbished annually, and used for several consecutive years. Incubation of the one to three eggs is carried out by both sexes, though with the female taking the greater part, and it lasts for about thirty days. At four to five weeks the young are able to feed themselves on prey brought in by the adults, and they fledge in about forty-five days.

A species of moist or swampy woodlands and wooded river valleys, the Red-shouldered Hawk (*Buteo lineatus*) breeds in eastern North America, from southern Canada and the eastern USA to central Mexico, with an additional isolated population inhabiting the river valleys of California. In the northern parts of its range the species is migratory, wintering as far south as the southern USA and Mexico. It appears to be far less active than the preceding species, apparently preferring to hunt from a tree perch rather than on the wing. Prey items are varied, and include small mammals, snakes, frogs, crayfish, small or young birds, and some large insects.

In the spring the Red-shouldered Hawk is a noisy and conspicuous bird, with pairs circling and soaring over the nesting area, calling loudly. Later, when breeding is under way, the birds are much less in evidence. If not utilizing an old squirrel, hawk or crow nest, the birds build a substantial, well-constructed nest of sticks, sited in a large tree. The average clutch of three eggs, laid at two- to three-day intervals, hatches after about twenty-eight days of incubation, which is shared by both birds. The staggered egg-laying results in some difference in the size of the young, which leave the nest after a further five to six weeks.

Jackal Buzzard and African Red-tailed Buzzard
Named on account of its distinctive jackal-like call, the Jackal Buzzard (1) can also be recognized (depending on race) by its white or chestnut underparts contrasting with the blackish upoperside. The African Red-tailed Buzzard (2) is identifiable by its rufous tail, dark upper breast, and spotted lower breast and belly.
(Maps 187 and 188)

Buzzards of Africa and Eurasia

Taking its name from its high-pitched yelping "*kyaah-ka-ka-ka*" call, which resembles that of the Black-backed Jackal, the Jackal Buzzard (*Buteo rufofuscus*) is a handsome buzzard of hilly, mountainous or open savanna country in Africa. It is distributed throughout much of that continent, south of approximately 15°N, with the apparent exception of extreme southern Angola, northern Namibia and much of Botswana. It is generally found at altitudes of between 3300 and 16,400 feet (1000 and 5000 metres), and approaches sea level only at the Cape. When hunting, the bird either pounces from a perch, or stoops from the hover, on to prey that includes medium-sized rodents, snakes, lizards, small ground-based birds, and insects, though it will also take carrion in the form of road casualties.

A bird of African savannas and forest edges, the African Red-tailed Buzzard (*Buteo auguralis*) is found from Sierra Leone east to western Ethiopia, and south through Zaire and Uganda to Angola. Northern populations are migratory, moving north into the Sahel zone in the wet season after breeding at more southerly latitudes. The nest, lined with green leaves, is formed of sticks, and although it is occasionally built on a rocky outcrop, it is most often sited in a tree, at any height from 33 to 115 feet (10 to 35 metres) above the ground. The two or three eggs may, in some cases, be incubated by both birds, and although positive information is currently unavailable, indications are that fledging occurs about twelve weeks after egg-laying. The species preys on frogs, lizards, snakes, insects and small mammals, but apparently not on birds.

Typically a bird of open tundra and mountains, with a virtually circumpolar range, the Rough-legged Buzzard (*Buteo lagopus*) is slightly larger than the Common Buzzard and has relatively longer wings and tail. In autumn the species withdraws south of its breeding range, wintering mainly from central Europe eastwards to Japan, southern Canada and the northern USA. In flight it exhibits great beauty and ease, making full use of wind and up-currents for soaring, gliding, and even hovering; it will occasionally quarter the ground, very much in the style of a harrier. It perches, either in an elevated position or, when a suitable perch is not available, even on the ground, and adopts a characteristically upright stance. Prey is usually caught by a short stoop, from either the perch or from the hover, and consists almost entirely of small mammals, especially lemmings in the Arctic. In its winter range it takes field mice, voles, rabbits and, when rodent numbers are low, more birds. In Scandinavia the breeding population fluctuates markedly in response to the four-year rodent cycle, and in "good" lemming years the species may nest farther south, and remain in the breeding area for longer than normal.

Shortly after arriving in their breeding area, the birds

Rough-legged Buzzard and Long-legged Buzzard
Most often seen in its winter range, the Rough-legged Buzzard (2) is distinguished from the slightly smaller Common Buzzard by its paler plumage is on head and neck, a white, dark-barred tail, and usually a brown breast-band. The well-feathered tarsi give the species its name. The dark or rufous general appearance of the Long-legged Buzzard (1), and its unmarked, similarly-coloured tail, help to identify this species.
(Maps 189 and 190)

perform a courtship display similar to that of the Common Buzzard, with much vocalization. The relatively small nest is usually placed on a ledge, but may be sited in a tree or, in tundra regions, directly on the ground. It is formed of sticks, with a lining of green vegetation. In years that offer a plentiful supply of food, three to four eggs are laid, and are incubated mainly by the female for about thirty days. The young fledge in a further 34 to 43 days, and become independent after a few weeks.

The Long-legged Buzzard (*Buteo rufinus*) is also very similar to the Common Buzzard but it is larger, with proportionally longer and broader wings. It is a bird of dry steppes and semi-deserts and mountains up to 13,000 feet (4000m), breeding from northern Africa through south-eastern Europe eastwards to Central Asia. The more northerly populations are migratory, wintering south to northern Africa and eastwards to northern India. The species preys mainly on small to medium-sized mammals such as gerbils and desert rats, and also on lizards.

HARPY EAGLE

Weighing up to 10 pounds (4.5kg), the Harpy Eagle (*Harpia harpyja*) is heavy, but not the heaviest of eagles, and its wing-span too is exceeded by many others. What does mark it out from all other eagles, however, is the immense size of its feet and talons, and the great girth of its legs. On this basis it is certainly the most powerful eagle in the world. Dwelling in the rainforests of Central and South America, the Harpy's prey includes big animals such as sloths and howler monkeys, but several eagles with less formidable armament take animals as large or larger. Probably the reason for the Harpy's exceptional leg and foot development is the way in which prey are captured. Most of its victims are arboreal, and sloths in particular have an exceedingly strong grip as they hang below branches high in the canopy. Film of the Harpy in action shows that it is able to tear a sloth off its branch almost without a check in flight as it rolls to pass below it. Weight and momentum must help, but great strength is essential too, and the thickness of the bird's leg-bones may also provide an important safety margin to reduce the risk of injury in such an attack. The relatively short wings are understandable too, for long wings would be a handicap to a bird plunging through the canopy in this way.

Like many eagles, Harpies have regular nest sites, used year after year, and much of our knowledge of the bird's breeding biology and way of life is based on just two of these in the Kanuku mountains of southern Guyana. The nests are situated at a great height in the crowns of silk cotton trees, about 165 feet (50m) above the ground.

Made of sticks up to 1.6 inches (4cm) thick, the nest is about 5 feet (1.5m) across and lined with green leaves and animal hair. Two eggs may be laid, but it is normal for only one young eagle to be reared. Periods of incubation and fledging are not known because both of the nests studied already held a well-grown young eagle when they were first visited. Although these birds were some eight to ten months old and capable of flight, they were still dependent on their parents. Although not confined to the nest, they still spent their time in its vicinity or in neighbouring trees, frequently uttering high-pitched hunger screams. Intervals between feeding were long – up to ten days in one case – and the screams became more insistent as the fast continued. Wing flaps flashing the white underwing coverts accompanied the calls. When food eventually arrived, the young bird chased the adult away almost immediately and "mantled" over its meal – that is, covered it from view beneath high arched wings. Mock killing behaviour was directed at one prey animal brought, but the young were not seen to make any attempts to make their own kills. Clearly, with such a long period of dependence the Harpy Eagle can breed only every other year at best, and this seems typical of most very large eagles other than sea eagles. Such a slow reproductive rate of course makes them very vulnerable to human persecution and habitat loss.

In order to study their behaviour more closely, researchers in Guyana took captive an adult female and a juvenile of each sex. Contrary to expectation, the adult was the more docile and trainable, and took food from the fist from the second day of her captivity. Two weeks later she could be flown free in the forest, and would still return for food. Pursuing prey, she kept below the canopy and flew at great speed, manoeuvring with amazing agility between branches, and sometimes seeming to climb almost vertically. Food requirements were found to average about 8 ounces (225 grammes) of meat per day. In practice this could be achieved by letting the bird gorge itself to full capacity every three days, and this is probably what happens in the wild, with a kill followed by a fast occurring about twice a week.

Harpy Eagle
The magnificent and unmistakable Harpy Eagle is still to be found in its New World primary forest habitat, although when at rest its rather sombre plumage makes it difficult to detect. When hunting, its short, broad wings allow it to travel through the trees with surprising speed and agility.
(*Map 191*)

Isidor's Eagle
Replacing the Harpy Eagle and Guiana Crested Eagle at higher altitudes, the handsomely-crested Isidor's Eagle, when on the wing, shows a unique underside pattern of black, white and chestnut.
(*Map 192*)

ISIDOR'S EAGLE AND GUIANA CRESTED EAGLE

Frequenting the more heavily-forested slopes of the Andes of South America, Isidor's Eagle (*Oroaetus isidori*) is a large, robust and handsome species with a short, spike-like crest, which is often held erect, even in flight. With a range extending from the Merida Andes of Venezuela to Colombia, and south through the Andes to northwestern Argentina, this rather uncommon eagle is found on relatively undisturbed, humid forested slopes, between 5250 and 9200 feet (1600 and 2800 metres) although it may occasionally be seen almost down to sea level. It is most often seen soaring above the tree-tops, from where it swoops down on its prey, which is reported to consist of arboreal mammals and birds, ranging from squirrels, woolly monkeys, sloths and racoons, through to large birds such as guans and curassows.

Built at least 65 feet (20m) up in a tree, most often an oak (*Quercus* sp.), the nest is usually a very large structure and may measure 7 feet (2m) or more across by 3 feet (1m) deep, probably reflecting the accumulated efforts of several seasons of use. It is built almost exclusively of live branches, which are collected on the wing – torn from the trees by the huge bird's weight and momentum as it rushes past. A single egg seems to comprise the normal clutch, which is almost certainly incubated solely by the female. The male

Guiana Crested Eagle
This rather rare and little-known eagle of the humid forests of Central and South America is smaller than the Harpy Eagle but closely related to that species. It is most readily identified by its long, broadly banded tail, and by its prominent, undivided crest.
(Map 193)

probably does most of the hunting, with the female caring for the young bird until it is large enough to tear up prey brought in to the nest. The young bird is estimated to fly when about sixteen weeks old.

Some doubt seems to hang over the bird's future, for although its habitat is difficult to penetrate, deforestation is proceeding at an alarming rate, and this does not bode well for an already somewhat thinly-distributed species.

Humid tropical forest from 1650 to 5250 feet (500 to 1600 metres) above sea level is the habitat of the large and impressive Guiana Crested Eagle (*Morphnus guianensis*). Ranging from Honduras in Central America south to Bolivia, northeastern Argentina and southern Brazil, it is today threatened by deforestation every bit as severely as the Isidor's Eagle. The bird is obviously a close relative of the larger and heavier-built Harpy Eagle, and whilst the Harpy has a divided crest, that of the present species is single, prominent, and pointed.

It is a generally uncommon to rare species, about which very little is known. It is reported to soar regularly above the tree-tops, but much of its time is spent perched motionless, but conspicuously, in tall forest trees. Locally, the bird is known as "Churuco", meaning "monkey", and it certainly preys on the smaller species, as well as taking opossums, birds, iguanas and other reptiles. The nest is claimed to be an enormous structure, sited high in a very tall forest tree, and to contain a single egg; unfortunately, further details concerning breeding behaviour, incubation and fledging are, as yet, not known. However, it can be assumed that as with all large eagles, individuals take several years to reach sexual maturity and even then have a very low reproductive rate. This, of course, is an additional handicap to a species facing the pressures imposed by man's exploitation of the environment.

LONG-CRESTED EAGLE

The distinctive long floppy crest, from which the Long-crested Eagle (*Lophaetus occipitalis*) derives its name, together with its tight, white-feathered "leggings" and relatively small yellow feet, make this a rather easy species to identify. It is a fairly common resident bird of the wooded and better-watered savannas of Africa south of the Sahara, apparently preferring short grassland or marshy areas, bordered by trees. It is more closely associated with man than any other African eagle, adapting well to cultivated areas where there are scattered mature trees, either introduced or indigenous. Normally sedentary, it is, nevertheless, probably nomadic, at least to some extent, in the non-breeding season, possibly moving in response to fluctuating prey numbers.

The bird often perches for long periods on a prominent tree, telegraph pole or fence post, intently scanning the ground below, and when prey is spotted it glides down, quickly seizing it in its talons. The unfortunate victim is then either swallowed whole, on the ground, or carried back up to the perch where it is dealt with and eaten. The majority of the bird's prey comprises small rodents, and a study in South Africa showed 86 per cent of its prey items to be Vlei Rats (*Ortomys* sp.). The bird does most of its active hunting in the early morning, and again towards evening. It may be seen soaring at other times of the day, or resting in the shady canopy of a tree during the heat of the day. It is often very vocal, calling both while perched and during display flights. The call is a high-pitched, screaming "*keeeee-eh*", or a prolonged series of sharp "*kik-kik-kik-kik-keee-eh*" notes may also be given.

At the commencement of the breeding season the species is extremely vocal, with single birds and pairs calling loudly from perches and while on the wing. Aerial displays seem to be less important in this species than in many other birds of prey, but the male may occasionally perform brief undulating flights, diving and then swooping up again, perhaps repeating the cycle several times. Either male or female may occasionally soar to heights of up to 650 feet (200m) above the breeding site. The male feeds the female during courtship, and copulation, accompanied by much calling, takes place in trees near the nest site. The nest, which may be used for several consecutive seasons, is rather small, and usually situated well within the shady leaf canopy of a tall tree, anywhere between 23 and 65 feet (7 and 20 metres) above the ground. It is built, or refurbished, by both sexes, and is constructed of sticks and twigs with a lining of green leaves. Occasionally a pair will take over and repair the old nest of another raptor.

Normally, two dull white eggs, with variable grey and dark red blotches, are laid, though sometimes, presumably as a response to unfavourable conditions, only a single egg is laid. Only the female has been observed incubating the clutch, and during the 40 to 42 days required for hatching the male normally feeds his mate near the nest. Nevertheless, there is some evidence that the female, at least in the early stages of incubation, does some hunting for herself. Where two young hatch there is apparently no sibling aggression, and there are a number of records indicating that two young are regularly reared. Initially, the male brings prey to the nest for the female to feed to the chicks. Later, when the young are about three weeks old, the female assists with bringing in prey, although the male is still the main provider. Prey is most often carried in the crop, regurgitated into the nest, and then torn up and fed to the young by the adult, until such time as the chicks are able to feed themselves. The young first fly at about fifty-five days, but stay in the vicinity of the nest, and continue to be fed by the adults, for some three or four months.

Long-crested Eagle
Known to sometimes attend bush-fires, to exploit the fleeing small animals, the Long-crested Eagle is one of Africa's less formidable eagles.
(*Map 194*)

THE HANDSOME AND AGGRESSIVE HAWK-EAGLES

A small, powerful, and heavily-built eagle, with a long tail and short rounded wings, Cassin's Hawk-eagle (*Spizaetus africanus*) is a little-known species of dense, high-level tropical rainforests of western and central Africa. Throughout its range the species is apparently very rare, and is seldom, if ever, seen perched, probably spending much of its time hidden in the canopy, quietly watching for prey. The few prey items that have been recorded include birds and squirrels, which it probably catches in the tree-tops. Occasionally it is reported soaring low over the forest, and it is only then that it becomes at all conspicuous.

The species was found breeding for the first time in 1970, when a nest was reported from northeastern Gabon. At least one other nest has been discovered since then, but still very little has been recorded about the species' breeding biology.

Across its extensive range, from India and Sri Lanka through tropical Asia to southern Indo-China, and in Indonesia, the Philippines, the Andamans and Lesser Sunda Islands, the appropriately-named Changeable Hawk-eagle (*Spizaetus cirrhatus*) has a confusing variety of plumages. Also, while typically the bird has a prominent long crest, some races are virtually crestless, others totally so, and one (*S. c. limnaetus*) is dimorphic, with a melanic (dark) form as well as a normal form. The bird frequents wooded or forested areas with reasonably clear patches suitable for hunting. Although the species is often seen soaring, it seems to spend the greater part of its day perched half-hidden in the foliage of a large tree, keeping a watch for prey moving in clearings on the ground below. Hares, young peafowl, partridges, squirrels, rats and lizards all figure in the bird's list of prey items; unfortunately, it is not popular around forest villages, where it is very destructive to poultry. Courtship display appears to be almost non-existent, and the large, leaf-lined stick nest is usually sited in excess of 40 feet (12m) up, in a large tree. It seems that the birds may not breed every year, and it is believed that the female incubates the single egg unaided.

The large, powerful, Mountain Hawk-eagle (*Spizaetus nipalensis*) is much larger than the preceding species, and is distributed from Sri Lanka, western India and the Himalayas, to southeastern China and the major islands of Japan. It is a forest species which may be seen soaring above the canopy, from where its calls frequently draw attention to itself. Typically the bird hunts from a tree perch providing a commanding view of an open glade below, swooping out and dropping swiftly down on to its unsuspecting victim. It takes mammals up to the size of hares, large gamebirds such as pheasants and domestic poultry, and occasionally lizards.

In spring, single birds or pairs soar over the breeding area, and perform vigorous undulating display flights. The huge nest is built of sticks and large branches in a forest tree, and in time may measure up to 7 feet (2m) across by more than 3 feet (1m) deep. Invariably a single egg is laid, and this is incubated solely by the female. During the early fledging period the male brings food for both the female and the young chick.

The unmistakable Blyth's Hawk-eagle (*Spizaetus alboniger*) is a handsome black and white hawk-eagle of hill and mountain forests in the Malay Peninsula, Sumatra and Borneo. The bird hunts in the canopy, taking arboreal mammals and birds, and occasionally bats.

The fairly common Black Hawk-eagle (*Spizaetus tyrannus*) lives in lowland forest from eastern Mexico south to northeastern Argentina, Paraguay, and southeastern Brazil. It is most often seen when soaring high over the forest, and at such times is often very vocal, uttering a rhythmical "*whit-whit-whit-wheeeeeeer*". Otherwise, its time is mainly spent perching inconspicuously within the canopy, or lower down, while presumably watching for prey, which is said to include birds, small arboreal mammals and bats.

***Spizaetus* Hawk-eagles**
The rather similar-looking Changeable Hawk-eagle (3) and much larger Mountain Hawk-eagle (2) both have obvious and floppy crests, though crestless, melanistic Changeables also occur. Despite being commonly seen, very little is yet known about Blyth's Hawk-eagle (5), and even less is known about the rare Cassin's Hawk-eagle (4). One of only two New World *Spizaetus* species, with no close relatives, the Black Hawk-eagle (1) is a fairly common lowland species, in suitable habitat.
(*Maps 195-199*)

Black and White Hawk-eagle and Ornate Hawk-eagle
Two forest species of South America are considered here. Despite its striking pied plumage, the Black and White Hawk-eagle (1) is rarely seen and little known; the handsome Ornate Hawk-eagle (2) is notable for the wide variety of its vocalizations.
(Maps 200 and 201)

HAWK-EAGLES OF SOUTH AMERICA AND THE FAR EAST

The handsome but rather small Black and White Hawk-eagle (*Spizastur melanoleucus*) is usually found near forest edges or clearings, and along rivers, in humid and wet tropical forests of South America, and is distributed from southern Mexico southwards to Bolivia, northern Argentina, Paraguay, and southern Brazil. Although a conspicuous and easily-recognized species, throughout most of its extensive range it is generally regarded as rare and local. It soars regularly, and sometimes may be seen perched conspicuously on a branch, when its short, bushy black crest and white-feathered legs are very obvious.

With similar habitat preferences to the preceding species, the strikingly-plumaged and unmistakable Ornate Hawk-eagle (*Spizaetus ornatus*) is distributed from eastern Mexico to western Ecuador, northern Argentina and southern Brazil, and is also found on Trinidad. It is a forest species with a preference for open areas and clearings. On warm days it may often be seen soaring, on horizontal wings, high over the surrounding forests; however, when cruising low over the tree-tops it is often noisy, giving a whistled "*whit, wheeeuuu, whep, whep, whep*". It preys on medium- to large-sized birds such as chachalacas, guans, quails and parrots, but also takes various small mammals.

As its name implies, the Java Hawk-eagle (*Spizaetus bartelsi*) is found only on the island of Java, where it is generally regarded as rare. Being restricted to wooded hills and mountains up to 6500 feet (2000m) mainly in the west of the island, it is now severely threatened by continuing deforestation, and is largely confined to forest reserves. With no information concerning the nest, eggs or habits of the bird currently available, it is difficult to envisage how any sort of conservation strategy can be developed, and at least for the present, the bird's future must remain precarious.

Found on the island of Sulawesi, and the off-shore islands of Buton, Muna, Peling and the Sula group, the Celebes Hawk-eagle (*Spizaetus lanceolatus*) ranges throughout the forested lowlands, up to at least 5000 feet (1524m) in

Hawk-eagles of the Southeast Asian Islands
These four more-or-less distinctly-crested Hawk-eagles, each with its own restricted island distribution, show very different underside patterns. In the Java Hawk-eagle (1) it is dark brown, with broad whitish bars; in the Celebes Hawk-eagle (2) it is narrowly barred black-and-white; in Wallace's Hawk-eagle (3) it is narrowly barred with buff and brown, whilst in the Philippine Hawk-eagle (4) it is rufous, with heavy brown streaks or blotches.
(Maps 202–205)

mountain forests. The bird is most often encountered gliding and sailing above the tree-tops, where it is assumed to take at least some of its prey. However, it seems to prefer hunting in clearings, and although details of its prey are lacking, one bird is known to have taken a chicken, though it is doubtful if it poses any serious threat to domestic fowl. A single, inaccessible nest has been located, some 65 feet (20m) up in an enormous tree at an altitude of around 5000 feet. The fledged young is said to be noisy, giving constant hunger-screams.

The rare and little-known Philippine Hawk-eagle (*Spizaetus philippensis*) is a forest species restricted to the Philippines, including the island of Palawan. The bird presumably has similar habits to other Asian hawk-eagles.

The continuing process of fragmentation of the lowland forests of peninsular Burma and the Malay Peninsula, Borneo and Sumatra, in which Wallace's Hawk-eagle (*Spizaetus nanus*) lives, poses an ever-increasing threat to the species' continued existence. It is a rare and very thinly-distributed species, and precious little is known concerning its breeding and life-history.

BOOTED EAGLE

The heavily-feathered legs of the Booted Eagle (*Hieraaetus pennatus*) give rise to its vernacular name, while another unusual feature of the bird's plumage is that it is dimorphic, occurring in both light and dark forms. Light phase birds are brown above and white below, with contrasting black flight feathers, while dark phase birds are uniform dark brown, except for a conspicuous pale brown diagonal band across the upper wing-coverts, similar to that of the pale form. In flight, both forms show a diagnostic pale wedge on the inner primaries and outer secondaries. Another useful character, seen when a bird is viewed head-on in flight, is a conspicuous small white patch at the junction of the leading edge of the wing and the body. Both phases also show a U-shaped pale rump patch.

The species' breeding range extends from the Iberian Peninsula and northwestern Africa, eastwards to western Siberia and southern Asia, with an additional isolated breeding population in Cape Province, South Africa. Although this species has an extensive range, no races are recognized. The Booted Eagle is typically migratory, with Western Palearctic populations moving south in the autumn to winter in Africa, mainly in Mali, Sudan and Ethiopia, and then southwards through eastern Africa. Some birds infiltrate farther south, into the range of the South African breeding population. The main migration routes of European-breeding birds are through the Caucasus, Bosporus and Gibraltar, both in spring and autumn. The more easterly populations also move south, wintering mainly in India and Burma. Those birds that breed in South Africa arrive on their breeding grounds in Cape Province in early August, and depart in March. In the non-breeding season, many of these birds are observed farther north, in the northern Cape and Namibia, and some even reach southern Angola.

The species prefers dry woodland with open areas in undulating, hilly country or mountainous areas. It soars regularly on flat or slightly drooping wings, and most of its hunting is carried out on the wing, from heights of 330 to 820 feet (100 to 250 metres) or more. When prey is spotted, the bird is able to stoop in quite spectacular fashion, often parachuting initially, and then plunging rapidly, extending the feet as it nears the ground. It may also dive swiftly down into trees, weaving its way with great agility through branches in pursuit of its quarry. At other times it may be observed perched for long periods, waiting for prey to reveal itself. It catches small to medium-sized birds such as larks, starlings, thrushes, doves and partridges; small mammals like susliks, rats, moles and young rabbits; and also large lizards, and occasionally insects.

Soon after arrival on their breeding grounds, the birds perform spectacular display flights, comprising steep dives and upward swoops, accompanied by much calling. The male may also dive repeatedly at the female, and she may roll in flight and present talons. Mating takes place on a cliff ledge, or on a branch of a tree near the nest. Nest building commences shortly after pairing, with both sexes participating. Usually placed in a tree, from 23 to 56 feet (7 to 17 metres) above the ground, the nest is constructed of sticks, and lined with green leaves. Occasionally, in areas where

Booted Eagle
The strongly migratory Booted Eagle is firmly attached to forested country north of the Equator during the breeding season. Migration, however, takes the birds to a vast area covering extreme southern Europe and many parts of the African continent. (*Map 206*)

trees are scarce, a nest may be built on a cliff. Two eggs, which are white with a few faint reddish speckles, are normally laid three to four days apart, and are incubated mainly by the female, for approximately forty days. During this incubation period she is fed at the nest by her mate. When the young hatch they are covered in white or grey down, depending upon whether they will develop into light or dark phase adults. The young fledge in seven to eight weeks, and after their first flight they may return to the nest to be fed, and usually remain in the vicinity of the nest for a further ten days or so.

THE *HIERAAETUS* HAWK-EAGLES

Although some 300 to 400 pairs are estimated to be resident in Spain, elsewhere in southern Europe numbers of Bonelli's Eagle (*Hieraaetus fasciatus*) are disturbingly low, as this powerful, medium-sized eagle has suffered much persecution by man for decades in its southern European breeding haunts. Fortunately, outside this area, across northern Africa, east to India and southern China, the species seems to be faring much better. It is a fine eagle, inhabiting wooded hills and rugged mountains, from sea level up to perhaps 8200 feet (2500m), and adults are often present all year round in the general vicinity of the breeding area. In soaring flight the rather long and broad wings are held flat, and the bird shows a noticeably protruding head, and a long tail with a black terminal band. An aggressive and agile hunter, often killing prey as heavy as, or even heavier than, itself, it preys on a wide variety of mammals and birds in about equal proportions – sometimes taking small snakes and lizards, and even domestic fowl if they are not adequately protected. It is swift enough to be able to catch birds as they fly up from the ground, or fly them down in longer chases.

Typically, the nest is built high up on a ledge in a steep gorge or on a rock face, but in the absence of such a site a large tree will be selected. The nest is an enormous structure of sticks, often measuring in excess of 7 feet (2m) across. It usually contains two eggs, which are incubated by both sexes although the female takes the greater share of the work. Following an incubation period of 40 to 45 days, the young fledge after a further 50 to 80 days, depending on local conditions. Birds breeding south of the Sahara are treated by some authorities as a separate species (*H. spilogaster*), while others regard it merely as a race of the present species.

Closely related to the Booted Eagle of Europe, the Little Eagle (*Hieraaetus morphnoides*) is a small, stocky eagle which also has both light and, more rarely, dark phase plumages. It is widely distributed in Australia, but is absent from Tasmania and the Cape York Peninsula and is scarce in New Guinea. However, it is non-migratory, probably only making local movements in response to fluctuations in prey abundance. It lives in open wooded country and hunts either on the wing or from a suitable tree perch with a commanding view. Its prey includes small mammals, reptiles, large insects and occasionally birds. On warm days it is often to be seen soaring in tight circles, on flat wings. In the breeding season this small eagle performs high, spectacular display flights, involving repeated steep climbs and dives, with wings closed, accompanied by much calling.

Resident in the forested and wooded areas of Africa south of the Sahara, Ayres' Hawk-eagle (*Hieraaetus dubius*) is a small, handsomely-marked, stocky eagle which is not often seen, and is generally uncommon to rare throughout its range. It often soars to great heights, or spends long hours perched in the canopy, where it is difficult to observe. In high soaring flight, when potential prey is spotted, it plummets at incredible speed, exhibiting a falcon-like profile. At tree-height it is able to weave skilfully in and out of branches in pursuit of birds, many of which are caught in flight. It takes medium-sized birds, from bulbuls and starlings up to pigeons and occasionally guineafowl, and also small mammals, such as tree squirrels.

The contrastingly-patterned Chestnut-bellied Hawk-eagle (*Hieraaetus kienerii*) is an unmistakable forest eagle with a discontinuous range, occurring in parts of south-western India, and in Sri Lanka, and then again from the eastern Himalayas to Burma, Malaya, Borneo and Indonesia.

The *Hieraeetus* Hawk-eagles
Foot development varies considerably in this group of bold and aggressive predators. Bonelli's Eagle (4) and the Little Eagle (2) have very powerful feet with an exceptionally long hind claw, while the Chestnut-bellied Hawk-eagle (1) has unusually long toes. Ayres' Hawk-eagle (3) is a small species, specializing on bird prey.
(Maps 207–210)

Philippine Eagle
One of the world's rarest eagles, the Philippine Eagle is now afforded legal protection, which hopefully will result in an improvement in its present precarious state. A captive breeding and release programme has also been instigated.
(*Map 211*)

Martial Eagle
Being Africa's largest eagle, the distinctively-plumaged Martial Eagle is impossible to confuse with any other. It is most often seen soaring on long wings, high above the African bush, in its search for prey.
(*Map 212*)

PHILIPPINE EAGLE AND MARTIAL EAGLE

Second only to the Harpy Eagle in size and power, the magnificent Philippine Eagle (*Pithecophaga jefferyi*) is sadly one of the most threatened birds of prey in the world. Its problems are not new; one of the first to speak out on its behalf was Charles Lindbergh, the pioneer aviator. However, continued deforestation, hunting, and illegal trapping have made its position increasingly precarious. Recent efforts by conservationists have succeeded in stirring concern for the bird among the Philippine people, and indeed the name by which it is introduced here reflects this. Formerly known as the Monkey-eating Eagle (a misnomer), it now ranks as a national symbol. Whether this will suffice to save it in a land plagued by political uncertainty and natural disasters remains to be seen.

Flying lemurs, not monkeys, are the principal prey of the Philippine Eagle, but small deer, hornbills and other large birds also figure in its diet. Even some snakes are taken. Still-hunting, that is, patient watching from a perch, is one of its foraging techniques. The other is to soar to the tops of forested mountains, then glide down low over the canopy, ready to seize prey. Mindanao is its main stronghold, but recent investigations have revealed that some of the other islands hold more birds than had previously been realized.

No information appears to exist about the displays of this bird, and we are still in ignorance about many features of its breeding biology. Nests are hard to find, as they are situated in the tops of forest giants, often shrouded by creepers, and close observation or filming is obviously a major undertaking. Only one egg is laid, as with many large eagles, apparently usually in November. With an incubation period of about nine weeks, and a further fifteen weeks for fledging, this ensures that the young eagle leaves the nest at the start of the dry season in late April. Both parents incubate, and bring sprays of fresh leaves to the nest throughout the breeding cycle. The female performed about 70 per cent of the incubation in one nest observed, while food finding was exclusively the job of the male. He continues to be mainly responsible for this while the young are reared. A young bird fitted with a tiny radio was tracked after fledging, and remained in its parents' home range for at least eighteen months, during which time it was probably dependent on them for much of its food. This extended period of dependency is typical of large eagles, and allows them to breed at most every other year. Such a slow reproductive rate is yet another factor making them vulnerable to habitat loss, persecution, and other adverse circumstances.

Arguably as impressive, if less powerfully built, is Africa's largest eagle, the Martial Eagle (*Polemaetus bellicosus*). A predator of open country, it is typical of savanna and bushveldt areas with scattered acacia thorn trees. Much of its day is spent in the air, whether actively seeking prey or

Crowned Eagle
In the forests of Africa south of the Sahara, the impressive Crowned Eagle fills the same ecological niche as the Harpy Eagle in South America – dashing through the tangled canopy as it hunts large prey such as antelopes, monkeys, rats and birds. Today it is most at risk from human disturbance, particularly as its crown feathers are much prized by some local tribes. (*Map 213*)

not, although display flights as such are not a prominent feature of its behaviour. Prey sighted from the air, often a long way off, is taken in a long, oblique, high-speed stoop. Birds such as guineafowl, francolins and bustards make up much of its diet, but large mammals such as hyraxes and small antelopes are also frequent victims. Even some mammalian predators such as small cats and mongooses are occasionally taken.

Typical eagle nests are built, piles of sticks up to 13 feet (4m) in diameter, sited typically in an African beech. One egg only is the normal clutch, and incubation is almost entirely by the female. Hatching after seven weeks, the eaglet is fed by the female for about nine weeks, after which it has to cope unaided with the prey brought to the nest. Fledging usually takes place about fourteen weeks.

Martial Eagles may breed several years in succession, then fail to do so for a time. All in all, their breeding rate is low, and they are vulnerable to persecution inflicted in order, supposedly, to protect farm stock.

CROWNED EAGLE

Although it is by no means Africa's largest eagle, the Crowned Eagle (*Stephanoaetus coronatus*) is nevertheless that continent's most powerful species. Its stout legs, and feet with huge hind-talons, are ideally suited to taking large prey, which the bird does either by dropping on to it from above, or by capturing it after a short, swift, aerial chase – the eagle's short wings allowing it to fly with considerable agility through the tangled branches and foliage of its woodland habitat. In the main, the bird's prey consists of small antelopes and other unexpectedly heavy animals, but other items include monkeys, hyraxes, mongooses, rats and even domestic cats. It also takes some reptiles and snakes, and the occasional bird. The relatively large size of much of this prey dramatically underlines the species' power and killing capabilities. The bird seems to divide its day approximately equally between soaring above the forest (when it causes much agitation among the local monkeys) and perching in a tree with a good view over some opening or clearing, from where it can swoop down on to its prey.

The species seems fairly well distributed throughout forested and well-wooded areas of Africa south of the Sahara, from sea level up to more than 11,500 feet (3500m), although it is certainly less common towards the south. It is an extremely noisy species, much prone to vocalization both when perched and when on the wing. In display, the male performs steep dives and ascents, sometimes as much as 3000 feet (915m) above the tree-tops, calling loud and long at the top of each ascent. When the female joins the display flight she will often roll over in mid-air and present her

Golden Eagle
When caught in sunlight, the golden nape and neck hackles of the Golden Eagle show how the species acquired its name. It is a bird of wild mountains and glens, so typical of the Scottish Highlands, although the bird is distributed throughout the Northern Hemisphere in similar habitats.
(*Map 214*)

Gurney's Eagle and Wedge-tailed Eagle
The least-known of all the true eagles (*Aquila* spp.), Gurney's Eagle (1) seems doomed to be the first to become extinct as its preferred habitat is the rapidly-diminishing lowland forest of New Guinea. Named on account of its distinctively-shaped tail, which is best seen in flight, the impressive, dark-plumaged Wedge-tailed Eagle (2) is Australia's largest raptor. It is wi persecuted, but seems to be holding its own in the wilder parts of its homeland.
(Maps 215 and 216)

talons to the male. The nest, which is used for many seasons, is sited anywhere between 40 and 150 feet (12 and 45 metres) up in a large tree. It is built of sticks, with a lining of greenery, and construction is carried out by both birds, although the female takes the major part. A well-established nest can measure up to 7 feet (2m) across by 10 feet (3m) deep. Incubation of the one or two eggs is usually shared by both birds. It lasts about fifty days, and during this time the female is fed on the nest by her mate, although in some pairs the roles can become temporarily reversed, with the female feeding the incubating male. If two young are hatched, the weaker one soon succumbs to the stronger, and the remaining chick is fed by both parents, again with the female taking the major part, until fledging at about 110 days. After this point there are considerable differences between families. In some, the young are dependent on their parents for so long that the adults are prevented from breeding in the following season; in others, the young mature more quickly and the adults are able to breed regularly, producing young each year.

GOLDEN EAGLE

Occurring in suitable habitats throughout the entire Holarctic region, with partial southerly winter migrations, the Golden Eagle (*Aquila chrysaetos*) is the most widespread and numerous large eagle in the Northern Hemisphere. However, it is nowhere common, and persecution pressures in many parts of its range are certainly putting its future in jeopardy.

It is a bird of open mountainous country, the wilder and more extensive the better, and over such terrain it spends many hours on the wing each day, performing all manner of graceful glides, side-slips, soaring ascents and dives, all performed apparently effortlessly and with virtually no wing-movements. It is also capable of spectacular steep dives, at speeds in excess of 100 mph (160kph). With such flying skills it easily captures a wide variety of mammals and gamebirds, invariably taking them on the ground in a swooping attack.

Although sometimes in a tree, the untidy nest of sticks and branches is most often built on a rocky crag, and over the course of many seasons it can grow to enormous size. Most pairs have a number of nests, which they use in rotation. Usually two eggs are laid, and these are incubated, most often by the female alone, for about forty-five days. Somewhat unusually, about 20 per cent of all second chicks survive to fledging, which usually takes about eighty days. In non-migratory populations, the young seem reluctant to leave their natal area, and even when driven off by their parents the following season, they move only a relatively short distance away.

THE *AQUILA* EAGLES

Besides the Golden Eagle, the genus *Aquila* contains eight other species, distributed throughout the Old World. All bear a general resemblance in build and plumage to the Golden Eagle, though only Verreaux's Eagle, considered in the next section, can match that species' powers of flight.

Australia's largest bird of prey, the Wedge-tailed Eagle (*Aquila audax*) is a handsome species resembling the Golden Eagle in adult plumage, but with a long wedge-shaped tail. Impressive looks have, however, been of little help to it in mitigating the effects of persecution. Intensive shooting and trapping campaigns have been directed against it as a supposed menace to lambs and other stock, yet the extent of the remaining wilderness in Australia has so far enabled it to survive. Ironically, its major prey today over much of Australia is the introduced rabbit, rightly considered a pest; in times past marsupials up to the size of medium-sized wallabies would have been its staple diet.

Early mornings or evening are the favoured times for hunting, which is usually done in low-level flight. During the heat of the day the bird may perch inactively, or soar to great heights, occasionally descending in a long stoop to take prey. Soaring and aerobatics are also a feature of the displays which herald the start of the breeding season. August or September are typical months for breeding. The huge stick nest may be sited anywhere from a tall tree-top down to near ground level, depending on the type of vegetation available. Even nests on the ground are occasionally

The *Aquila* Eagles of Eurasia and Africa
Both the Lesser Spotted Eagle (1) and Greater Spotted Eagle (2) derive their names from their light-spotted plumage as immature birds; the adults are virtually unmarked and can sometimes be very similar to each other in colour, making identification difficult. The white shoulder-patch and tawny nape make the Imperial Eagle (3) an easily-identified bird. Although extremely variable in colour, the generally brown plumage, combined with its medium size, should identify the Tawny Eagle (4), whilst the sepia-brown plumage and occipital crest are good field guides to identifying Wahlberg's Eagle (5).
(Maps 217–221)

recorded. Two eggs are usually laid, and both young are frequently reared to fledging, which is rather unusual in eagles. Fledging occurs from about ten weeks, but the young continue to be dependent on their parents for a considerable time after their first flight.

Gurney's Eagle (*Aquila gurneyi*) is another Australasian species, but one that is much less well known and possibly also much closer to extinction. It inhabits New Guinea, the Aru Islands and the northern Moluccas, and unlike most other *Aquila* species it is a forest-dweller. Unfortunately, the forest it prefers is that of the coastal lowlands, where forest destruction for cultivation is at present most intense. Gurney's Eagle is probably the least well-known member of the genus, and information is so scarce that it is difficult to assess the bird's status or future prospects.

Two smaller Eurasian species are the Greater Spotted Eagle (*Aquila clanga*) and Lesser Spotted Eagle (*Aquila pomarina*). Difficult to distinguish in the field, especially as adults, when they are unspotted, they can be differentiated to some extent by habitat. The Greater Spotted Eagle is typically a bird of marshy valleys and the sides of lakes or rivers, near to woodland but not within it. The Lesser Spotted is more thoroughly a woodland bird, with no particular need to be near water. Both are efficient general hunters of medium-sized birds and mammals, those taken by the larger species including a good many waterbirds. Hunting is usually carried out by quartering at tree-top height, or from a perch. Both species are migratory, moving south in winter to northeast Africa or the Middle East.

Piracy on other predators is a regular habit of the Tawny Eagle (*Aquila rapax*) though it is quite capable both of hunting efficiently for itself and of scavenging on carrion. With such versatile habits it is perhaps not surprising that it is one of the most numerous and successful of the *Aquila* eagles, with a range including eastern Europe, much of Asia, and most of Africa. Northern populations are migratory, and often travel in very large flocks. In Africa the Tawny Eagle is most likely to be confused with Wahlberg's Eagle (*Aquila wahlbergi*), a bird of wooded savanna or bushveldt. A hunter of small gamebirds, small mammals and reptiles, it forages by making short flights from tree to tree, pouncing on prey taken by surprise.

Only slightly smaller than the Golden Eagle, but more handsomely marked, is the Imperial Eagle (*Aquila heliaca*). Although it has a wide distribution through Central Asia, its European populations are under threat, as it prefers the open lowland country in which man's activities are most intense. Birds of the Spanish race, characterized by their striking white shoulders, are particularly at risk. Less agile in flight than the Golden Eagle, this is nevertheless a bold and skilful hunter.

VERREAUX'S EAGLE

Unrivalled in its powers of flight, and majestic in appearance, this bird has so captured the imagination of African ornithologists that it has been described as probably the world's most intensively studied eagle. *Aquila verreauxi*, also known as the Black Eagle, commemorates in its name a French naturalist who, with his brother, studied the flora and fauna of the Cape in the early nineteenth century. Rocky mountains, cliffs and gorges are this eagle's habitat, where updraughts and air currents provide conditions in which it can soar effortlessly for hours on end. Such flights serve to mark territories rather than to seek food, though actual physical aggression between neighbouring pairs is rare. During the heat of the day, time may be spent on a cliff perch, resting or preening.

Occurring in suitable areas from the Cape to Ethiopia,its staple diet in most places consists of hyraxes. "Dassies", as these animals are widely known in Africa, live in colonies among rocks, and are usually taken by eagles quartering low over hill slopes to surprise them sunbathing or feeding in the open. In Somalia and Ethiopia a more varied diet is recorded, including small antelopes and hares up to a weight of about 22 pounds (10kg). Birds such as francolins and guineafowl are also occasionally captured.

Detailed knowledge of the Black Eagle's breeding biology has been amassed by a long-continued survey of some fifty pairs in the Matopos Hills of Zimbabwe. Aerial displays mark the approach of breeding, and as might be expected from such a master of the air they are extremely spectacular. Undulating display flights with alternating dives and upward swoops are performed by many eagles, but in this species the dives are steeper than most and the upward swoops longer, estimated at up to 1000 feet (over 300 metres). At the top of each swoop the eagle may execute a roll or somersault. Both sexes may perform undulating flights, but a variation in which the bird swings, pendulum-fashion, between two points in the sky seems to be exclusive to the male. Mock battles and talon-grappling between male and female are both occasionally seen.

Nests are usually placed on cliffs, sometimes on trees, particularly euphorbias. Each pair maintains up to five nests, though usually only one or two. The nest is of sticks, and measures up to 8 feet (2.4m) across, the central cup being about 3 feet (1m) across, and lined with green leaves. Nest building and repair is carried out by both sexes. Two eggs are usually laid, at three-day intervals. Only the female incubates at night, but some males take a large share of the task during daylight hours. Hatching after just over six weeks, the eaglet from the first-laid egg will be some three days older than its sibling, and the strange "Cain and Abel" battle then ensues, more intensively perhaps than in any

Verreaux's Eagle
Alternatively known as the Black Eagle, Verreaux's Eagle is, for many ornithologists, the ultimate eagle. Certainly its mastery of the air is unsurpassed, and this, combined with its black and white plumage, set off by yellow facial features, cannot fail to impress all who see it in the dry, mountainous regions of Africa.
(*Map 222*)

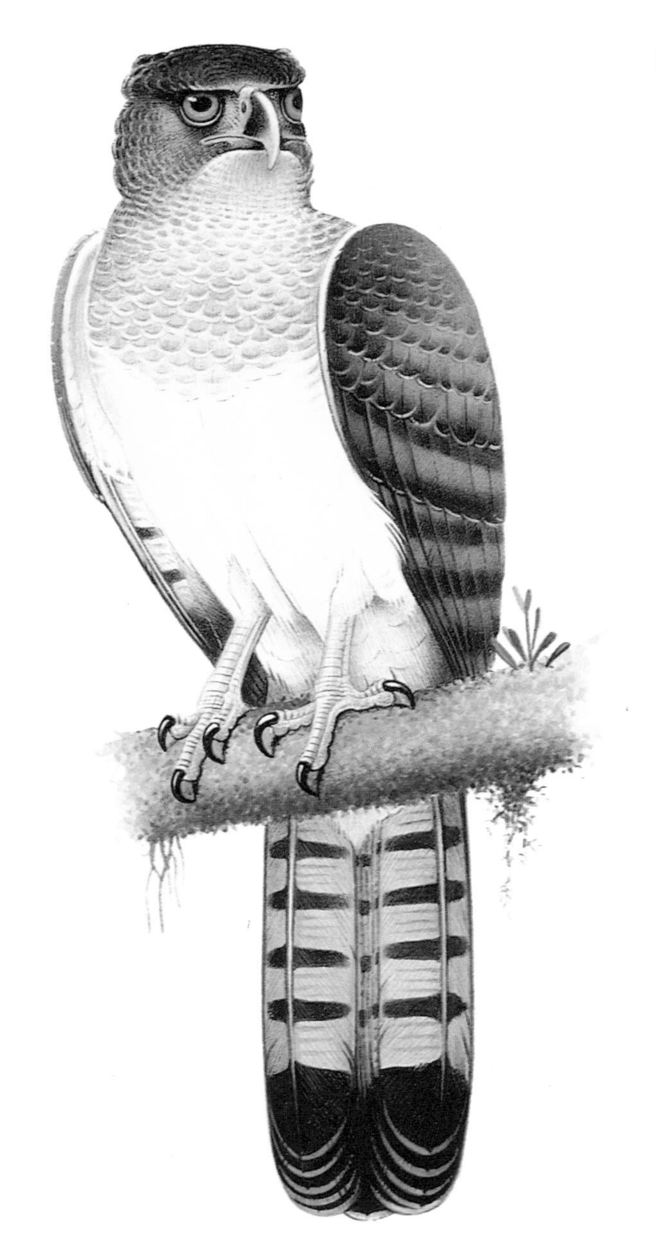

New Guinea Harpy Eagle
Ranking as one of the world's most spectacular eagles, the New Guinea Harpy Eagle is today unfortunately under considerable threat. Deforestation of its New Guinea habitat, and the demand for its decorative wing- and tail-feathers, are imposing pressures on its ever-dwindling population from which it may never recover.
(*Map 223*)

other eagle species. In one set of 650 breeding records there was only a single confirmed case of two chicks being reared; normally the elder kills the younger, the parents making no attempt to intervene. A detailed record was kept of one such battle, which ended in the usual way after 72 hours. During this time, the elder chick pecked the younger 1569 times in 38 bouts lasting a total of 187 minutes out of the 34 daylight hours available. The end result was inevitable.

The first feathers to appear on the chick are the primary wing quills at about thirty days, and the eaglet has feathers covering most of the down after sixty days. At first the young bird is brooded by the female almost continuously, but by three weeks old this has dwindled to 30 per cent of the time, and soon after this it ceases, apart from short periods when the female will shelter the chick from rain or sun. For the first thirty days, the male brings most of the food, but after this both parents take roughly equal shares in hunting. Making its first flight at about thirteen weeks, the young bird is dependent on its parents for a further fourteen to fifteen weeks, after which they drive it out of the nesting territory to fend for itself. Breeding success varies considerably from year to year, recorded extremes in the Matopos study ranging from 46 per cent to 89 per cent. Weather appears to be a crucial factor, with good breeding results following hot dry years, and poor results following years of above-average rainfall.

New Guinea Harpy Eagle

Despite being rather common on the island of New Guinea, and on some of its low off-shore islands, the New Guinea Harpy Eagle (*Harpyopsis novaeguinae*) is not very well known at all. Mostly, it seems to be encountered in lowland forest, and on lower beech-wooded mountain slopes, up to about 10,000 feet (3050m), where it is often to be seen soaring above the tree-tops, or occasionally perched in some large tree. When observed in this situation it can often be seen craning its neck at strange angles, peering this way and that in its search for prey. Possibly its erected ruff is being used as an aid to hearing prey in such instances. Once prey is located this large eagle can move about on the ground with surprising speed, using its rather long legs to good advantage and employing flaps of its half-opened wings to assist in the chase.

The species' feeding preferences are not adequately recorded, but it is known to take tree kangaroos and ground wallabies, while unconfirmed reports claim that it will also prey on piglets. We seem to know almost nothing about the bird's breeding habits, but one nest, some 65 feet (20m) up in a large tree, was very big, built of sticks, and contained a single nestling. The local people maintain that the same nests are re-used each year.

Unfortunately, this handsome and impressive bird is, like so many others, under considerable threat. Its wooded lowland haunts are being rapidly clear-felled for their valuable timber, and the eagle is being driven more and more into the mountains. Unfortunately, it is not safe even there, because large numbers are killed annually and sold in the local markets to satisfy the demands of the New Guinea highlanders, who greatly prize the wing and tail feathers for use in their head-dresses. Certainly the species' continued existence is a cause for great concern.

Indian Black Eagle
Exceptionally long wings are the distinguishing feature of this Asian forest predator. Combined with the bird's very low body weight they permit the unusually slow flight over the forest canopy which the bird uses as its main hunting technique. *(Map 224)*

INDIAN BLACK EAGLE

With highly specialized wings featuring long and flexible primaries, and equally specialized feet, in which the outer toe is considerably shortened and the talons on the others are much longer and straighter than normal, the Indian Black Eagle (*Ictinaetus malayensis*) is unique among the eagles. When observed in its natural habitat of forested mountain country from India through Southeast Asia to Sulawesi and the Moluccas, the reasons for these specializations soon become apparent. When hunting, the bird soars in wide circles, at an extraordinarily low speed. It does this on motionless, slightly up-tilted wings, the long, splayed primaries of which undoubtedly allow the bird to achieve an exceptionally low stalling speed. The body too is small in relation to the wing-area, resulting in an unusually low wing-loading. All this allows the bird to fly extremely slowly over, and even through, the canopy, inspecting everything closely in its search for lizards, small mammals and birds, and in particular for nestlings and eggs. Here is where the birds' specialized feet come into their own, for although eggs or nestlings may be snatched from a nest, the bird will also frequently take the entire nest, the shape of the talons undoubtedly facilitating this while the power of the huge wings allows the whole structure to be torn free from its anchorage. The nest is then carried away to a convenient perch where the contents are dealt with at leisure. Curiously, despite being adapted for slow flight, the bird is also capable of considerable speed, either when swooping on to tree- or ground-based prey, or even when swooping into dark caves to catch swiflets or bats.

The bird's speed is also shown during its display flight, which involves spectacular high-speed dives, often in excess of 10,000 feet (3050m), with fully-folded wings, often ending in an upward swoop. The birds also indulge in high-speed acrobatic chases through the canopy. The rarely-discovered nest is sited high in a large and often creeper-festooned tree, and is constructed of small sticks, with a lining of stout green leaves. Usually one egg is laid, occasionally two, but further details of incubation and fledging are unknown.

Family Sagittariidae

Secretary Bird

One species

The Secretary Bird – *Sagittarius serpentarius*

Clerks of bygone days were evidently in the habit of keeping quill pens tucked behind their ears, for it is this bird's strikingly plumed head which reminded early ornithologists of secretaries, and so determined its name. The Latin *Sagittarius*, however, recalls an archer with his quiver of arrows. Whatever their origins, unusual names seem well-merited by this very unusual bird. Eagle-sized, with very long legs, long central tail feathers, and the unmistakably ornamented head, the Secretary Bird is like no other bird of prey. In addition to its distinctive outer appearance it also has various anatomical peculiarities, and doubts have often been voiced as to its relationship with other raptors. Chief contenders as possible relatives are the seriemas of South America – birds, allied to the cranes and rails, which resemble the Secretary Bird in appearance and way of life. However, for the present this unique species is retained among the raptors, but classified in a family of its own.

Grassland, bushveldt and sparsely wooded savanna are the Secretary Bird's preferred habitats. Although it can fly well it spends most of its day on foot, patrolling its territory at a steady pace in search of prey. Now and then it bursts into a quicker, stamping gait – probably to try and startle prey into moving. Once spotted, most victims are seized in the bill after a quick dash, but larger animals may be killed with blows from the feet. Secretary Birds have a reputation for taking snakes, and these do indeed form part of its food. However, small mammals, lizards and large insects make up most of the diet, and young birds or eggs are often taken from ground nests. Ground blackened by a recent grass fire is searched for small victims of the flames, but large carrion is ignored. Pairs and family parties may hunt together, and the territory of up to 4000 acres (1600ha) of grassland is vigorously defended against intruding neighbours. In arid areas, territorial instincts are subdued in the vicinity of water-holes, where gatherings of twenty or more birds may occur. Secretary Birds roost on the tops of flat-topped acacia trees where available, usually leaving them an hour or two after dawn and returning about an hour before sunset.

Overhead, a Secretary Bird shows a distinctive silhouette, with broad wings, and the long tail and legs projecting behind. Courtship displays offer a chance to observe this outline at leisure, as the birds, singly or together, soar high in the sky uttering strange groaning calls.

Switchback nuptial flights like those of many other large raptors are also sometimes seen. Courtship chases on the ground also occur, the two birds dashing in zig-zag fashion through the grass with their wings raised above their backs. The nest is a huge flat stick platform up to 8 feet (2.4m) across. Interestingly, the sticks are carried in the bill; presumably the bird's feet are too weak to carry them in the usual manner of hawks and eagles. A territory usually includes one or two old nests which may or may not be re-used. Two or three greenish-white eggs are laid, hatching after about forty-five days of incubation, which appears to be entirely by the female. The young are brooded, again mainly by the female, for three weeks or so while the male brings most of the food. In the later stages, roles are reversed and the female does most of the hunting. Food is always carried in the crop and regurgitated – a habit shared with vultures but not with other raptors which always carry it in the feet. At first the food is a liquid mush of half-digested insects; solid food fed to the chicks later may be held with the foot and torn into smaller pieces with the bill as it is by other birds of prey. At ten to eleven weeks old the young finally leave the nest, though they are able to fly only very weakly for some two weeks after that. The family party may hunt together for a time after this, but only until the young are competent at securing their own food.

Secretary Bird
Deriving its name from its supposed resemblance to an old-time lawyer's clerk with a bunch of quill pens behind his ear, the unique Secretary Bird is becoming less common in its African plains habitat. Most often seen on the ground hunting prey, especially at bush-fires, it is, nevertheless, a rather graceful flyer.
(*Map 225*)

Family FALCONIDAE

Caracaras and Falcons

Sixty-one species in ten genera

CRESTED CARACARA

Introducing the family Falconidae is the first of a number of South American species which are in many respects atypical of the family. Typical falcons are small to medium in size, and have pointed wings. However, the Crested Caracara (*Polyborus plancus*) is a decidedly large bird, with broad eagle-like wings: indeed it is sometimes called the Mexican Eagle and is the national bird of Mexico. Despite its impressive appearance it is actually a scavenger, like all caracaras, and thus very different from most members of the family in behaviour. Another difference is that caracaras build their own nests, like the hawk family but unlike all other members of the falcon family whose nesting habits are known.

Distributed from the southern USA south to Tierra del Fuego and the Falkland Islands, the Crested Caracara is absent only from the rainforests of Amazonia. Elsewhere it is present wherever there is food to be scavenged. It exhibits a good deal of geographic variation, and has sometimes been subdivided into three species. The form occurring in the USA is sometimes called Audubon's Caracara.

Although often seen with vultures, and somewhat resembling them in habits, the caracara's methods of finding food differ from them in a number of ways. It does not soar, but moves quite efficiently in flapping flight, so it is not dependent on thermals to keep it airborne and enable it to seek food. Consequently it is on the wing from first light, and is likely to be first on the scene at road casualties or other overnight fatalities. It is also more actively predatory and opportunistic than any vulture, quick to seize weak or disabled animals up to the size of sheep or goats. The latter habit has earned it a bad reputation in sheep country, and it is often shot. Its close relative, the Guadalupe Caracara (*Polyborus lutosus*) suffered the ultimate penalty of extinction for its similar habits. Confined to the island of Guadalupe off Baja California, this bird was regarded as a menace to Angora goats reared on the island, and was deliberately exterminated; not long after, the island was abandoned! The Crested Caracara occasionally pursues prey in groups, and also indulges in "kleptoparasitism" – pursuing and harassing other birds to make them disgorge their food. Vultures and pelicans are frequent victims of this treatment. It is also fond of fish, and digs out turtle eggs after watching the adults lay. The long legs and flat-toed feet are ideal for scratching under fallen branches or cowpats, but less useful for carrying food, so the bill is more usually employed. When scratching and excavating, the bird is looking for dung bettles or other insects, and it may be these rather than carrion that attract it to some of the extensively decomposed corpses frequented by vultures. Agile in flight when occasion demands, it is said to seize pieces of food held out from moving trains in Brazil.

No well-marked displays appear to precede the Crested Caracara's breeding cycle, although there are records of fights between males. The nest is a large stick structure with a deep central cup lined with pellets, dung and rubbish. It may be placed in the crown of a palm, a cactus or a tree, and in totally treeless areas it will be placed on rocks or even on the ground. Nests are added to and re-used year after year. Two or three eggs are laid, and incubated by both adults for about four weeks. The fledging period appears to be very variable, but is at least two months. Both parents take part in caring for the young, and assist in feeding them until they are quite well grown. There is some evidence that the Crested Caracara may at times rear more than one brood in a year.

CARACARAS OF SOUTH AMERICA'S MOUNTAINS AND RAINFORESTS

Besides the Crested Caracara, eight other species inhabit South and Central America, and they are grouped into three genera. They resemble the preceding species in being scavengers or opportunists, rather than being truly raptorial. Two species in particular are about as far from the image of the falcon family as can be imagined. Dwelling in dense rainforest, these are the members of the genus *Daptrius*, lumpy black and white birds with brightly coloured bare skin on the face, more resembling the South American gamebirds called currassows than birds of prey. Somewhat the better-known of the two, the Red-throated Caracara (*Daptrius americanus*) occurs from southern Mexico south to Peru and Brazil. Usually found in parties of three to six, its presence is generally announced by a chorus of harsh screams and cackles, often from high in the forest canopy. Wasp larvae make up most of its diet, varied with a few fruits and seeds, and it displays surprising agility for so clumsy-looking a bird when breaking into a wasps' nest. Surprisingly, even the most dangerous wasps merely swarm round it without attacking, and some form of natural chemical repulsion has been suggested. When a wasps' nest is too thin and papery to support the bird, it may tear pieces off and carry them to a more comfortable perch to feed. Particularly noisy at the start of the breeding season, the Red-throated Caracara builds a nest of twigs, and lays two or three eggs. Beyond this, however, its breeding habits are unknown.

Mainly an Amazonian species, the Yellow-throated

Crested Caracara
Related to the falcons, the Crested Caracara is a specialized carrion-feeder, as witnessed by its bare face. Nevertheless, it is widely omnivorous, taking live or dead fish, mammals, insects and larvae, birds' eggs and young, as well as vegetable matter, feeding wherever and whenever the opportunity arises. (*Map 226*)

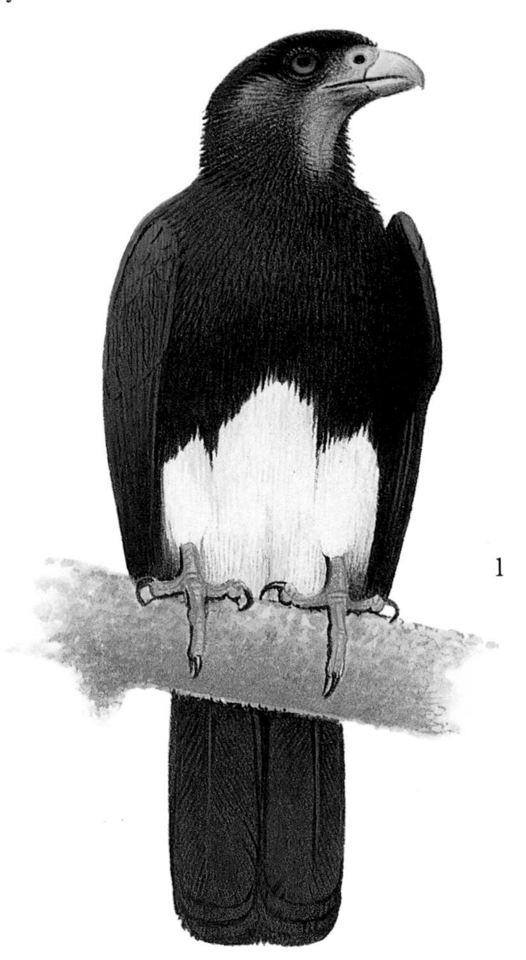

1

2

Yellow-throated Caracara and Red-throated Caracara
The unfeathered skin of the face and chin gives these birds their vernacular names, being lemon-yellow in the Yellow-throated Caracara (2), and pink to reddish in the Red-throated Caracara (1). Both are opportunistic feeders and scavengers of the South American forests.
(Maps 227 and 228)

Caracara (*Daptrius ater*) resembles the Red-throated in many ways, but appears to have a more varied diet. Whether it also attacks wasps' nests is not known, although it certainly eats ants. Also consumed are insects, spiders, nestling birds, fruits and some carrion. More inclined to be solitary than its relative, it also ventures out at times into other habitats such as savanna or mangroves. It is one of many tropical forest birds whose nests have never been seen and described by ornithologists.

A totally different habitat is chosen by the four southern South American species that make up the genus *Phalcoboenus*. They are birds of open treeless or mountainous country, including the High Andes. The Carunculated Caracara (*Phalcoboenus carunculatus*) lives in the Andes of Ecuador and Colombia, and has been little studied, but its habits appear to be similar to those of the better-known Mountain Caracara (*Phalcoboenus megalopterus*). Living from 3300 feet (1000m) up to the highest elevations, it finds food while wandering about on foot on high-altitude cattle pastures or moorlands. Large insects, rodents, nestling birds and carrion make up its diet, and it has learned to exploit man in places, visiting Indian villages, and following cars to glean food scraps thrown from the windows. Around Lake Titicaca it forages in farmed areas. Breeding on cliffs, it may build little or no nest, or a substantial stick structure. Two eggs are laid.

Lower altitudes, from the slopes of the Andes through Patagonia, are chosen by the White-throated Caracara (*Phalcoboenus albogularis*). Similar to others of the genus in most ways, it is the only one that ventures at all into woodland, in this case forests of *Nothofagus* or Southern Beech. First described by Charles Darwin, it is alternatively known as Darwin's Caracara.

Occurring as it does on the Falkland Islands, as well as on Tierra del Fuego, Forster's Caracara (*Phalcoboenus australis*) is probably the best-known member of the genus. It is a scavenger around colonies of penguins and other seabirds, but also attacks weak lambs, and has been extensively shot as a result. Nests are placed in grass tussocks or on rock ledges.

Two small caracaras are included in the genus *Milvago*. The Chimango Caracara (*Milvago chimango*) lives in the southern half of South America, and is a bird of open country, reaching very high population densities on the Argentinian pampas. Another opportunistic species, its diet includes such varied items as insects, eggs and nestlings, vegetable matter and carrion. It prefers cultivated areas, and can sometimes be seen in large numbers following a tractor as gulls do in the USA and Europe. It has earned unpopularity by attacking weak lambs, and pecking at saddle sores on horses.

The Yellow-headed Caracara (*Milvago chimachima*) has a generally more northerly range, extending from Panama south to northern Argentina. It inhabits more wooded areas than the preceding species, including savanna, brush and clearings in forest. Particularly fond of cattle country, it is known for its habit of picking ticks from the backs of stock, though as with the Chimango Caracara it will also attack sores. Both species build fairly large stick nests, usually in trees, though the Chimango Caracara will also nest on the ground in open pampas.

Savanna, Woodland and Mountain Caracaras
The Carunculated Caracara (1), Mountain Caracara (2), White-throated Caracara (3) and Forster's Caracara (6) replace each other southwards down the west side of South America, with Forster's, the southernmost, occurring on several off-shore islands. They seem to partially replace Crows, feeding on virtually anything, including refuse and carrion, as well as preying on birds, eggs, insects and small mammals. Widely distributed throughout South America, with some overlap, the Chimango Caracara (4) and Yellow-headed Caracara (5) are usually thought to form a superspecies: the male Chimango has bluish-grey legs, whilst those of the female are yellow.
(*Maps 229-234*)

Laughing Falcon
Distinctive both visually and audibly, the Laughing Falcon is one of South America's most renowned snake-eating birds, taking venomous and non-venomous species with equal relish.
(*Map 235*)

Forest Falcons
An astonishing range of plumage variations makes the Barred Forest Falcon (1) one of the most confusing of South American raptors. Sclater's Forest Falcon (2) is a rare species with a short tail. The Slaty-backed Forest Falcon (3) is one of the few raptors known to deliberately provoke mobbing by small birds in order to catch them. Known only from a few specimens, Traylor's Forest Falcon (4) has relatively smaller feet than other members of this group.
(Maps 236–239)

Laughing Falcon

Dawn in a South American rainforest is marked by a chorus of bizarre sounds from the hoarse roaring of howler monkeys to the repeated "*hanaquoi*" calls of the gamebirds called chachalacas. Joining in with at first a single note, then a double one, repeated more and more frequently, the Laughing Falcon's voice is one of the major ingredients of this glorious cacophony. Often, a second bird will join in, the combined effect rising to a crescendo of excitement. The performance is repeated at dusk, and intermittently at other times of day. At other times, such as when disturbed, the Laughing Falcon utters various cackling calls which sound even more like laughter than its usual clarion call.

Found over most forested parts of Central and South America, the Laughing Falcon (*Herpetotheres cachinnans*) prefers clearings, edges or watercourses to unbroken woodland. Were it not for its voice it would often be missed, since it is fond of perching on a high, exposed branch, screened from below by the canopy. Long periods may be passed on the same perch, for the Laughing Falcon is a "still hunter" of great patience, and the prey for which it waits are snakes. Once a snake is seen, the falcon drops on it like a stone, hitting the ground with a distinct thud. Snakes are seized in the bill, just behind the head, which is sometimes bitten off, and the kill is usually swift. However, some accounts mention the bird using one wing to fend off the strikes of a snake, while manoeuvring to deliver the *coup de grâce.* Snakes taken include even highly venomous species such as coral snakes, and range in size from small to quite large. Small ones are swallowed tail-first, while large ones are torn to pieces before being consumed. Some lizards are also taken, and a few other creatures such as small mammals and centipedes. Laughing Falcons fly relatively infrequently, and when they do, it is usually just a short move between perches or a return to a perch with newly caught prey. Snakes may be carried in the bill if small, otherwise they are carried with the feet, holding the snake in line with the bird's body. Flight action consists of alternating flaps and glides, and the bird usually raises and lowers the tail a few times after alighting.

Relatively few nests of this species have been studied, but

Collared Forest Falcon
Specialized for hunting in thick cover, the Collared Forest Falcon is prepared to pursue prey either by running after it or by flying, according to circumstances. It displays astonishing manoeuvrability in both forms of locomotion.
(Map 240)

it is evidently prepared to use a variety of sites. Constructing no nest as such, it most commonly uses a cavity in a tree where the top of a limb has snapped off, anywhere from 33 feet (10m) above ground to 100 feet (30m) or more. Old nests of other birds are sometimes used, and cavities in a cliff face were used at one Mexican site. Perhaps the oddest site discovered was a scrape hollowed out within an epiphytic fern growing in a tree fork. Only one egg appears to be laid, but there is no information on incubation length, or the shares taken by the parents in this duty. All observations so far have been made on nests that already contained well-grown young, which in several cases were in cavities so shallow they could be seen from the ground.

At one such nest in Costa Rica, a downy young bird was seen in early March. It was cared for by the female, which spent much of her time in or near the nest cavity. A snake was brought by the male early in the morning, and this was the signal for a loud calling duet between the two parents. The snake itself was not fed to the young bird until the afternoon. Sadly, this promising series of observation was brought to a premature close the next day, when the nestling was killed by a tayra (a mammal related to weasels and stoats) which had climbed the tree after apparently seeing the nestling from the ground. The female seemed half-hearted in her attempts at defence, although the mammal was driven off – too late – by human shouts. Subsequently, the female ate her dead nestling. Cannibalism of this kind is quite common in birds of prey; only a live nestling can evoke parental responses, and once it has died it is perceived only as a food item. Such behaviour may seem unpleasant, but has obvious survival value in times of food shortage.

FOREST FALCONS OF CENTRAL AND SOUTH AMERICA

Represented by five geographical races across its extensive range, stretching from southeastern Mexico down to Colombia, Ecuador, Peru, Bolivia, northern Argentina and Paraguay, and across Brazil to the Guianas, the Barred Forest Falcon (*Micrastur ruficollis*) is to be found in most American sub-tropical and tropical forests. It is a short-winged, long-tailed falcon which, more than any other, preys on parties of birds following army ants, dashing from cover in order to take its victims by surprise. Although birds form the bulk of its diet, it is not averse to taking mice or small lizards. Surprisingly, although it is a fairly common species, details of its breeding habits seem not to have been recorded.

Much rarer than the preceding species, Sclater's Forest Falcon (*Micrastur plumbeus*) has a much more restricted range, extending from western Colombia to northwestern Ecuador. It is known to inhabit lowland, and perhaps sub-tropical forests, but nothing else seems to have been recorded about the species. A study of this bird could prove rewarding, even if only to discover how it interacts with the preceding species where their ranges overlap.

Despite having an extensive South American distribution, the Slaty-backed Forest Falcon (*Micrastur mirandollei*) is nevertheless a rare species, apparently restricted to uninterrupted lowland rainforests of eastern Costa Rica, down to eastern Peru, across the Guianas and Brazilian Amazonia to Para. It is reported to have a variety of calls and vocalizations, and within its chosen habitat to make considerable movements. If this is true, then it is probably in response to prey-movements, since climatic conditions are unlikely to affect the species greatly. However, until more information becomes available, this can only be speculation.

An extremely rare species, long confused with the Collared Forest Falcon (*Micrastur semitorquatus*), Traylor's Forest Falcon (*Micrastur buckleyi*) is virtually unknown in the wild; most of our knowledge comes from about ten specimens in collections. It is a small-footed forest falcon, at present known to occur only in northeastern Peru and Amazonian Ecuador. Adults can be distinguished from those of *Micrastur semitorquatus* by having four instead of six white outer tail-feather bands, but other details of the species' lifestyle, and how it compares with its congeners, are for the present totally unknown.

The relatively long legs and striking plumage of the attractive little Collared Forest Falcon (*Micrastur semitorquatus*) make it an easy bird to identify, except in the small area of overlap with the smaller, and much rarer, Traylor's Forest Falcon (*M. buckleyi*). The present species has an extensive American distribution, ranging from central Mexico down through eastern Bolivia and the

African Pygmy Falcon
The delightfully attractive African Pygmy Falcon is sexually dimorphic – the male lacking the chestnut-brown back-patch of the female. Pairs are often seen perched together quite prominently, and in such situations are easily mistaken for large shrikes.
(*Map 241*)

Fielden's Falconet and Spot-winged Falconet
With chestnut head and back, the female of Fielden's Falconet (1) appears brighter than the male. The Spot-winged Falconet (2) of South America, despite its name, is actually larger than some of the true falcons of the genus *Falco*.
(Maps 242–243)

greater part of Paraguay to northern Argentina, and is to be found in suitably dense tropical forest, up to attitudes of about 8200 feet (2500m).

The species has a variety of calls, the most common being a slow and oft-repeated "*ahr*", which fades and falls, and has been likened to the groans of a person in constant pain. Not infrequently a pair will call alternately, sometimes for as long as three-quarters of an hour. The bird's preferred habitat is dense, almost impenetrable, vegetation, and it is extraordinarily adept at moving through dense cover with agility and at high speed, both on the wing and on foot. It is noticeably crepuscular, being active during very early morning and late evening; its prominent eyes, large ear-openings and facial ruff apparently being adaptations to this way of life. When resting, the bird is remarkably lethargic, and sometimes allows quite close human approach. In marked contrast to this it is bold and aggressive when hunting prey, its speed and agility allowing it to take a variety of birds (including the occasional domestic fowl), small mammals, lizards, snakes and large insects. Prey is always captured in the feet, and vertebrates are despatched with a swift bite to the neck.

Surprisingly, despite being fairly common, the species' nest has never been found, and nothing is known of its display (if any) or breeding biology. However, birds are seen in pairs at all times of the year, which possibly indicates that they pair for life.

AFRICAN PYGMY FALCON

A bird of African thornbush country and desert, the African Pygmy Falcon (*Polihierax semitorquatus*) has two distinct areas of distribution; one from southern Sudan through Ethiopia, Somalia, Kenya and Uganda to northern Tanzania; the other from southern Angola through Zambia, Zimbabwe, Namibia and Botswana to northern South Africa. Throughout its range, this charming little bird cannot be confused with any other, and it has often been described as looking like a shrike with red legs and cere, and a falcon's bill. Although mostly silent, it occasionally gives a shrill, high-pitched "*tu-tu-tu-tu*" call, building up to a crescendo.

Being a sedentary species, not known to migrate, the bird is usually to be found daily in the same rather restricted area. It is often to be seen perched on some vantage point, such as a tree, fence post or bush, from where it dashes out in pursuit of its favoured prey of flying insects. Also included in the bird's diet are small lizards, snakes and birds.

The bird seems to have a predilection for the nests of other birds, particularly those of weavers and starlings, for not only does it use them for roosting, and for sheltering from rain, but it also uses them for breeding. Surprisingly, the bird only takes over an unoccupied nest, rarely, if ever, displacing the nest's rightful owner. Nests of Buffalo Weavers (*Dinemellia dinemelli*) containing either a starling's nest, or a lining of grass formed by some other species, are the most highly prized nesting sites. The female is said to incubate the two or three eggs unaided, and to be fed by the male during this period. Other details of the breeding cycle appear not to have been recorded, and the display, if any, has never been observed.

THE DIMINUTIVE FALCONETS

With a Far Eastern distribution extending from Burma eastward to South Vietnam, the little-known Fielden's Falconet (*Polihierax insignis*) is an uncommon and local inhabitant of light savanna woodlands and open country. It is known to feed on insects and small birds, with some small

Asian Forest Falconets
Occupying similar ecological niches but with virtually no geographical overlap, these diminutive birds of prey are easily identified by their plumage. Despite some rufous feathering on the thighs, neither the Red-legged Falconet (1) nor the Black-legged Falconet (2) have red legs: they are best identified by their facial patterns. The Bornean Falconet (3) has a white crown, whilst the very similar Philippine (4) and Pied (5) Falconets are again differentiated by their facial patterns.
(Maps 244–248)

snakes and frogs, and to have a weak, fluttering, parrot-like flight. Vitrually nothing is known of the species' breeding habits, although it is reported to use a stick-nest, which is assumed to be that of some other species. The bird's generally greyish colour, combined with its small size, make it clearly distinguishable from any other raptor occurring in its range. Its general lifestyle may prove to be similar to that of the African Pygmy Falcon (*Polihierax semitorquatus*) since it appears to be the eastern representative of that species.

The sole member of its genus, the Spot-winged Falconet (*Spiziapteryx circumcinctus*) is found in semi-desert and savanna country with scattered large trees, in western and northern Argentina. Although occasionally seen sunning itself on bushes or telegraph poles, the bird most often perches inconspicuously about 30 feet (9m) up in a tree, and when disturbed it prefers to hop or climb, parrot-like, further up the tree rather than fly away. In flight, it is also somewhat parrot-like, although it intersperses wing-beats with glides. Nothing else seems to be known about the species, although local natives claim that it hunts birds.

The tiny, sparrow-sized, Red-legged Falconet (*Microhierax caerulescens*) is found from the Himalayas east through Burma as far as Indo-China, and is essentially a bird of forests. Its behaviour is extremely like that of a flycatcher – darting out from a tree-perch to catch insects, and returning to eat them on the perch. It may also take a few small birds. It roosts and nests in the same abandoned woodpecker or barbet hole, and although it is known that four or five eggs are laid, on a bed of insect remains, details of its incubation and fledging periods have not been recorded.

Extremely similar to the preceding species, the Black-legged Falconet (*Microhierax fringillarius*) is distributed from southern Burma through Malaya, Sumatra, Borneo and Java, as far as Bali, and since the two birds' ranges abut, this species is sometimes considered to be a race of *Microhierax caerulescens*. Its lifestyle is virtually identical, although the Black-legged Falconet will sometimes nest in holes under the eaves of buildings.

Another falconet about which very little is known, the Bornean Falconet (*Microhierax latifrons*) has a range restricted to northwestern Borneo, where it is found in forested country, inhabiting clearings up to about 5000 feet (1524m). The bird may be encountered singly, in pairs, or in family groups. It feeds on insects, particularly dragonflies, catching them in flycatcher style, and is said to attack other birds entering its territory.

Found either singly or in pairs, though occasionally in small parties on the larger Philippine Islands, the Philippine Falconet (*Microhierax erythrogonys*) seems to have habits very similar to other species in its genus. It is a bird of high open forest, inhabiting clearings or the banks of watercourses, where it feeds on insects, preferring butterflies and moths. It nests in disused barbet or woodpecker holes, usually not less than about 26 feet (8m) from the ground.

The largest species in its genus, and by far the most aggressive, the Pied Falconet (*Microhierax melanoleucus*) has a range extending from Assam across southeastern China and into upper Laos and the northern Annam region of Vietnam. It is found in deep forest, between 3300 and 6600 feet (1000 and 2000 metres) above sea level, frequenting clearings, either in pairs or small groups, where it preys on insects, small reptiles and mammals. It will even stoop, like a true falcon, on to birds considerably larger than itself. Old woodpecker or barbet holes, 115 feet (35m) or more above the ground, are used to rear the three or four young.

PEREGRINE

Impressive powers of flight, and spectacular hunting methods, have made the Peregrine (*Falco peregrinus*) one of the most renowned of all birds of prey. Ironically, it is also one that has suffered greatly from a whole variety of human activities, and even now remains under threat in many parts of the world.

In flight or at rest, the Peregrine's compact build conveys an impression of power and helps distinguish it from other falcons of similar size. Its wings are broad at the base and sharply pointed, but proportionately shorter than in many falcons, while the tail is also relatively short. The usual flight action consists of short bursts of shallow wing-beats alternating with brief glides. At close range, the barred underparts are characteristic of adults, although young birds are streaked below. The head is always dark, with a prominent "moustache" streak. Despite the many threats that face it, the Peregrine still has a worldwide distribution, and shows great geographical variation. Northern forms are the largest and generally palest, while southern races are often smaller, and tend towards darker or brighter colouring. Two races occurring in northern Africa and the Middle East are sometimes separated as a distinct species called the Barbary Falcon or Shaheen; they are paler, with more rufous heads, and are less stocky in build than typical Peregrines. The largest of all races, sometimes called Peale's Falcon, occurs in Alaska, and is notable for producing great amounts of powder down, probably as an adaptation to its very damp environment. Spread over the plumage, the powder gives the bird a strong bluish "bloom", and acts as a waterproofing agent.

Cliffs and crags are the essential feature of the Peregrine's habitat in most parts of the world, usually in open country.

Peregrine
A superbly efficient bird-hunter, the Peregrine is one of the world's fastest and most aerial predators, with physical adaptations for aerial hunting unsurpassed by any other species. Its stoop, and the lethal blow delivered with the hind claw of the open foot, are among the most dramatic of all raptor hunting techniques. *(Map 249)*

Sea cliffs are favoured, especially where colonies of seabirds provide a ready food supply. In all situations, birds are the main prey, and it is the manner in which they are taken that has earned the Peregrine such fame. Nearly all its victims are captured in flight, and having seen its prey, the falcon gains height above it, then half closes its wings and stoops at its quarry at tremendous speed. The lethal blow is delivered with the powerful hind claw, and frequently the victim is allowed to fall freely to the ground before the Peregrine descends to collect it. Pigeons and gamebirds are favoured prey, though the smaller southern races tend to take correspondingly smaller birds. Occasionally mammals or birds are taken from the ground, and there is even a record of a Peregrine taking a fish, but such cases are exceptional.

The breeding season commences with spectacular display flights, both birds stooping at each other and sometimes passing food in the air, accompanied by loud, harsh screaming. A bare cliff ledge is the typical nesting place, though sometimes the old nest of another bird such as a Raven or buzzard is selected. Three or four eggs are usually laid, hatching after four weeks of incubation, mainly by the female. The male's job is to provide food for his mate, and after hatching, for the young or "eyasses". Intruders near the nest are attacked vigorously, with much raucous screaming. The young finally leave the nest after about six weeks, and for a time the whole family may occasionally be seen in the air together, often stooping at each other in play.

Peregrines have long been highly esteemed for falconry, and in past centuries the taking of young birds for this purpose probably caused little harm. However, other pressures have gradually increased. Persecution by gamekeepers in such areas as grouse moors became a problem with the rise of the great estates in Britain and Europe in the last century. This pressure may have relaxed in wartime, but was replaced in the Second World War by the systematic annihilation of the species in southern Britain because of its supposed threat to carrier pigeons. Recovery from this onslaught was soon halted by the worst danger of all – the disastrous effect of pesticide residues on breeding success. At present, controls on these chemicals have led to a welcome recovery in many places, but this magnificent bird still faces the threat of widespread illegal capture, usually for financial gain, and constant vigilance is still essential to safeguard its future.

COMMON KESTREL

Hovering overhead or perched on a telegraph pole, the Common Kestrel's predilection for hunting near motorway verges has made it by far the most familiar European raptor. Counting Kestrels to while away the miles need not be the prerogative of European motorists however, for not only is this species widespread throughout the Old World, but close relatives with similar habits also occur in every other continent except Antarctica. They form a well-marked group within the genus *Falco*, distinguished by foraging habits and a number of plumage features. Predominantly ground feeders, insects and small mammals or reptiles constitute the prey of many species, although some are fully capable of taking birds in flight as well. Because so much of their prey is terrestrial, they seek it by watching from a vantage point. Tree perches are a common choice, but most species, like the European, are adept at hovering, which enables them to seek prey in more open areas as well. Several Kestrels show a more marked plumage difference between the sexes than is usual among falcons, and in the majority the females and juveniles at least have rufous upperparts and tails with dark bars. Size ranges from very small to medium.

With a range embracing most of Europe, Asia and Africa, the Common Kestrel (*Falco tinnunculus*) is one of the world's most widely distributed and abundant birds of prey. Twelve geographical races are recognized, varying in depth of colour and barring, and in the differences between male and female, but all are very similar in proportions and habits to the European form. Kestrels breeding in Eastern Europe and Central Asia are strongly migratory, but even British-bred birds have travelled as far as North Africa, as shown by ringing (banding) recoveries.

Kestrels are among the most intensively studied of all birds of prey, partly due to their convenient readiness to accept nest boxes and other artificial sites in which to breed. Detailed studies of a large breeding population were first carried out in Holland, using a network of nest boxes on poles, spaced out in a grid on reclaimed marshland – excellent habitat for hunting, but entirely lacking in natural nest sites. Such studies still continue in the Netherlands, Britain and elsewhere, and have added greatly to our understanding of the relationship between breeding success

The Common Kestrel
Small mammals detected while hovering or perched are the Common Kestrel's typical prey, but the species is also a skilled bird hunter, at times employing stealthy tactics like those of the Sparrowhawk to surprise birds such as House Sparrows and young Starlings. Where voles are the main prey, Common Kestrel breeding success may be closely linked to the fluctuations in numbers of those rodents.
(*Map 250*)

and environmental factors in birds of prey.

Nest site selection and courtship displays may occur any time from late winter onwards. In flight displays the male circles round the female, who may be in flight or perched, and dives close past her. If she is airborne, she may roll over and present talons. Later, courtship feeding of the female by the male may take place, often at the selected nest site, and this is frequently followed by mating. Apart from nest boxes, a wide variety of natural sites may be selected, but cavities in trees are a common choice where available. Old crows' nests, haystacks or rock ledges are also used, and in urban areas buildings provide many substitutes for the latter.

Breeding time is very variable in the Common Kestrel, even within a small region, though it will generally start earlier in more favourable habitats. First eggs may be laid any time from late March to early June, and subsequent ones at intervals of two or three days. Incubation may start with any egg from the first to the last, so that some broods of young may show a considerable age range while others are nearly all the same age. The number of eggs laid is related to the starting date; early clutches are commonly of five, quite often of six, and rarely of seven eggs. Later clutches may consist of three or four eggs, and very late ones may contain only one or two.

Incubation and fledging each last for about four weeks, and after a short period spent with the parents in the nest vicinity, the young birds disperse for distances which vary enormously, from a few miles to many hundreds. Northern populations are truly migratory, but even within Britain there is a tendency for Scottish birds to travel farther than birds from southern England. Longer journeys and higher mortality are likely when a good breeding season is followed by poor conditions in autumn and early winter.

THE KESTRELS: MASTERS OF HOVERING FLIGHT

The Mediterranean countries and Central Asia make up the breeding range of the Lesser Kestrel (*Falco naumanni*), a highly gregarious species. Plains, grasslands and deserts are its preferred habitats, and its hunting techniques are very much like those of the Common Kestrel, with hovering an essential skill in treeless country. Bouts of hovering are generally more frequent, but briefer than in the Common Kestrel, and the Lesser Kestrel tends to fly closer to the ground – usually at about 30 to 50 feet (9 to 15 metres). Additionally, because of its social habits, it is often seen hunting in flocks or small parties. This is especially so when the bird is on migration to its wintering quarters, mainly in Africa, when it travels in large flocks, sometimes numbering several thousands. Nesting colonially, in numbers up to a hundred pairs or more, the birds favour tall buildings such as churches and castles as breeding sites.

Lesser Kestrels arrive at their breeding places about two weeks before egg laying. Although there is little display as such, the birds spend much of their time during this fortnight soaring in noisy flocks. Colonies commonly number about fifteen to twenty pairs, though they may sometimes contain over a hundred. Clutch size ranges from three eggs to six, and incubation is performed mainly by the female. Prey is brought entirely by the male at first, and that fed to the young appears to consist entirely of insects, especially grasshoppers.

Another social species is the Red-footed Kestrel (*Falco vespertinus*) of central Europe and Asia, which solves the problem of colonial nesting by appropriating the old nests of another gregarious species, the Rook (*Corvus frugilegus*). In its African winter quarters it also roosts communally, sometimes in gatherings of 4000–5000 birds. It hovers frequently, though it is rather slower on the wing than the Common Kestrel, and prefers open country with scattered woods and trees, where it also uses the perch-hunting technique quite often. Taking amphibians and small mammals in the breeding areas, it switches to an insectivorous diet in its winter quarters, where flying termites and grasshoppers are important food sources.

Remarkably, this species' breeding colonies are not found in totally abandoned rookeries, but in disused Rooks' nests scattered among occupied ones. Red-footed Kestrels lay their eggs while the Rooks are rearing their young, so perhaps this difference in timing explains how the two species are able to coexist without problems. A study in Hungary found that 13 per cent of Rooks' nests were occupied by the falcons in the colonies investigated. Both sexes incubate in equal shares during daylight, and at a little over three weeks the incubation period is rather short for a kestrel of this size. The Hungarian study found that 48 per cent of eggs laid actually resulted in fledged young, losses being mainly due to non-hatching, though a few eggs are lost to predators, including Rooks.

Two typical Kestrels resident in Africa in addition to the Common Kestrel are the aptly named Fox Kestrel (*Falco alopex*), an all-rufous bird with a very long tail, and the Greater or White-eyed Kestrel (*Falco rupicoloides*), the largest member of the group. The latter species has the habit of caching prey, usually beneath grass tussocks or clods of earth. Although this behaviour may occur at any time of year, it is often noted during incubation, when the female caches surplus food brought by the male.

Only one species of kestrel is found in the New World. The American Kestrel (*Falco sparverius*) is a highly successful species ranging from Canada south to Tierra del Fuego. A good deal smaller than the Common Kestrel, it nevertheless resembles it in habits, and has developed similar ways of exploiting man-made environments. Though varying a great deal geographically, it is generally one of the most brightly coloured of the kestrels and unusually the sexes have clearly distinct plumages even as juveniles. Studies of the bird's breeding behaviour have, as with the Common Kestrel, made good use of nest boxes, though of a different type as this species likes to nest in old woodpecker holes which the American boxes are designed to simulate. Banding of young kestrels has indicated an annual mortality rate of 57 per cent, with relatively few living for more than four years. Sadly, shooting has accounted for most of the bodies recovered.

)ld World and New
Vorld Kestrels
:he Red-footed Kestrel of
:urasia (1) is a versatile
unter, though in parts of its
ange frogs may make up 75
er cent of its diet. The
.esser Kestrel (2), also of
:urasia, frequently roosts in
ucalyptus groves on its
nnual migration to Africa.
ı Africa the Fox Kestrel (3)
reeds in rocky gorges, while
ıe Greater or White-eyed
:estrel (4) prefers the
:attered acacias and scrub
f the bushveld. Alone in the
Iew World, the American
.estrel (5) has a range
xtending from Canada to
ıe tip of South America,
ith several different races
arying greatly in the
itensity of their plumage
ɔlouring.
Aaps 251-255)

Grey Kestrel and Dickinson's Kestrel
Two African kestrels with atypical plumage, these species are also both remarkable for their unusual nesting habits, the Grey Kestrel (1) depending on the old nests of the Hamerkop, a stork relative, while Dickinson's Kestrel (2) prefers the crowns of certain palms.
(Maps 256 and 257)

AFRICAN KESTRELS AND ISLAND SPECIES

Two kestrels found in Africa are distinguished by their largely greyish rather than rufous plumage. The Grey Kestrel (*Falco ardosiaceus*) is the only all-grey falcon apart from the larger and darker Sooty Falcon. Although it specializes in taking prey from the ground like other kestrels, its habits differ from them in many other ways. It never hovers, preferring either to seek prey from a high perch, or from low-level flight over grassland. In the latter case it will at times pursue and seize small birds startled into flight, rather in the manner of a Merlin (*Falco columbarius*). Otherwise, its chief prey are lizards and large insects.

A bird of lowland savannas or open areas surrounded by woodland, its distribution is influenced by that of a quite unrelated bird. Related to storks and herons, the Hamerkop (*Scopus umbretta*) is a bird of strange appearance and habits, noted among other things for its extraordinary nests. These are huge domed structures of sticks, weeds and mud, having a narrow side entrance leading to a central chamber. A typical nest is about 5 feet (1.5m) deep, built in a tree fork overhanging water. New nests are frequently built, yet their structural strength ensures that they last for a very long time, and it is in these old nests that the Grey Kestrel breeds. Occasionally it may drive out the rightful owners to obtain a nest site, but there are usually plenty of old nests to be had. Although there have been reports of Grey Kestrels nesting in holes in trees, these are unconfirmed, and its reliance on the Hamerkop seems to be virtually complete.

Dickinson's Kestrel (*Falco dickinsoni*) is less uniformly coloured than the preceding species and has a boldly barred tail. Swampy lowland savannas and cultivated areas are its preferred habitats, and it shows a strong liking for the vicinity of certain palms. Although also mainly a perch hunter, it does occasionally hover, and takes a varied assortment of prey, from small mammals, lizards and insects to frogs and crabs. A few small birds and bats are recorded as prey, indicating that some captures may be made in flight. Like many raptors it is attracted to grass fires to seek prey escaping from the flames. Typical nest sites are the hollow crowns of dead palm trees, although one pair have been recorded using a Hamerkop's nest like the Grey Kestrel.

Another greyish species, but with boldly barred underparts, is the Madagascar Banded Kestrel (*Falco zoniventris*). Confined to the island after which it is named, its habits are little known, but appear similar to those of Dickinson's Kestrel. Madagascar is the home of another species also, the Madagascar Kestrel (*Falco newtoni*). With typically rufous kestrel plumage it is a good deal smaller than the Common Kestrel, while two other species from the Indian Ocean islands are smaller still. Roughly the size of a Song Thrush (*Turdus philomelos*), the Seychelles Kestrel (*Falco araea*) is the smallest member of the genus *Falco*, while the somewhat larger Mauritius Kestrel (*Falco punctatus*) is one of the world's rarest and most endangered birds.

Closely similar to the Common Kestrel in size, plumage and habits are the Moluccan Kestrel (*Falco moluccensis*) of the East Indies, and the Nankeen Kestrel (*Falco cenchroides*) of Australia and New Guinea. Like the Common Kestrel, the Nankeen has adapted well to man's world, and has colonized urban and surburban areas in addition to its natural habitat of grasslands and open bush country. Equally fond of hovering, it is also a familiar roadside sight, either suspended in mid-air or perched on a telegraph post. The wide variety of prey taken includes mammals up to the size of a baby rabbit, lizards, spiders, scorpions and all kinds of large insects. Some birds are taken, including the introduced European Starling (*Sturnus vulgaris*), a regular prey of the Common Kestrel in its native range. When feeding young, its capture rate may be remarkable; one account mentions 74 food-carrying visits in three and three-quarter hours to a brood of three young.

Island-dwelling Kestrels
Island species, whether of birds or of other animals, frequently have specialized features and small populations. Indian Ocean island species shown here include the smallest kestrel (the Seychelles Kestrel, 2), the rarest species (the Mauritius Kestrel (1), the Madagascar Kestrel (3) and the Madagascar Banded Kestrel (4). By contrast the Moluccan Kestrel (6) and the Australian or Nankeen Kestrel (5) are both wide-ranging and successful raptors.
(Maps 258–263)

Red-headed Falcon and Merlin
A lively and dashing little predator, the Red-headed Falcon (1) is distinguished by its chestnut-marked head from all other falcons in its African and Indian distribution areas. A rather similarly-sized, and equally energetic falcon, the more sombrely-coloured Merlin (2) has a worldwide Northern Hemisphere distribution. Typically, it hunts in fast, low-level, horizontal flight, flushing small birds by surprise. *(Maps 264 and 265)*

COLOURFUL MEMBERS OF THE FALCON FAMILY

A fairly common bird of tree-scattered open country in India south of the Himalayas, but much less common in Africa south of the Sahara, usually in high-rainfall, low-lying and often swampy savannas, the Red-headed Falcon (*Falco chicquera*) is a distinctive species, usually found in pairs, both at rest and when hunting. Seldom straying far from its breeding site, it is a small and very active falcon, which takes birds in flight, and occasionally bats, as well as ground-based vertebrates such as lizards. Although there appears to be no nuptial display, the birds become very noisy and obvious in the vicinity of the nest, which in India is usually the disused nest of a crow or kite, and in Africa among the leaf-bases of *Borassus* palms. Claims that the birds actually build a nest need confirmation. Usually four eggs are laid, and apparently these are incubated solely by the female.

With an extensive northern Holarctic range, the Merlin (*Falco columbarius*) breeds across northern North America, and across Europe and Asia from Iceland and the British Isles through Scandinavia and Russia to Mongolia and Kamchatka. The birds all migrate south in the winter, with American populations moving south to Ecuador, Venezuela and the West Indies, while Old World birds are to be found in North Africa and Arabia, and from Iraq across northern India and China east to Korea and Japan. Throughout its range, this delightful tiny falcon is associated with open country, where it boldly hunts birds, occasionally somewhat larger than itself, as well as small mammals, lizards, snakes and insects, especially dragonflies. Its usual method of hunting is in low, erratic, ground-level flight, and the species is not known to make spectacular stoops at prey. In open or thinly-wooded country, the nest is a ground-scrape, or if a woodland site is selected, disused nests of birds such as crows are utilized. Normally, five or six eggs are laid, and are incubated for 28 to 32 days, mainly by the female, with the male taking a small share of the work. The young hatch at intervals, since this is how the eggs are laid, and are fledged at about twenty-seven days. They remain in the vicinity of the nest for some five to six weeks before setting out on their southerly migration.

As its name implies, the Bat Falcon (*Falco rufigularis*) specializes in preying on bats, which are caught on the wing, though it also takes small birds such as swallows, swifts and hummingbirds. The species is found from Mexico south to Ecuador, Peru, Bolivia, Paraguay and northern Argentina. It also occurs down the entire eastern side of South America, and on Trinidad, occurring in humid tropical woodland, usually below 5000 feet (1524m). Nests are usually in a tree-cavity, perhaps as high as 115 feet (35m), and the usual clutch appears to consist of three or four eggs. The incubation period appears not to be known, but fledging takes about thirty-five to forty days.

Probably the tropical American equivalent of the Peregrine (*Falco peregrinus*), the uncommon Orange-breasted Falcon (*Falco deiroleucus*) is found mainly in cooler, damp, mountain forest or scrub, from Mexico down through Central America to Peru, northern Argentina and Paraguay, up to about 5000 feet (1524m). This powerful species feeds almost exclusively on birds, with doves, caciques and parrots all being recorded as prey. The nest and clutch-size need confirmation, as do many other aspects of the species' breeding habits.

Recorded mostly from dry areas of Africa, the very rare Taita Falcon (*Falco fasciinucha*) occurs from southern Ethiopia to the Zambezi River, where it is found in mountainous country, usually between 6500 and 13,000 feet (2000 and 4000 metres). In appearance and habits it is much like a tiny Peregrine, which makes its rarity even more puzzling, for its habitat contains plenty of suitable birds for it to prey on. One nest observed was on an inaccessible, deep ledge, some 500 feet (150m) up a sheer cliff, and seemed to lack any nest-material. The clutch appears to consist of at least three eggs, but other breeding details remain to be discovered.

A bird of light forest or open country from the southwestern USA (where it is now extremely rare) down to the tip of South America, the Aplomado Falcon (*Falco femoralis*) is migratory at the extreme north and south of its range, and a passage migrant through Central America. It is a graceful, rapid flyer, catching birds and insects on the wing but also taking some small mammals and lizards on the ground. The two or three eggs are laid in the old nest of some other bird, and are incubated by both sexes. However, little else has been recorded about this rare species' breeding habits.

Falcons of America and Africa
Though resembling each other closely in plumage, the Bat Falcon (4) and Orange-breasted Falcon (2) of the New World differ in size and proportions, the former recalling the hobbies, while the latter is Peregrine-like in build. Another New World species with somewhat similar colouring, the Aplomado Falcon (3) is less stocky in shape. The very short-tailed Taita Falcon (1) of Africa is essentially a diminutive Peregrine in structure and habits.
(Maps 266–269)

Eleanora's Falcon
Named after a mediaeval Sardinian princess, this fine species well merits its distinguished name. Long-winged and buoyant, its powers of flight are the match of any falcon, though its smaller size limits it to lesser prey than the Peregrine and Lanner Falcon. It is one of several birds of prey occurring in both dark and light colour forms.
(*Map 270*)

THE SOMBRE-PLUMAGED FALCONS

Eleanora's Falcon (*Falco eleanorae*) is confined as a breeding bird to the Mediterranean area and the Canary Islands. Highly gregarious, it breeds in colonies, and on migration may travel in large flocks. All members of the species, even those breeding in the Canaries, follow the same migration route down the Red Sea and the coast of East Africa to the wintering quarters in Madagascar. New breeding colonies are still being discovered, so it is difficult to give even an estimate of its total numbers. It seems possible that the species may be extending its range. It breeds mainly on islands in the Mediterranean, nesting on steep sea cliffs, and the large colony at Cape Formentor in Mallorca is particularly well known to visitors.

Eleanora's Falcon does not begin breeding until early autumn. This is because it has specialized in feeding its young almost exclusively on migrants passing through on their way to Africa. Warblers, shrikes, chats, Nightingales, Golden Orioles and Hoopoes are among the most frequently taken species. The numbers of migrants available at this time may be huge, the autumn passage being swollen by the year's intake of young birds, and the proportion taken by the falcons is relatively insignificant. Sadly, human hunters in the Mediterranean area do much more damage! Outside the breeding season, insects form the birds' staple diet. Of medium size, Eleanora's Falcon appears very long-winged and long-tailed, and flies with a deceptively leisurely wing action. However, its exceptional speed and agility are displayed often enough in aerial play around the colonies. It occurs in two colour phases, a pale form and an almost black form.

Comparatively little is known about the lifestyle, breeding habits, distribution or migration of the Sooty Falcon (*Falco concolor*). It is known to breed from Libya to the Red Sea and Arabia, and to migrate to southern East Africa and Madagascar in winter. Like the preceding species it breeds in colonies, though it is generally more strongly territorial and less gregarious. Also like the previous species it times its breeding to coincide with the autumn migration. Bee-eaters, Hoopoes and Golden Orioles are favourite prey items in the breeding areas, but on migration and in its winter quarters it feeds on insects, small birds and bats. At all times of year it seems to prefer to hunt at dawn or dusk. It is smaller than Eleanora's Falcon, and like that species it has a dark colour phase, though this is quite rare and seldom seen.

Occurring in Australia, the Grey Falcon (*Falco hypoleucos*) is one of the continent's most beautiful but rarest and least-known birds of prey. Thinly distributed over most of central and eastern Australia, it favours lightly timbered plains and open hill country, and timbered watercourses in desert areas. Highly adapted for desert life, it is nomadic in habit, and it appears that members of a pair stay together at all

Sooty, Grey and Black Falcons
The uniformly slate-grey Sooty Falcon (1) breeds in some of the world's driest and most inhospitable regions in Africa and Arabia. In Australia, the rather large and striking Black Falcon (3) is unusual in having the soft parts bluish, or bluish-white. In the Grey Falcon (2), the rarest of the six Australian *Falco* species, these parts are bright orange, in sharp contrast with the generally pale grey plumage.
(Maps 271–273)

times of year – an important arrangement for a species whose members may be thinly scattered over a vast area at any given time. Although capable of high-speed flight, and of catching birds up to the size of pigeons, it also takes much of its prey from the ground, locating it in low-level flight with slow wing-beats interspersed with glides.

Another Australian falcon of arid regions is the Black Falcon (*Falco subniger*). With a particular fondness for areas near waterholes, this species performs local movements which appear to follow those of the button quails (*Turnix* spp.), which are one of its major prey items. A fast and active hunter, it takes birds in flight or on the ground, as well as mammals and insects. It will also fly low through bushes to try and flush out likely prey. Rarely inactive for long, it is an audacious species which has learned to exploit man when hunting. Farmers in Victoria tell how Black Falcons will often appear during a quail shoot or stubble burning, ready to take any quail fleeing from the guns or the flames.

THE HOBBIES AND THEIR RELATIVES

Typical hobbies are small falcons with swift and agile flight, but two larger species with very different habits are thought to be related to them. Australia and New Guinea are the home of the Brown Falcon (*Falco berigora*) which is second only to the Nankeen Kestrel as Australia's most abundant raptor. Quite unlike the true hobbies in lifestyle, it takes most of its prey from the ground, finding them either by still hunting from a perch, or while sailing round in low flight, with wings angled upwards almost like a harrier. Grasshoppers and other large insects are taken as well as lizards, snakes, small birds and mammals. Three races are recognized, and there is a commonly-seen melanistic (dark-plumaged) form.

Also considered related to the hobbies is the New Zealand Falcon (*Falco novaezeelandiae*). Its actions, power and aggressiveness are more in keeping with the larger falcons, and its flight action, though sometimes like that of a hobby, is at some times reminiscent of a kestrel, at others of a Peregrine. Numbers have been severely reduced by the expansion of human activities in New Zealand, and it is now restricted to offshore islands and on the mainland to high-altitude forest. Swift and aggressive when hunting, it pursues prey tenaciously if it fails to take it by surprise, sometimes even following it into buildings. Birds up to the size of a duck or gull are taken, but the falcon is not averse to taking ground prey such as insects, lizards and small mammals. It is also said to rob nests.

With a range covering almost the entire Palearctic, the European Hobby (*Falco subbuteo*) is a migrant, moving south from September onwards to winter in Africa,

Brown Falcon and New Zealand Falcon
Gliding and quartering on upwardly slanted wings, Australia's Brown Falcon (2) sometimes looks more like a harrier than a relative of the hobbies. Varying its flight technique according to its prey, the New Zealand Falcon (1) can resemble various other falcons, but the bird's adaptability has not saved it from dwindling sharply as a result of man's activities.
(Maps 274 and 275)

southern China and northern India, returning in April and May to breed. One of the most beautiful of all falcons, its elegance of plumage is matched by an unsurpassed grace and skill on the wing. Flying extremely fast, it moves on rapid, shallow wing-beats, interspersed with short glides. Its flight silhouette has been likened to that of a large swift, and its speed and agility are such that swifts and swallows do indeed form a proportion of its diet, albeit a small one. As well as birds, it also catches bats and large insects, dragonflies being particularly favoured. Recent studies in England indicate that the species is considerably more abundant there than formerly supposed. Nesting as it does in old crows' nests in scattered farmland trees, and hunting over a wide area, it can be inconspicuous and difficult to locate. This may be no bad thing, as in many parts of its range it has had the misfortune to attract the unwelcome attentions of egg collectors.

Distinguished by its deep chestnut underparts, the African Hobby (*Falco cuvieri*) is slightly smaller, but just as accomplished on the wing as the European Hobby. In addition to small birds, flying termites are a much-favoured food item. It is a bird of the savanna belt south of the Sahara, occurring in a narrow band across central Africa and much of East Africa. It performs some local movements but is not a truly migratory species.

With a wide distribution across tropical Asia, the Oriental Hobby (*Falco severus*) is a bird of dense woodland or forest, where it hunts in natural clearings. Although feeding on insects, especially large beetles, and small birds, it also takes bats, and some individuals specialize on them almost exclusively. Rather unusually for a hobby, prey are not caught in continuous flight but in swift sallies from a perch at the edge of a clearing.

Called the Little Falcon in many Australian bird books, the Australian Hobby (*Falco longipennis*) is a close counterpart of the European Hobby in habits and lifestyle, though it is even more of a bird specialist. With a varied repertoire of tactics, from long high-speed stoops, to level flight pursuit, or a series of short stoops at agile and elusive prey, no two hunts are ever quite the same. The introduced European Sturling (*Sturnus vulgaris*) is a frequent prey, as it is for the European Hobby in its original home. Roost-bound Starlings are taken in the half-light of dawn or dusk. Many other species figure on the bird's menu, however, and it is fond of riverside habitats in which it captures many birds that come to drink or to bathe.

THE SAKER AND ITS RELATIVES

Inhabiting plains, steppes, high-altitude plateaux and deserts are four of the largest and most impressive falcons. The Saker Falcon (*Falco cherrug*) ranges from central Europe eastwards to China as a breeding bird, and occurs in the Middle East and East Africa as a migrant. Not all birds migrate, and of those that do, some do not move far or for very long; southern populations are away from their breeding areas for only two to three months at most.

Appearing deceptively sluggish in flight for much of the time, the Saker is actually capable of great speed and power, and is greatly prized in falconry. For much of the time however, it is content to hunt ground prey such as susliks and other small rodents, patrolling at about 50 to 100 feet (15 to 30 metres) above the ground and not infrequently hovering. Birds feature more prominently in its diet in the winter quarters, and in East Africa it is often seen around the margins of lakes, where it preys on waders and ducks. Even larger species up to the size of small bustards are taken, and as an Arab falconer's bird it is used in conjunction with saluki dogs to hunt gazelles.

Prairies and plains of western North America are the home of the Saker's New World counterpart – the Prairie Falcon (*Falco mexicanus*). This is another fast and agile hunter, capable of catching birds such as swifts in flight, although like the Saker it obtains much of its food from the ground,

The Hobbies
A closely-knit group of four species, the typical hobbies are short-tailed, scimitar-winged hunters of small birds and insects, renowned for their speed and agility. Evenings are a favourite time for hunting insects in the European Hobby (1), the African Hobby (2) and the Oriental Hobby (3), and the European species is notable for the great heights at which it often flies. Australian Hobbies (4) are recorded diving into a flock of birds and seizing one in each foot.
(Maps 276–279)

Saker Falcon
A favourite hunting bird of Arab falconers, because of its power and aggression in the hunt, the Saker Falcon is a large, rather pale-looking falcon, due to its light head and underparts, and lack of distinct moustachial stripe. *(Map 280)*

including mammals, lizards and large insects. Although fast enough to catch many birds in level pursuit, it also stoops like a Peregrine at times, and often hovers when hunting ground prey. It regularly harasses other birds of prey near its breeding sites, and at high altitude can outfly a Peregrine due to its lighter wing-loading. Although some birds remain in the same area all the year round, most migrate south as far as Mexico. Some decline in the Prairie Falcon's numbers has been noticed due to human disturbance and pollution, but it has not been affected by pesticides to the same extent as the Peregrine, and has even colonized places from which the Peregrine has disappeared from this cause.

Returning to the Old World, the Lanner Falcon (*Falco biarmicus*) inhabits southern Europe, the Middle East and much of Africa, and several well-marked races are recognized. In Europe it is found in mountainous areas, on cliffs above meadows, and on sea cliffs. In Africa it tends to inhabit semi-deserts and savannas. Although young birds may wander from the breeding areas, the species is not migratory. The European population is declining rapidly, probably due mainly to the effect of pesticides and the taking of young birds for falconry.

Although less powerful than the Saker, the Lanner Falcon is an excellent flier, and takes much of its prey on the wing. Birds up to the size of guineafowl are captured, and it has a particular fondness for fruit bats. It is the only falcon known to attack flying birds head-on, that is, travelling in the opposite direction to itself – a feat requiring exceptional timing and coordination. However, not all its prey is aerial; in northern Ethiopia it takes great numbers of small rats of the genus *Arvicanthis* which are often found in plague numbers. It captures them by flying at high speed, low over the ground to take them by surprise at the mouths of their burrows. In the deserts of northwest Africa, it takes substantial numbers of the large and powerful spiny-tailed *Uromastix* lizards.

Resembling a smaller and duller-plumaged version of the Lanner is the Laggar Falcon (*Falco jugger*) of the Indian subcontinent. Another fine aerial performer, the Laggar Falcon remains paired throughout the year, and the two birds will sometimes hunt co-operatively, one capturing birds flushed into the open by the other. Inhabiting cultivated areas as well as open country, it is unafraid of man and will sometimes breed in towns. Like the Black Falcon of Australia it takes advantage of human hunters, and will often attend shooting parties to seize wounded birds, or even dead birds that have been discarded or lost.

GYR FALCON

Largest of all the falcons, size alone makes the Gyr Falcon *(Falco rusticolus)* impressive enough, while many High Arctic breeders have an almost pure-white plumage which confers on the bird an appearance of majesty rivalled only by the larger eagles. As a falconer's bird it is harder to train than the Peregrine, and less inclined to make spectacular stoops at prey; nevertheless, its regal aura has made it

'rairie, Lanner and .aggar Falcons
Jnusually amongst the 'alconidae, both the Lanner 'alcon (2) and the Laggar 'alcon (3) occasionally build heir own nests, rather than tilize a natural site, or the lisused nest of some other ird. Compared to body-size, he Prairie Falcon (1) of North America has roportionally the largest yes of any falcon; the exact ignificance of this, however, s not clear.
Maps 281–283)

desirable as a status symbol for some, and collecting young birds for the sport has at times given cause for concern. Fortunately, the remote nature of its breeding places, coupled with improved international law enforcement, have kept the numbers in captivity to a minimum. Probably the greatest threat to its future will arise through increased development and exploitation of the Arctic wilderness.

Distributed around the North Pole in the high latitudes of North America, Europe and Asia, the Gyr Falcon's plumage varies considerably from mainly grey to mainly white, with a few black spots. In the past, several races have been described and even given English names, such as Iceland Falcon and Greenland Falcon. It is nowadays considered best to regard this simply as a highly variable species, with pale forms most abundant in the northern parts of its range and dark ones in the south. It preys mainly on large birds such as ptarmigan and various wildfowl, but unlike the Peregrine it routinely captures prey by overtaking it in level flight. Though this may look less spectacular, it indicates exceptional speed, and this may well be the swiftest of the falcons.

At the southern edge of their range, Gyr Falcons may occur in lightly wooded country, but most breed north of the tree line, and their main habitat requirement is a cliff or crag to provide a nesting ledge. Old nests of Ravens or Rough-legged Buzzards are also often used, both on cliffs and occasionally in trees. As with most falcons, the start of the breeding season is marked by nuptial flights, with the two birds stooping at each other and talon-grappling. Three to five eggs are laid, mainly within a short period in late April and early May imposed by the unforgiving shortness of the Arctic summer. They are incubated almost entirely by the female, who is supplied with food by the male. The incubation period is 28 to 29 days, similar to that of the smaller falcons, but the fledging period, at 46 to 49 days, exceeds that of any other member of the genus *Falco*. In the first week or two after hatching, the female remains at the nest, feeding the young on food brought in by the male, but eventually she has to assist him in hunting. Gyr Falcons, somewhat surprisingly, are less aggressive than Peregrines towards human intruders near the nest, despite their greater size, perhaps because they have few natural enemies. After fledging, young Gyr Falcons remain near the nest site practicing their hunting skills on the new flying young of waders and other summer visitors to the Arctic.

Like many Arctic species, Gyr Falcons show regular fluctuations in breeding activity; in some years not breeding at all, in others rearing three or four young at most sites. Crucial factors appear to be food supply during the preceding winter, and ptarmigan numbers during the breeding season itself. Except for young birds in their first winter, Gyr Falcons take few mammals, so they are not directly affected by the extreme cyclical fluctuations of lemming numbers as are some Arctic predators such as Snowy Owls and skuas.

Gyr Falcon

Possibly the most impressive of all the falcons, the powerful Gyr Falcon is seen by relatively few ornithologists since it inhabits the cold arctic and sub-arctic zones, and only moves south into more temperate latitudes in winter.
(Map 284)

Distribution Maps

The maps on the following pages show the overall geographical range of each species. However, the exact distribution of a bird within its range will depend on the availability of suitable habitat, and may therefore be much more patchy than these maps can indicate. In addition, it must be remembered that for many species, especially those living in the tropics, information is very scarce and our knowledge sometimes based solely on a handful of museum specimens. Moreover, the activities of man are at the present time altering habitats on a vast scale, and at an alarming rate, and the distribution of the birds depending on them is also likely to change drastically.

Most birds of prey are residents, so the majority of the maps show a single year-round range. In the case of migratory species, solid lines of colour are used to indicate the limits of distribution outside the breeding season. Fuller details of the birds' movements are given in the text.

Year-round range of resident birds, and breeding range of migrant species.	Limits of distribution of migrant species outside the breeding season.

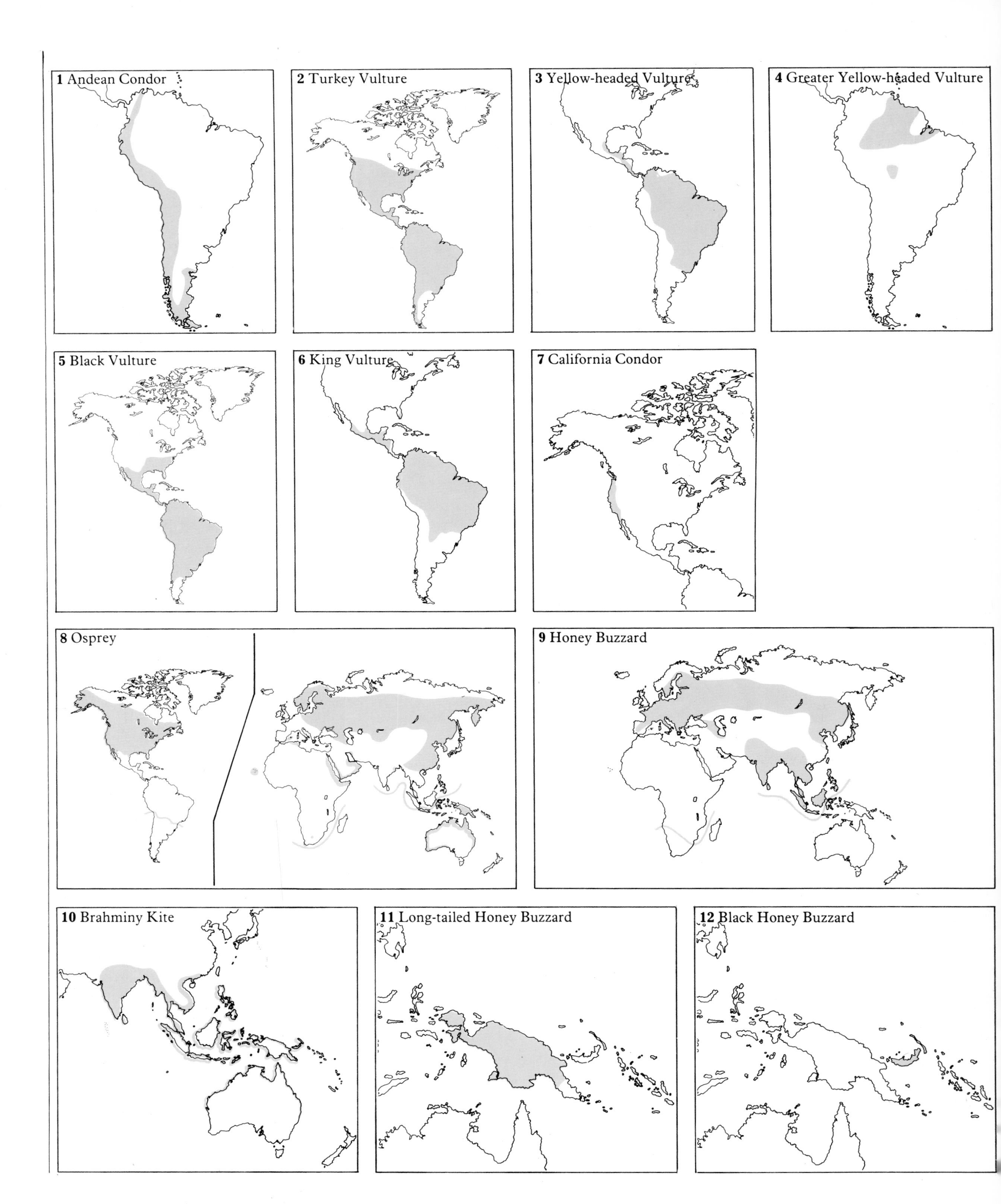
1 Andean Condor
2 Turkey Vulture
3 Yellow-headed Vulture
4 Greater Yellow-headed Vulture
5 Black Vulture
6 King Vulture
7 California Condor
8 Osprey
9 Honey Buzzard
10 Brahminy Kite
11 Long-tailed Honey Buzzard
12 Black Honey Buzzard

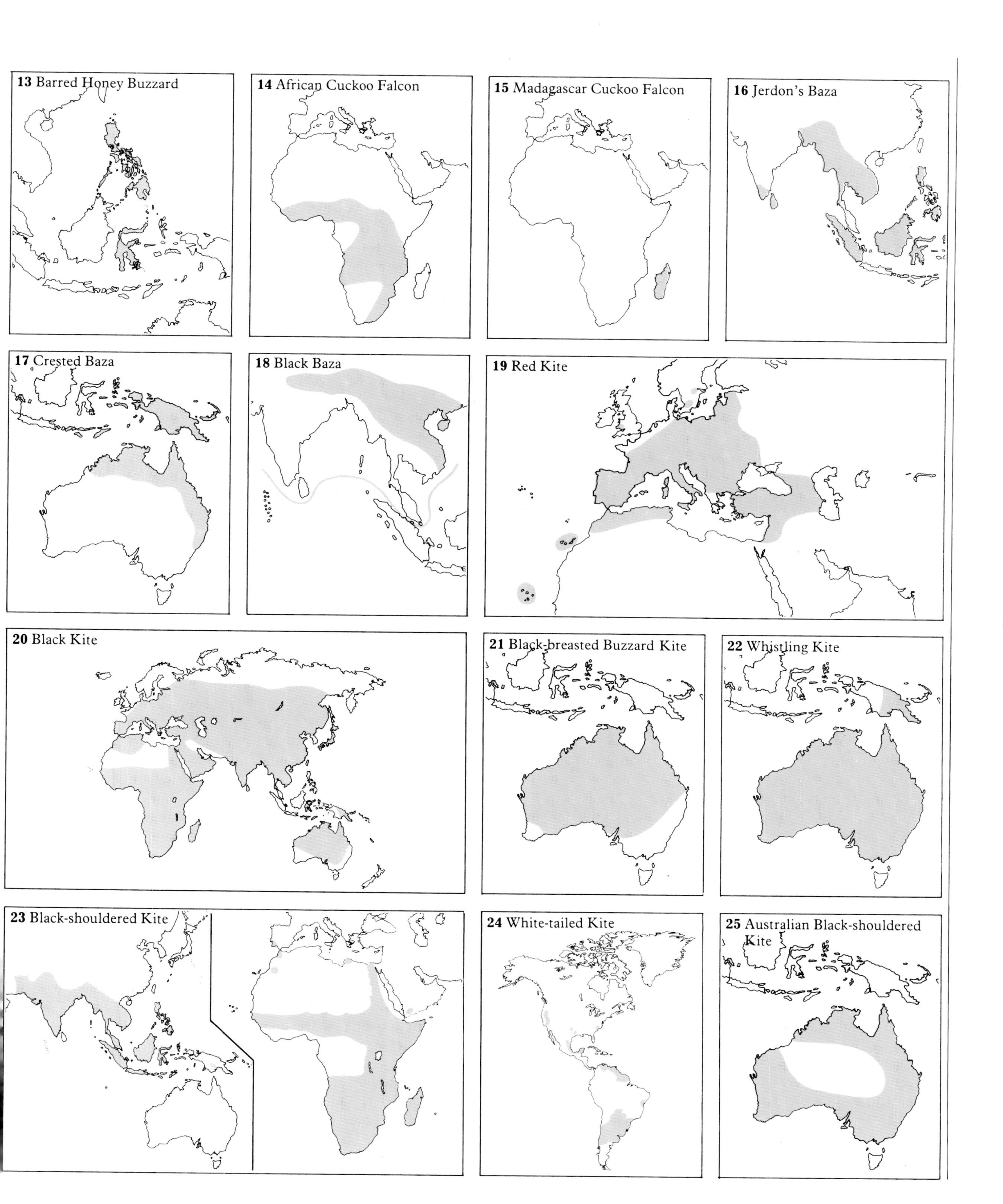

13 Barred Honey Buzzard
14 African Cuckoo Falcon
15 Madagascar Cuckoo Falcon
16 Jerdon's Baza
17 Crested Baza
18 Black Baza
19 Red Kite
20 Black Kite
21 Black-breasted Buzzard Kite
22 Whistling Kite
23 Black-shouldered Kite
24 White-tailed Kite
25 Australian Black-shouldered Kite

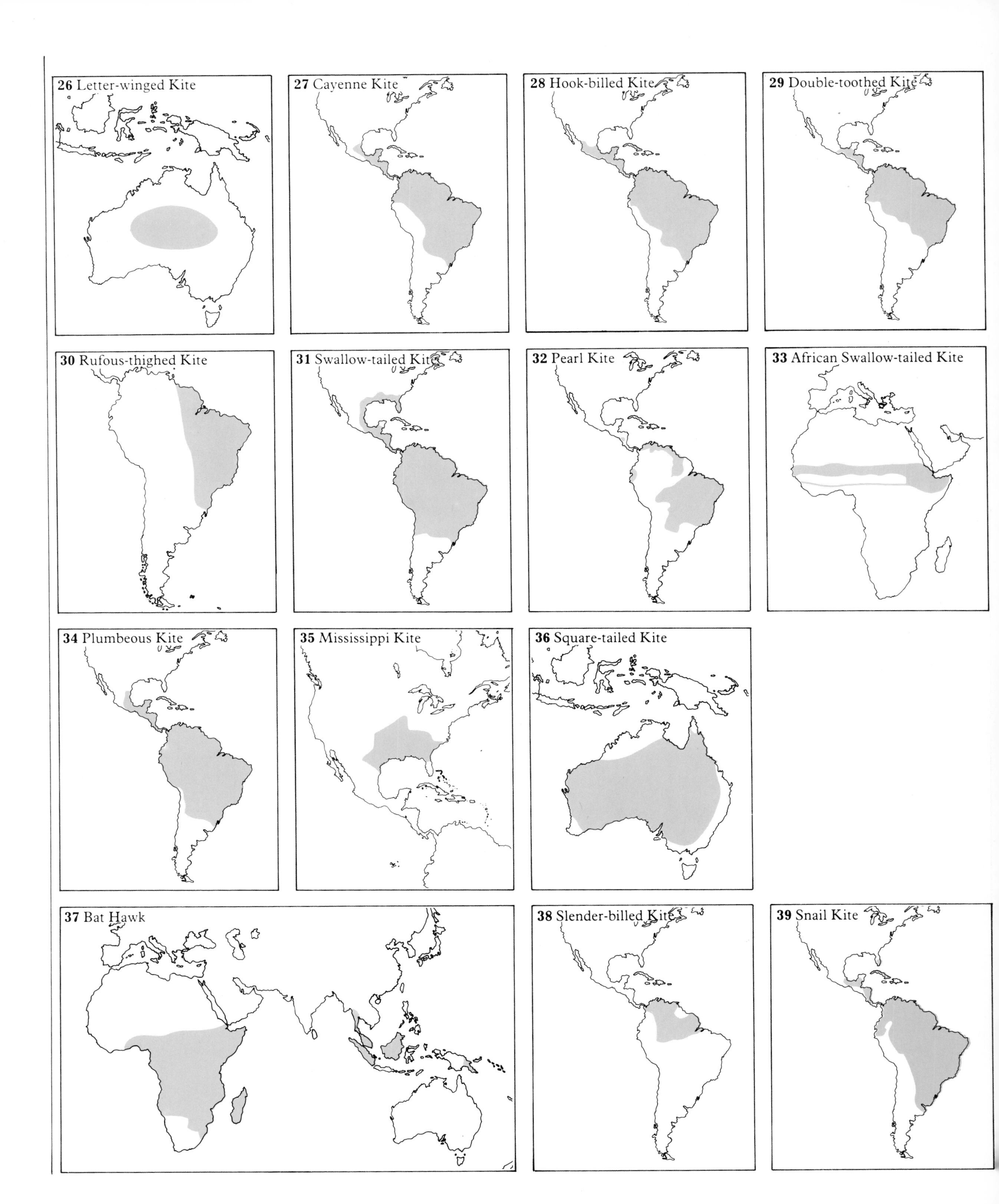
26 Letter-winged Kite
27 Cayenne Kite
28 Hook-billed Kite
29 Double-toothed Kite
30 Rufous-thighed Kite
31 Swallow-tailed Kite
32 Pearl Kite
33 African Swallow-tailed Kite
34 Plumbeous Kite
35 Mississippi Kite
36 Square-tailed Kite
37 Bat Hawk
38 Slender-billed Kite
39 Snail Kite

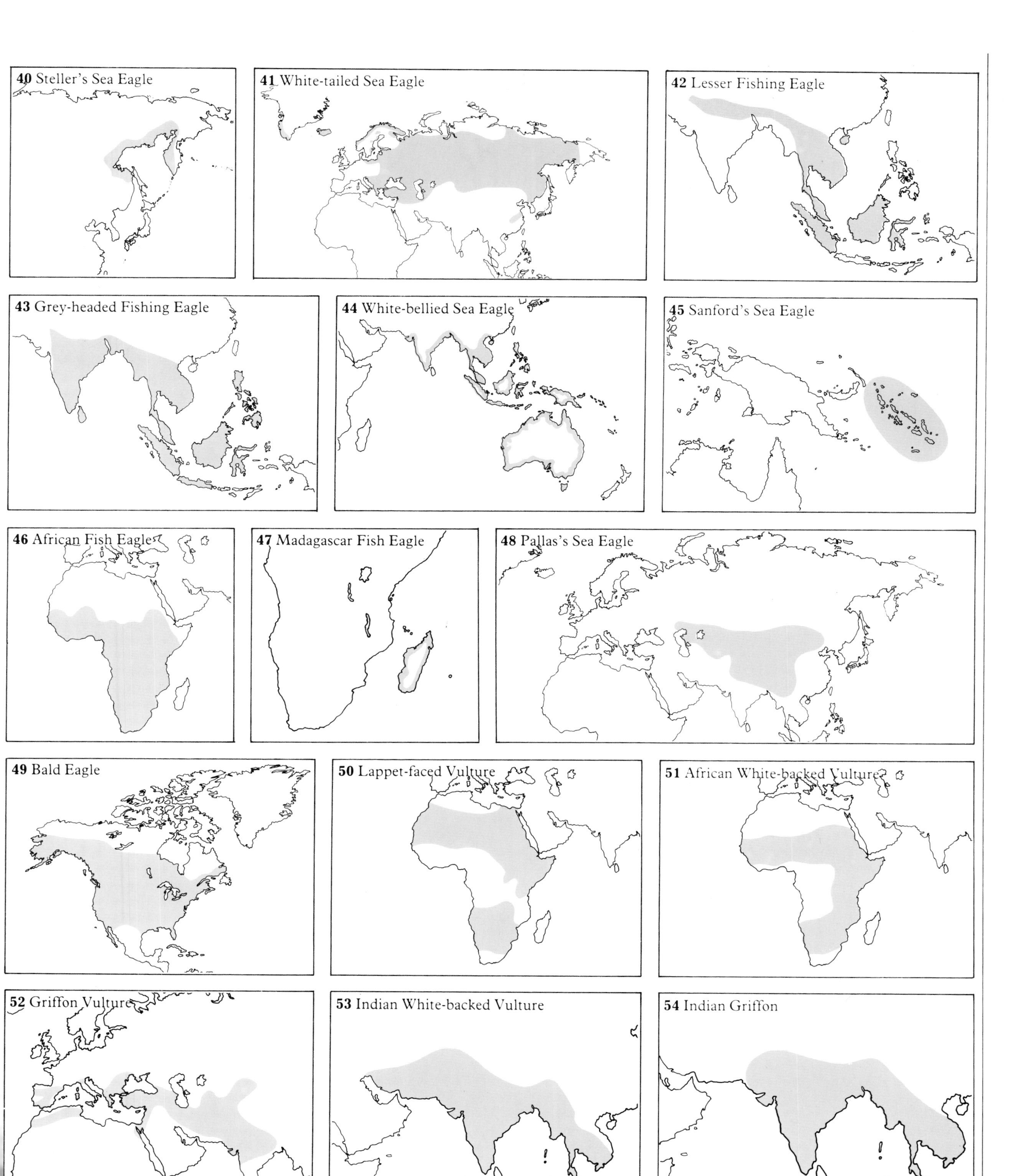
40 Steller's Sea Eagle
41 White-tailed Sea Eagle
42 Lesser Fishing Eagle
43 Grey-headed Fishing Eagle
44 White-bellied Sea Eagle
45 Sanford's Sea Eagle
46 African Fish Eagle
47 Madagascar Fish Eagle
48 Pallas's Sea Eagle
49 Bald Eagle
50 Lappet-faced Vulture
51 African White-backed Vulture
52 Griffon Vulture
53 Indian White-backed Vulture
54 Indian Griffon

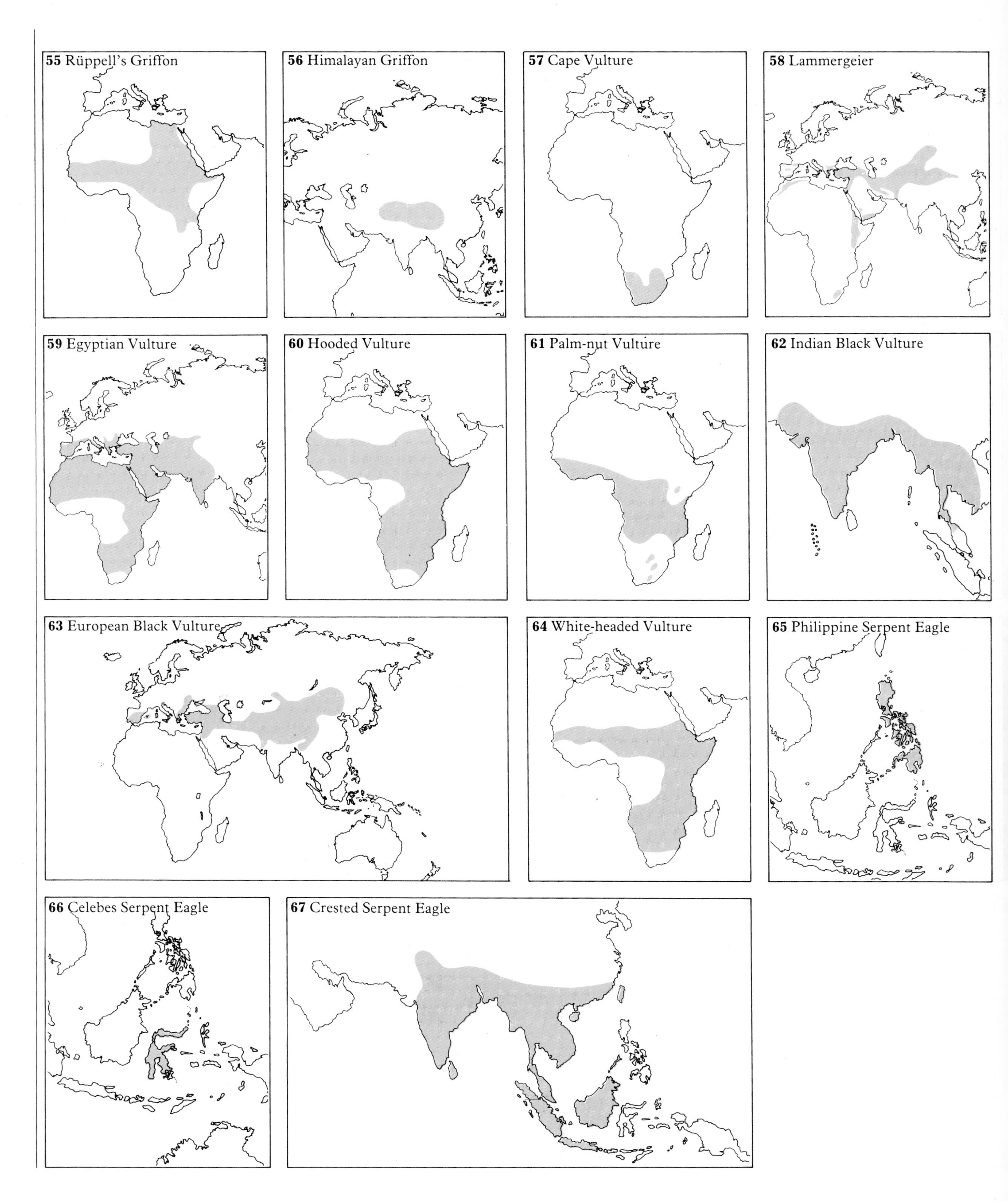
55 Rüppell's Griffon
56 Himalayan Griffon
57 Cape Vulture
58 Lammergeier
59 Egyptian Vulture
60 Hooded Vulture
61 Palm-nut Vulture
62 Indian Black Vulture
63 European Black Vulture
64 White-headed Vulture
65 Philippine Serpent Eagle
66 Celebes Serpent Eagle
67 Crested Serpent Eagle

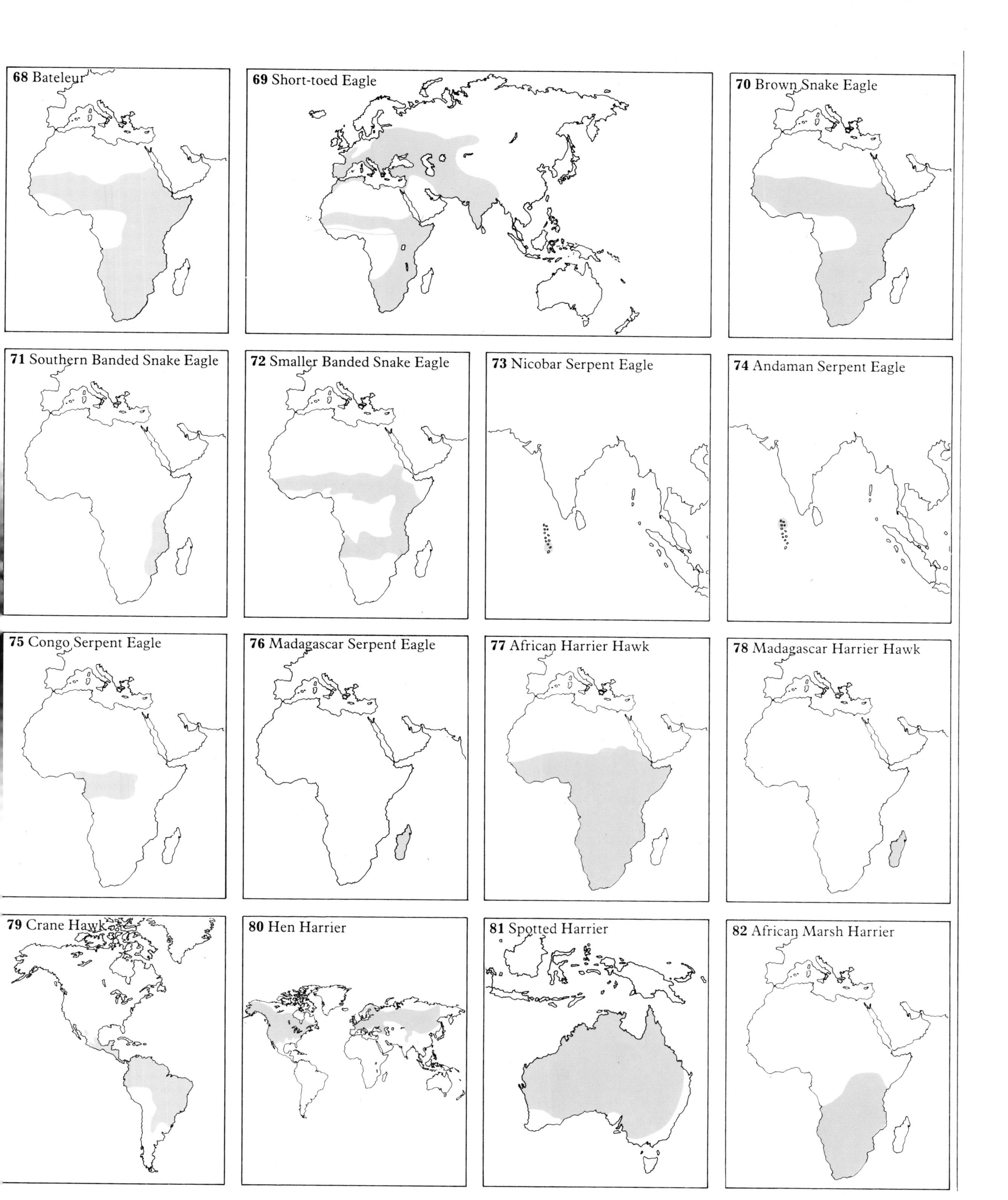
68 Bateleur
69 Short-toed Eagle
70 Brown Snake Eagle
71 Southern Banded Snake Eagle
72 Smaller Banded Snake Eagle
73 Nicobar Serpent Eagle
74 Andaman Serpent Eagle
75 Congo Serpent Eagle
76 Madagascar Serpent Eagle
77 African Harrier Hawk
78 Madagascar Harrier Hawk
79 Crane Hawk
80 Hen Harrier
81 Spotted Harrier
82 African Marsh Harrier

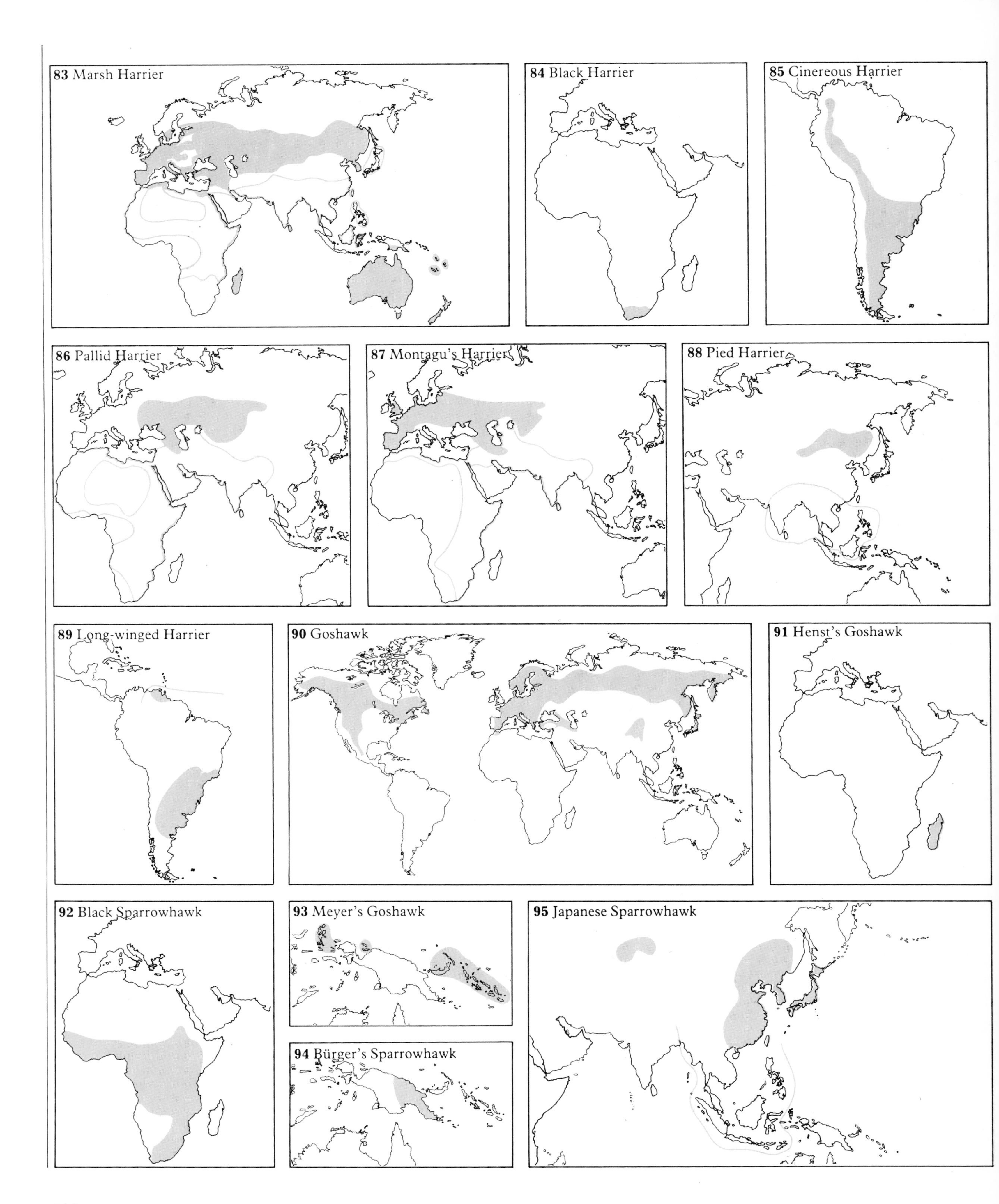
83 Marsh Harrier
84 Black Harrier
85 Cinereous Harrier
86 Pallid Harrier
87 Montagu's Harrier
88 Pied Harrier
89 Long-winged Harrier
90 Goshawk
91 Henst's Goshawk
92 Black Sparrowhawk
93 Meyer's Goshawk
94 Bürger's Sparrowhawk
95 Japanese Sparrowhawk

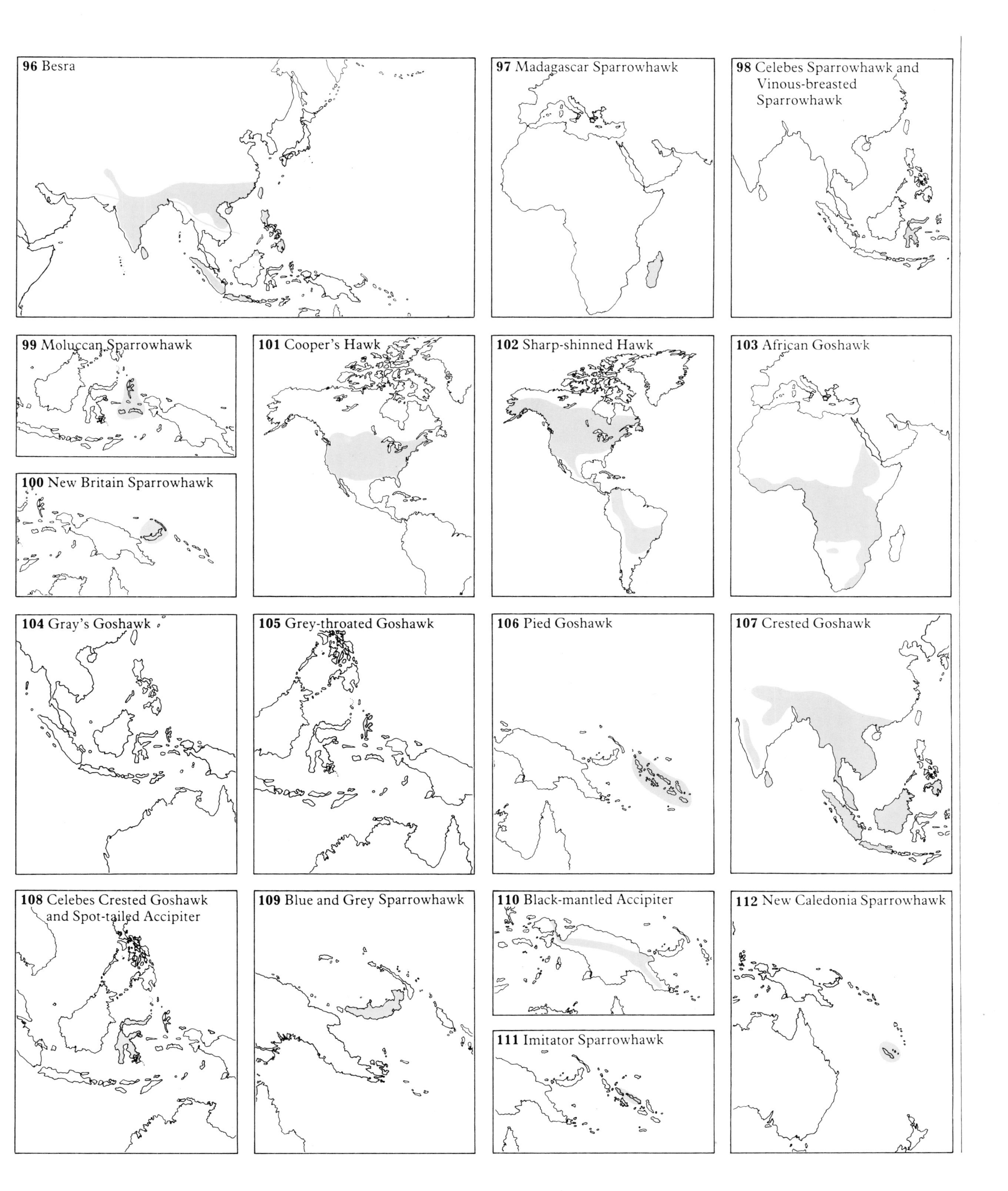
96 Besra
97 Madagascar Sparrowhawk
98 Celebes Sparrowhawk and Vinous-breasted Sparrowhawk
99 Moluccan Sparrowhawk
100 New Britain Sparrowhawk
101 Cooper's Hawk
102 Sharp-shinned Hawk
103 African Goshawk
104 Gray's Goshawk
105 Grey-throated Goshawk
106 Pied Goshawk
107 Crested Goshawk
108 Celebes Crested Goshawk and Spot-tailed Accipiter
109 Blue and Grey Sparrowhawk
110 Black-mantled Accipiter
111 Imitator Sparrowhawk
112 New Caledonia Sparrowhawk

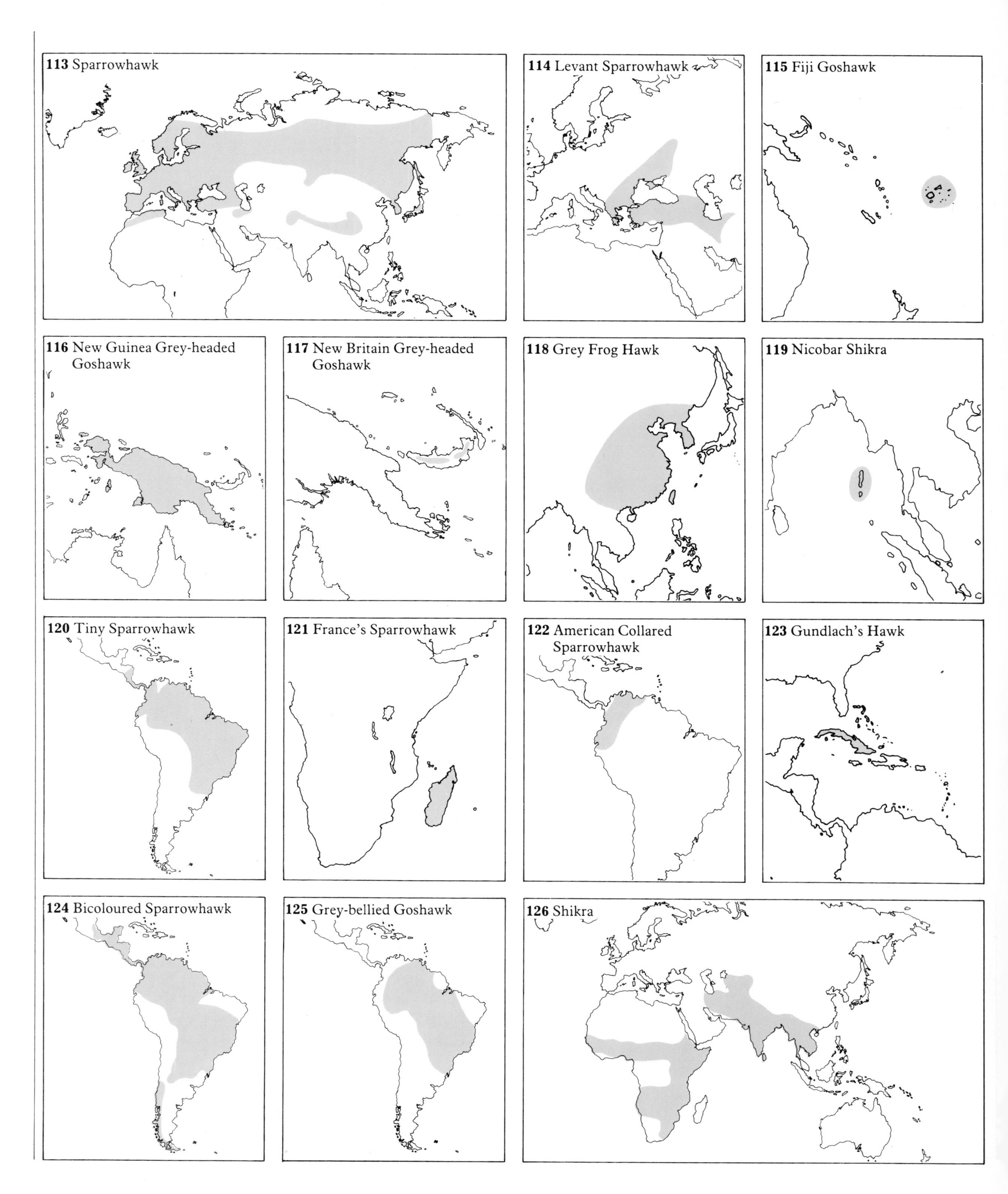
113 Sparrowhawk
114 Levant Sparrowhawk
115 Fiji Goshawk
116 New Guinea Grey-headed Goshawk
117 New Britain Grey-headed Goshawk
118 Grey Frog Hawk
119 Nicobar Shikra
120 Tiny Sparrowhawk
121 France's Sparrowhawk
122 American Collared Sparrowhawk
123 Gundlach's Hawk
124 Bicoloured Sparrowhawk
125 Grey-bellied Goshawk
126 Shikra

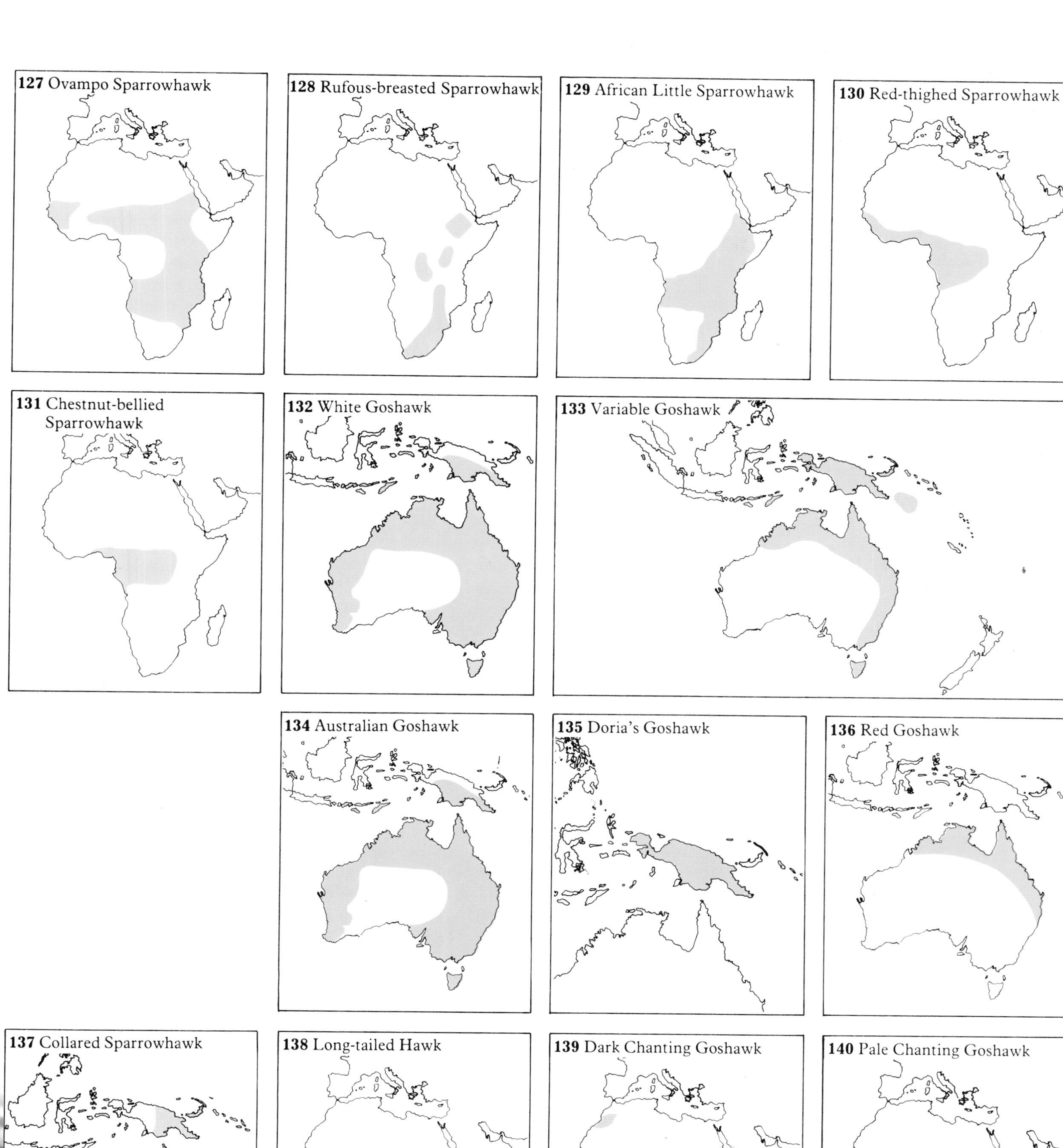

127 Ovampo Sparrowhawk
128 Rufous-breasted Sparrowhawk
129 African Little Sparrowhawk
130 Red-thighed Sparrowhawk
131 Chestnut-bellied Sparrowhawk
132 White Goshawk
133 Variable Goshawk
134 Australian Goshawk
137 Collared Sparrowhawk
138 Long-tailed Hawk

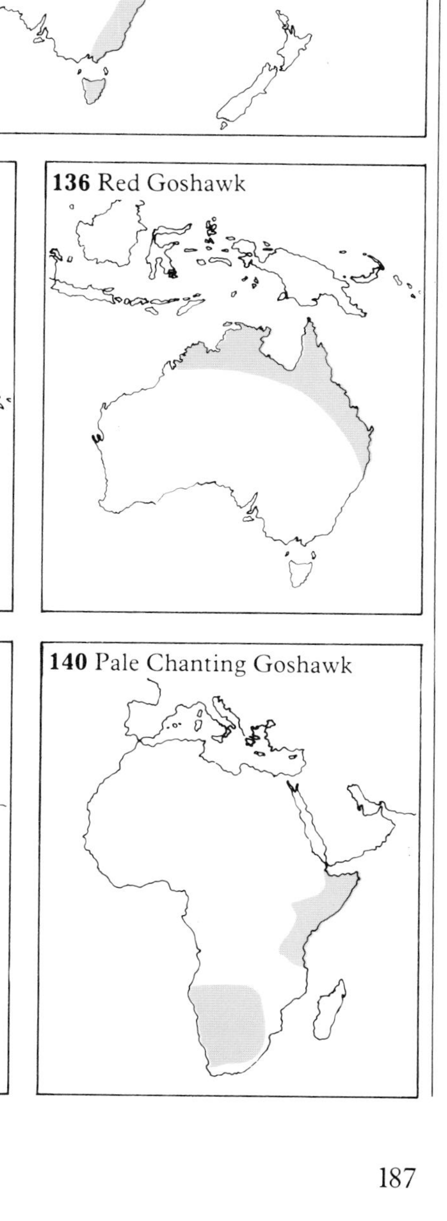

135 Doria's Goshawk
136 Red Goshawk
139 Dark Chanting Goshawk
140 Pale Chanting Goshawk

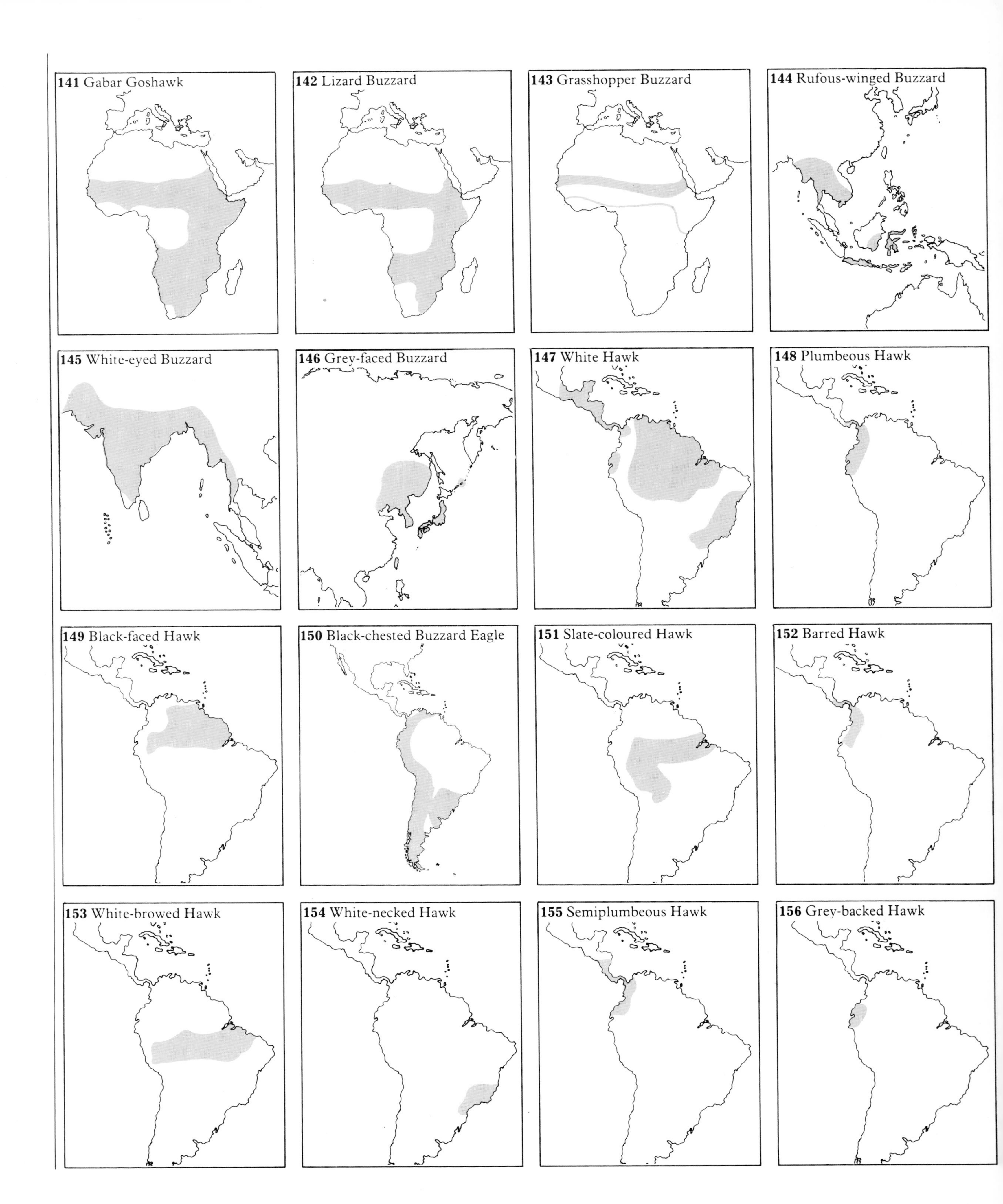
141 Gabar Goshawk
142 Lizard Buzzard
143 Grasshopper Buzzard
144 Rufous-winged Buzzard
145 White-eyed Buzzard
146 Grey-faced Buzzard
147 White Hawk
148 Plumbeous Hawk
149 Black-faced Hawk
150 Black-chested Buzzard Eagle
151 Slate-coloured Hawk
152 Barred Hawk
153 White-browed Hawk
154 White-necked Hawk
155 Semiplumbeous Hawk
156 Grey-backed Hawk

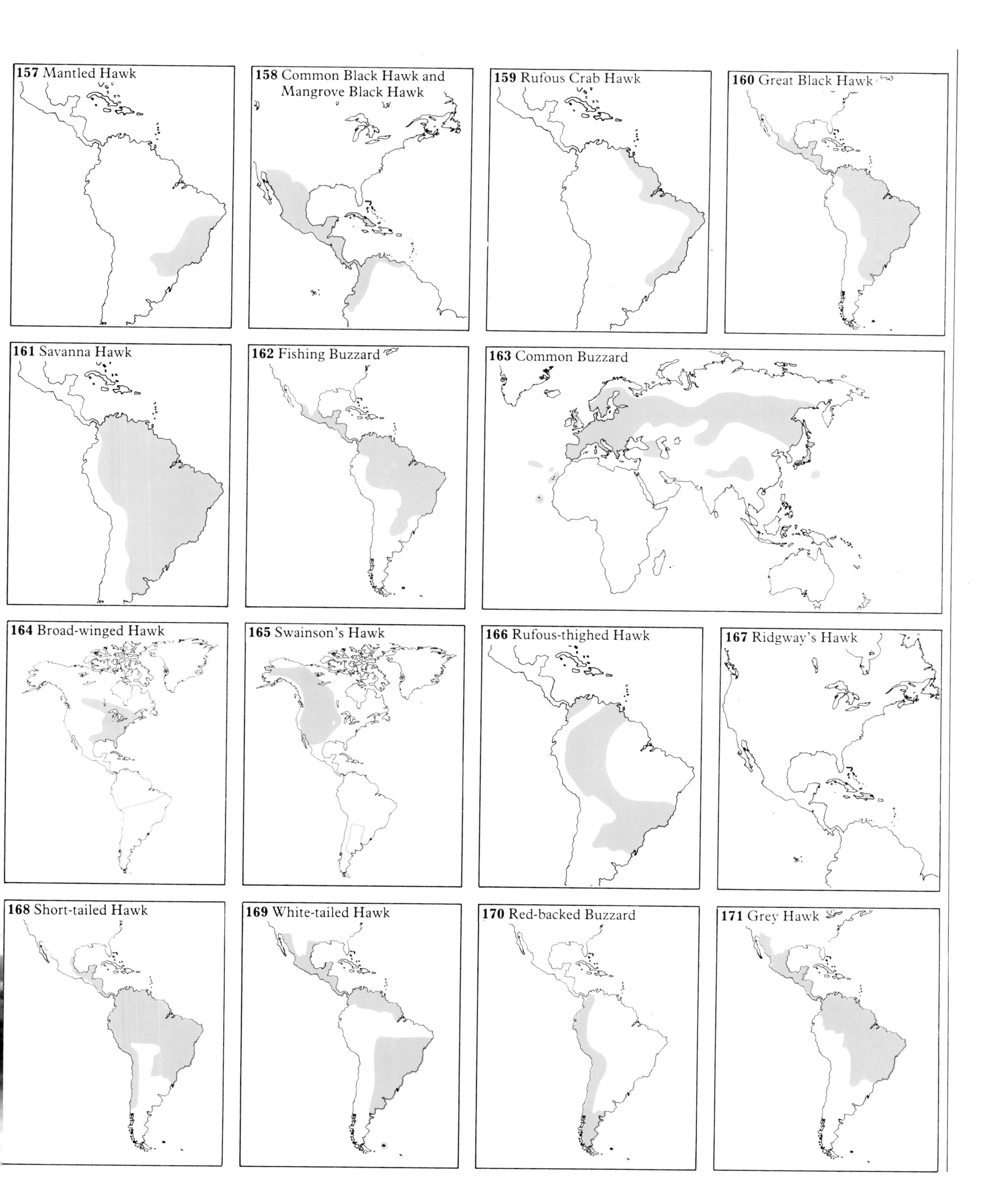
157 Mantled Hawk
158 Common Black Hawk and Mangrove Black Hawk
159 Rufous Crab Hawk
160 Great Black Hawk
161 Savanna Hawk
162 Fishing Buzzard
163 Common Buzzard
164 Broad-winged Hawk
165 Swainson's Hawk
166 Rufous-thighed Hawk
167 Ridgway's Hawk
168 Short-tailed Hawk
169 White-tailed Hawk
170 Red-backed Buzzard
171 Grey Hawk

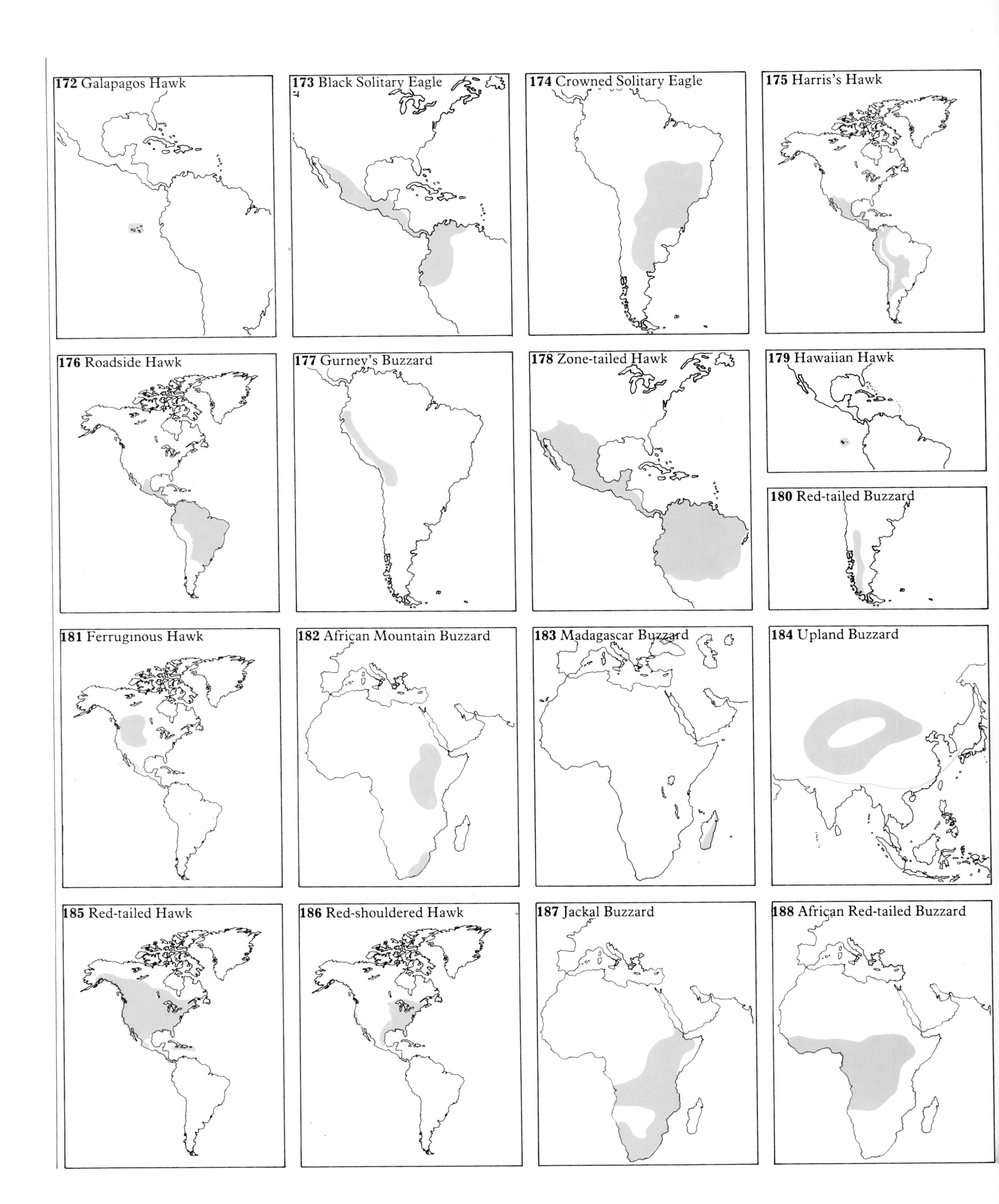
172 Galapagos Hawk
173 Black Solitary Eagle
174 Crowned Solitary Eagle
175 Harris's Hawk
176 Roadside Hawk
177 Gurney's Buzzard
178 Zone-tailed Hawk
179 Hawaiian Hawk
180 Red-tailed Buzzard
181 Ferruginous Hawk
182 African Mountain Buzzard
183 Madagascar Buzzard
184 Upland Buzzard
185 Red-tailed Hawk
186 Red-shouldered Hawk
187 Jackal Buzzard
188 African Red-tailed Buzzard

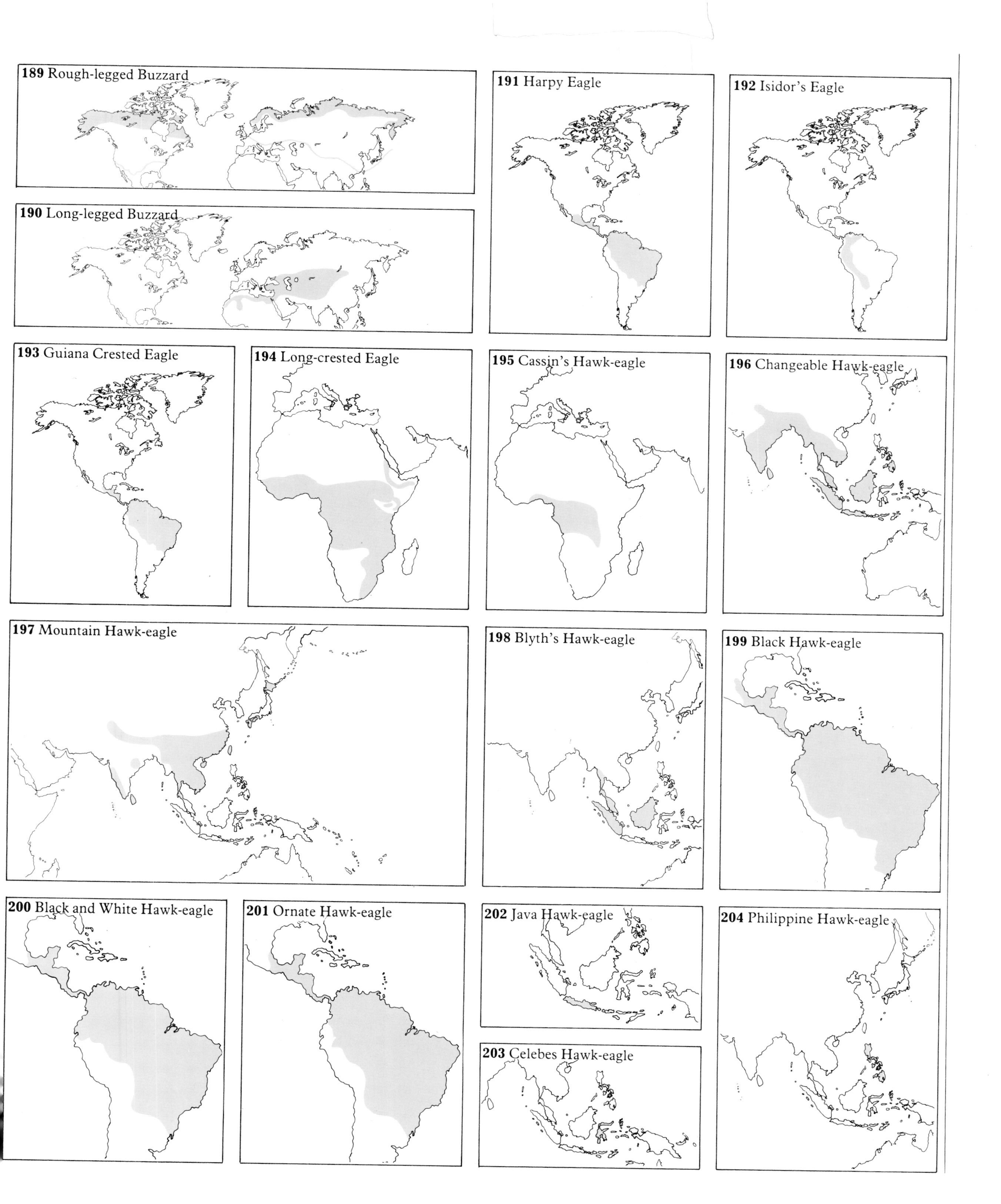
189 Rough-legged Buzzard
190 Long-legged Buzzard
191 Harpy Eagle
192 Isidor's Eagle
193 Guiana Crested Eagle
194 Long-crested Eagle
195 Cassin's Hawk-eagle
196 Changeable Hawk-eagle
197 Mountain Hawk-eagle
198 Blyth's Hawk-eagle
199 Black Hawk-eagle
200 Black and White Hawk-eagle
201 Ornate Hawk-eagle
202 Java Hawk-eagle
203 Celebes Hawk-eagle
204 Philippine Hawk-eagle

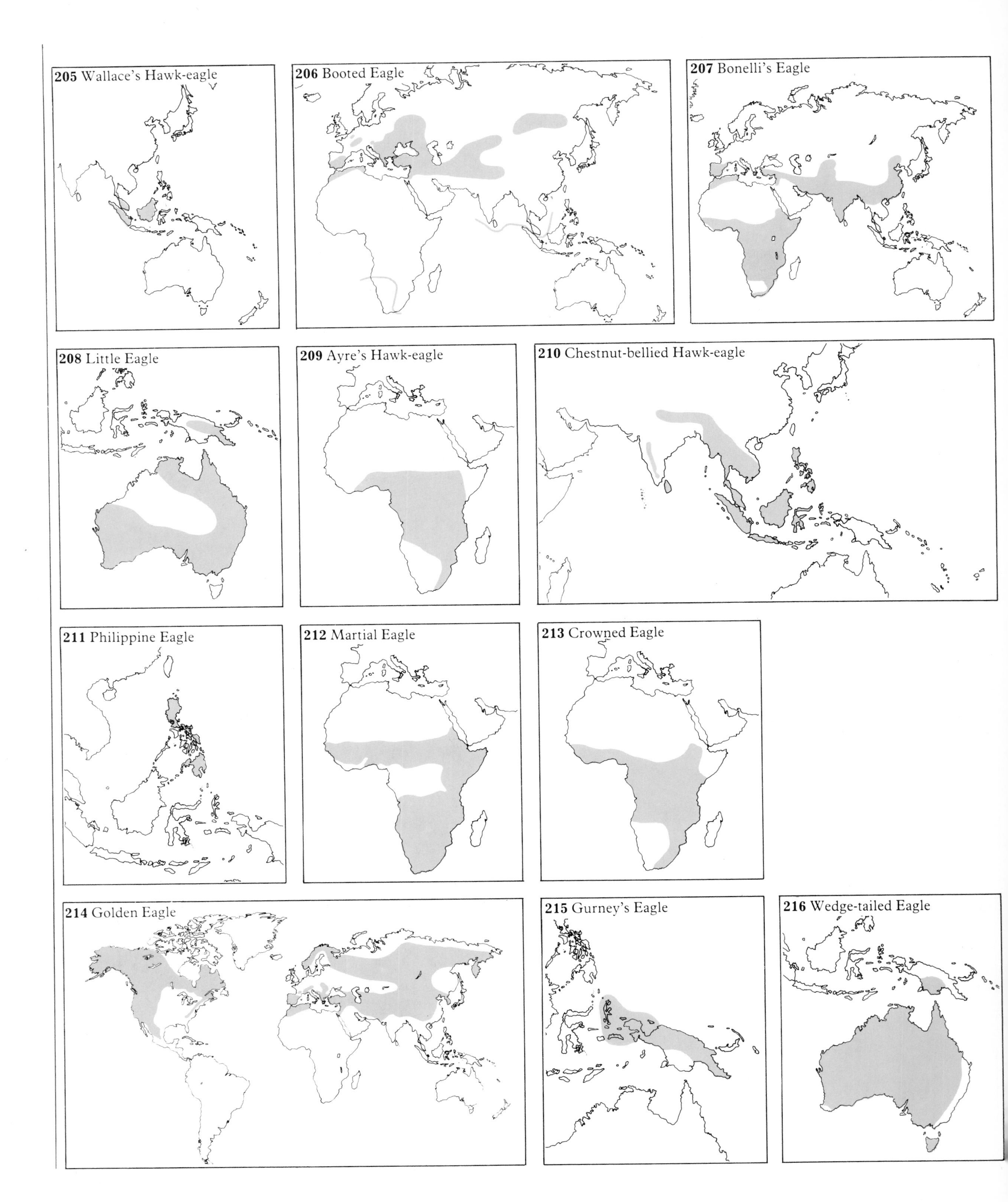
205 Wallace's Hawk-eagle
206 Booted Eagle
207 Bonelli's Eagle
208 Little Eagle
209 Ayre's Hawk-eagle
210 Chestnut-bellied Hawk-eagle
211 Philippine Eagle
212 Martial Eagle
213 Crowned Eagle
214 Golden Eagle
215 Gurney's Eagle
216 Wedge-tailed Eagle

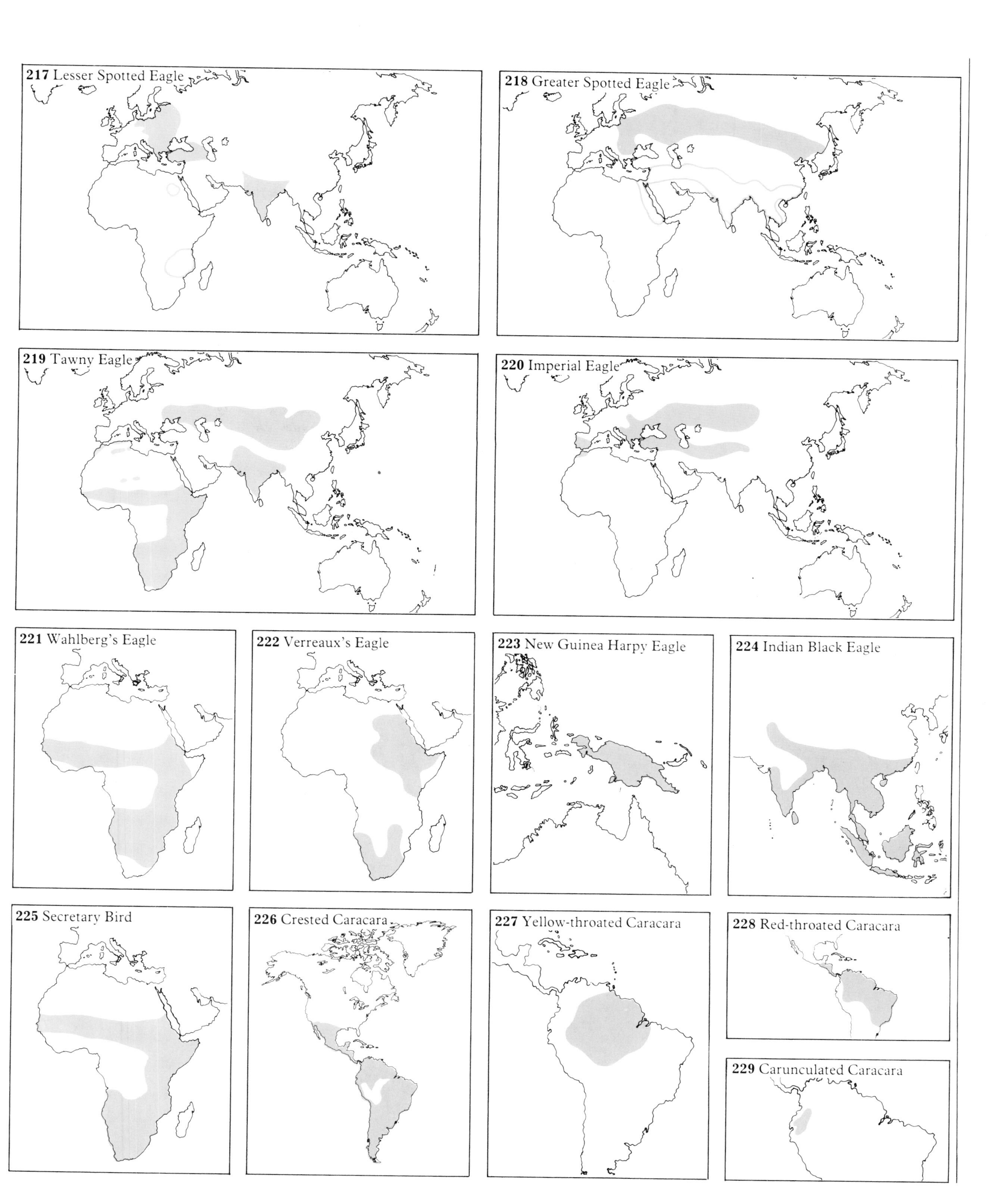
217 Lesser Spotted Eagle
218 Greater Spotted Eagle
219 Tawny Eagle
220 Imperial Eagle
221 Wahlberg's Eagle
222 Verreaux's Eagle
223 New Guinea Harpy Eagle
224 Indian Black Eagle
225 Secretary Bird
226 Crested Caracara
227 Yellow-throated Caracara
228 Red-throated Caracara
229 Carunculated Caracara

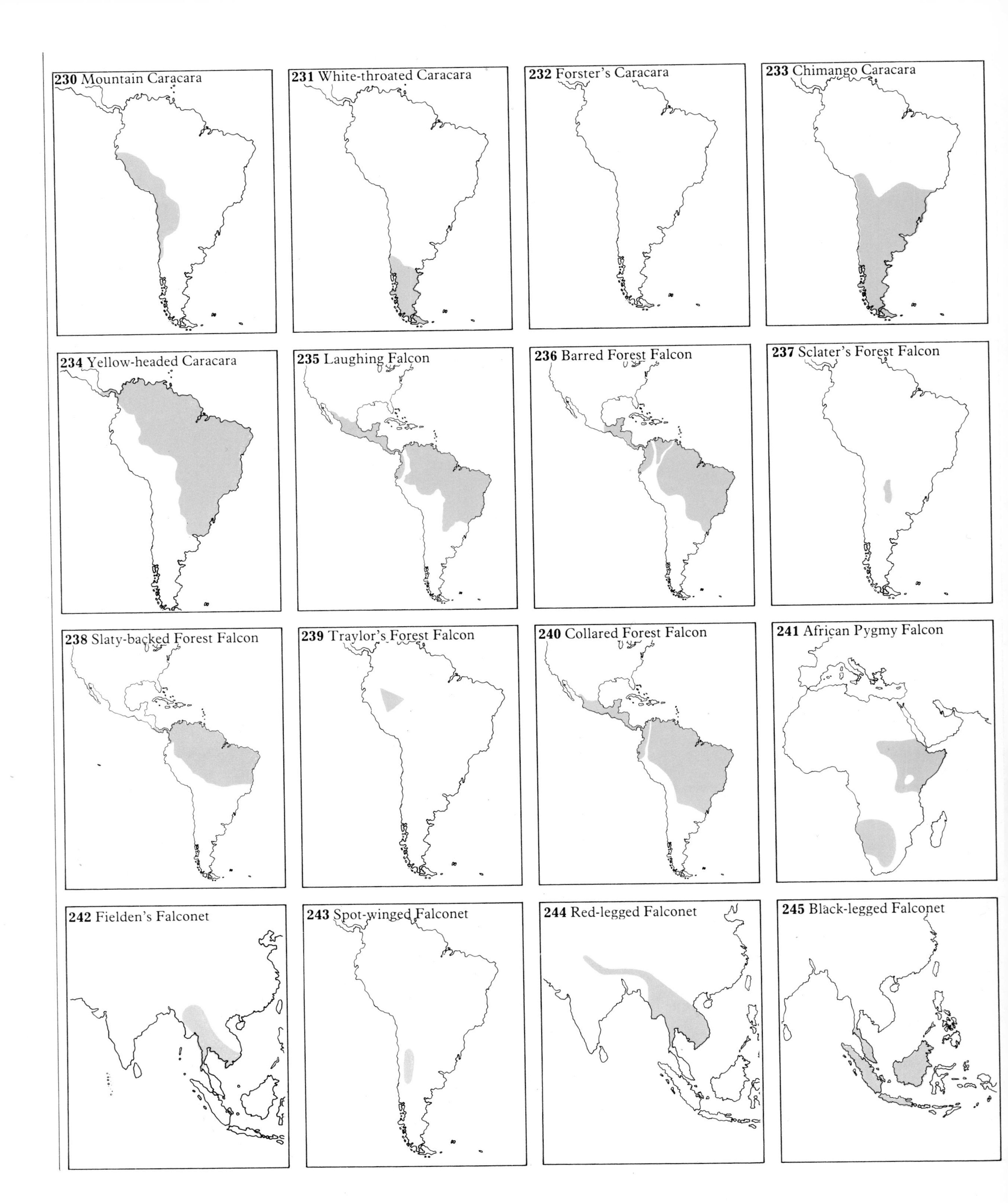
230 Mountain Caracara
231 White-throated Caracara
232 Forster's Caracara
233 Chimango Caracara
234 Yellow-headed Caracara
235 Laughing Falcon
236 Barred Forest Falcon
237 Sclater's Forest Falcon
238 Slaty-backed Forest Falcon
239 Traylor's Forest Falcon
240 Collared Forest Falcon
241 African Pygmy Falcon
242 Fielden's Falconet
243 Spot-winged Falconet
244 Red-legged Falconet
245 Black-legged Falconet

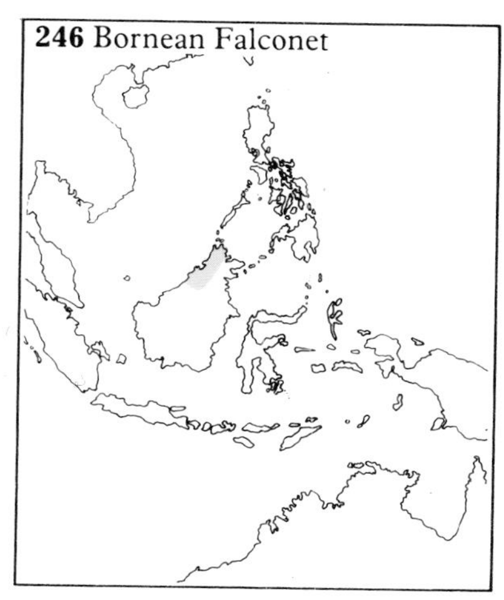
246 Bornean Falconet

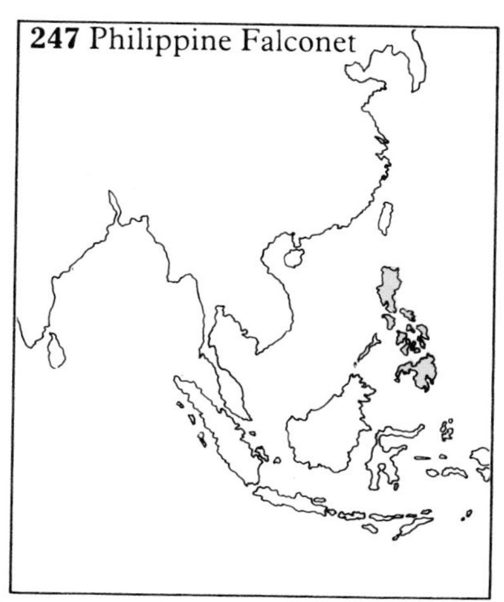
247 Philippine Falconet

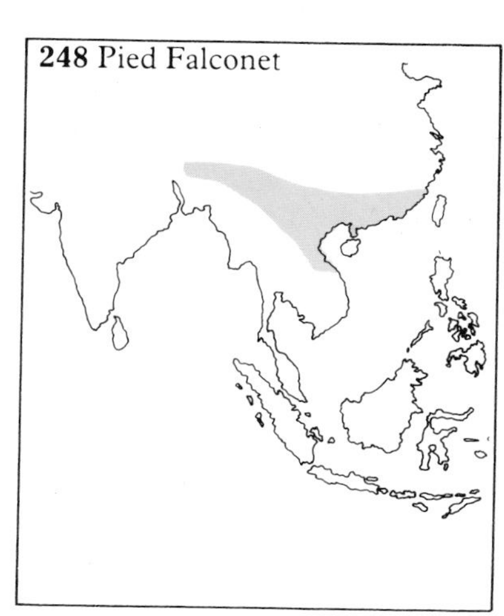
248 Pied Falconet

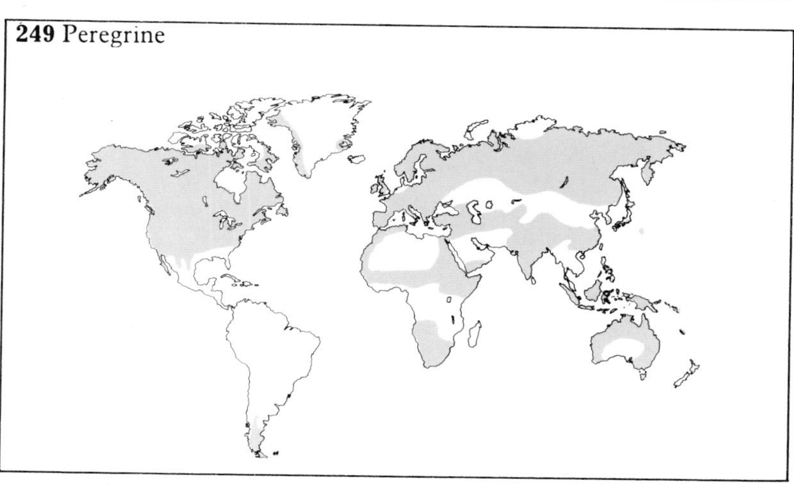
249 Peregrine

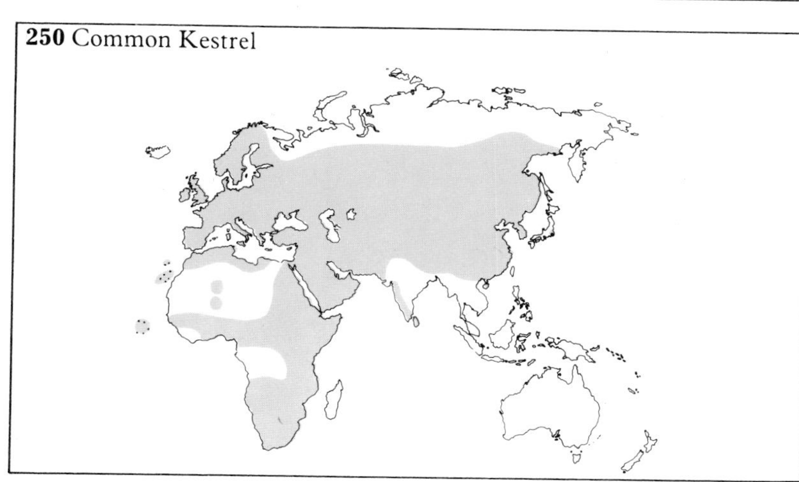
250 Common Kestrel

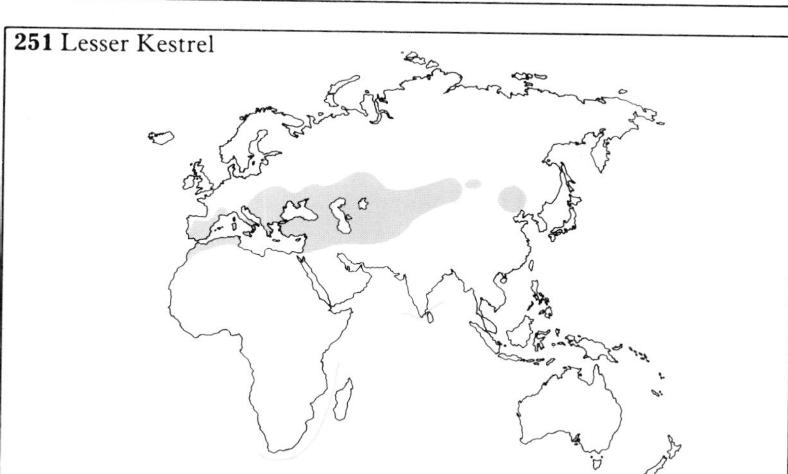
251 Lesser Kestrel

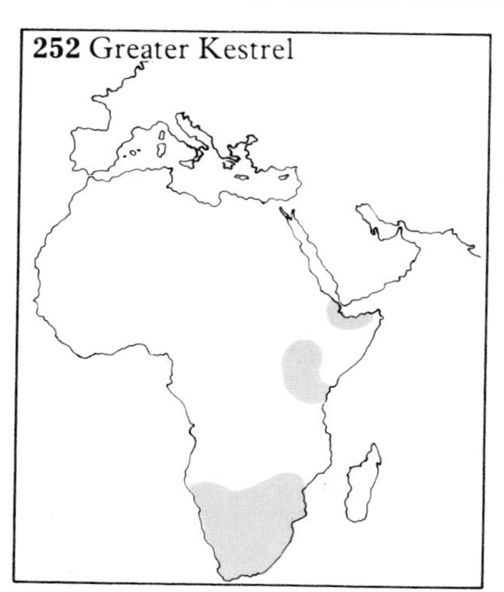
252 Greater Kestrel

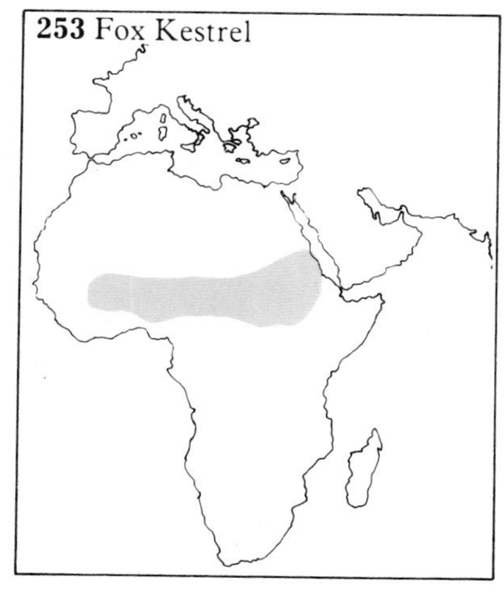
253 Fox Kestrel

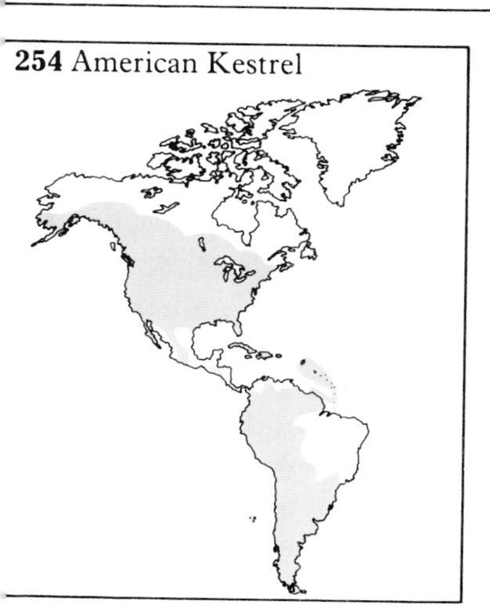
254 American Kestrel

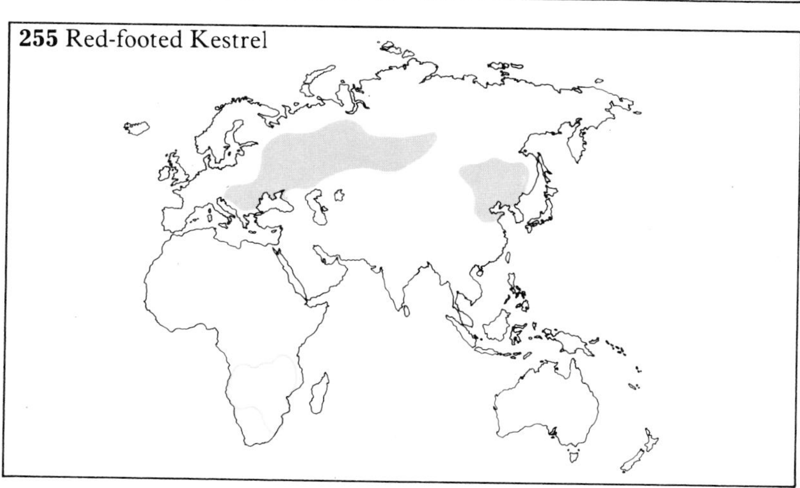
255 Red-footed Kestrel

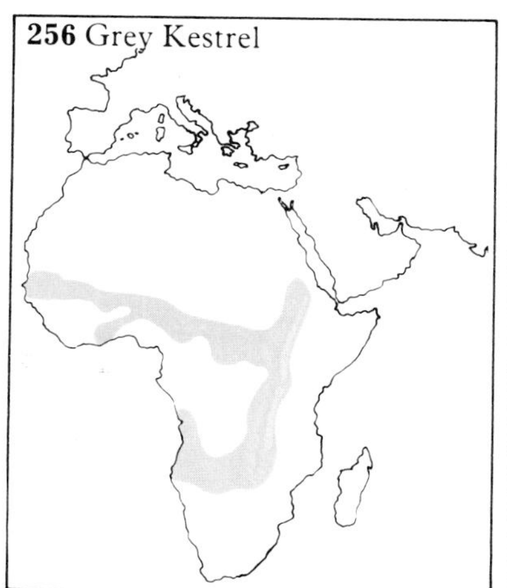
256 Grey Kestrel

257 Dickinson's Kestrel
258 Madagascar Kestrel
259 Mauritius Kestrel
260 Seychelles Kestrel
261 Moluccan Kestrel
262 Nankeen Kestrel
263 Madagascar Banded Kestrel
264 Red-headed Falcon
265 Merlin
266 Bat Falcon
267 Orange-breasted Falcon
268 Taita Falcon
269 Aplomado Falcon

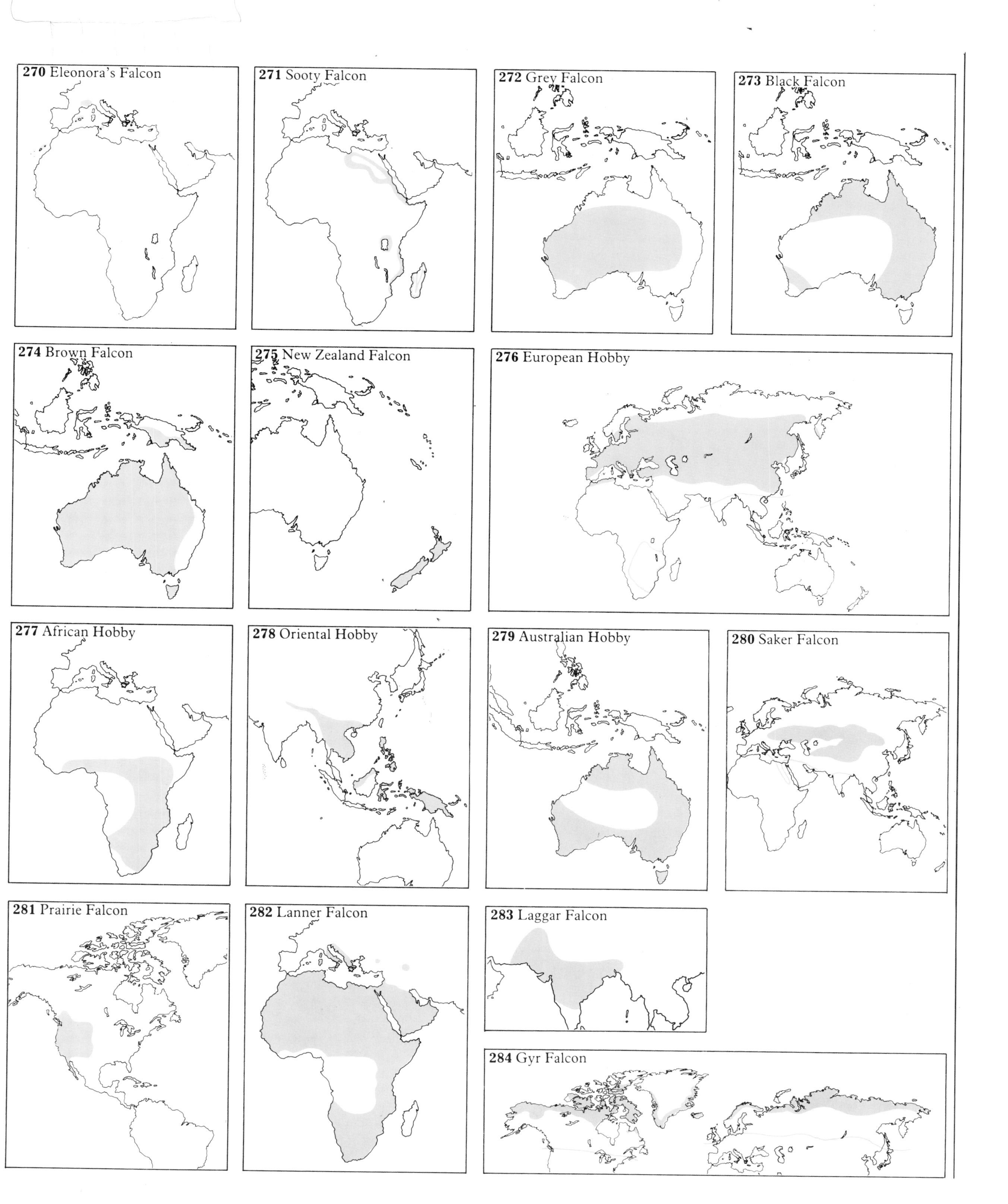
270 Eleonora's Falcon
271 Sooty Falcon
272 Grey Falcon
273 Black Falcon
274 Brown Falcon
275 New Zealand Falcon
276 European Hobby
277 African Hobby
278 Oriental Hobby
279 Australian Hobby
280 Saker Falcon
281 Prairie Falcon
282 Lanner Falcon
283 Laggar Falcon
284 Gyr Falcon

Systematic List and Measurements

FAMILY **Cathartidae:**	*Length*	*Wing*	*Distribution*
Andean Condor *(Vultur gryphus)*	42″ (107cm)	32″ (812mm)	Andes
Turkey Vulture *(Cathartes aura)*	25″ (63cm)	21″ (533mm)	North and South America, from southern Canada southwards
Yellow-headed Vulture *(C. burrovianus)*	30″ (76cm)	19½″ (495mm)	Central America (local) and southern South America
Greater Yellow-headed Vulture *(C. melambrotus)*	33″ (84cm)	20″ (508mm)	Northern South America
Black Vulture *(Coragyps atratus)*	22″ (56cm)	17″ (431mm)	Middle North America south to Patagonia
King Vulture *(Sarcorhamphus papa)*	30″ (76cm)	19½″ (495mm)	Central and South America
California Condor *(Gymnogyps californianus)*	49″ (124cm)	34″ (863mm)	California; formerly more widespread, now gravely endangered

FAMILY **Pandionidae:**			
Osprey *(Pandion haliaetus)*	22″ (56cm)	19″ (482mm)	Worldwide, except Arctic and Antarctic

FAMILY **Accipitridae:**			
African Cuckoo Falcon *(Aviceda cuculoides)*		11-13″ (279-333mm)	Southern half of Africa
Madagascar Cuckoo Falcon *(A.madagascariensis)*		12½-13″ (318-333mm)	Madagascar
Jerdon's Baza *(A. jerdoni)*		12-13″ (305-333mm)	South-east Asia and East Indies
Crested Baza *(A. subcristata)*		13-14″ (333-356mm)	Tropical Australia, New Guinea, Moluccas, Solomon Islands
Black Baza *(A. leuphotes)*	14-17″ (36-43cm)	9-10″ (228-254mm)	Lower Himalayas, migrating to India and South-east Asia
Cayenne Kite *(Leptodon cayanensis)*		12½″ (318mm)	Central and South America
Hook-billed Kite *(Chondrohierax uncinatus)*		11″ (279mm)	Central and South America, Caribbean
Long-tailed Honey-Buzzard *(Henicopernis longicauda)*		13-17″ (333-432mm)	New Guinea
Black Honey-Buzzard *(H. infuscata)*		14″ (356mm)	New Britain
Honey-Buzzard *(Pernis apivorus)*	20-23″ (51-58cm)	16″ (406mm)	Europe and Asia, migrating to Africa and southern Asia
Barred Honey-Buzzard *(Pernis celebensis)*		14½″ (368mm)	Sulawesi (Celebes) and Philippines
Swallow-tailed Kite *(Elanoides forficatus)*	24″ (61cm)	16½″ (419mm)	U.S.A., Central and South America
Bat Hawk *(Machaerhamphus alcinus)*		15½″ (393mm)	Tropical Asia, New Guinea and Africa
Pearl Kite *(Gampsonyx swainsonii)*		6″ (152mm)	Northern half of South America
White-tailed Kite *(Elanus leucurus)*	15½″ (39cm)	12″ (305mm)	Southern U.S.A., Central and South America
Black-shouldered Kite *(E. caeruleus)*	13″ (33cm)	11″ (279mm)	Spain, Africa and southern Asia
Australian Black-shouldered Kite *(E.notatus)*	14″ (36cm)	11½″ (292mm)	Australia
Letter-winged Kite *(E.scriptus)*	14½″ (37cm)	12″ (305mm)	Australia
African Swallow-tailed Kite *(Chelictinia riocourii)*		9½″ (241mm)	Northern half of Africa
Snail Kite *(Rostrhamus sociabilis)*	18″ (46cm)	14″ (356mm)	Southern U.S.A. Central and South America
Slender-billed Kite *(R. hamatus)*		11″ (279mm)	Northern South America and eastern Panama
Double-toothed Kite *(Harpagus bidentatus)*		8½″ (216mm)	Central and South America
Rufous-thighed Kite *(H. diodon)*		8″ (203mm)	South America
Plumbeous Kite *(Ictinia plumbea)*		11½″ (292mm)	Central and South America
Mississippi Kite *(I. misisippiensis)*	14″ (36cm)	12″ (305mm)	Southern U.S.A., wintering in Central and South America
Square-tailed Kite *(Lophoictinia isura)*	22″ (56cm)	18″ (457mm)	Australia; absent from Tasmania
Black-breasted Buzzard Kite *(Hamirostra melanosternon)*	22″ (56cm)	18″ (457mm)	Australia
Black Kite *(Milvus migrans)*	22″ (56cm)	17″ (432mm)	Europe, Asia, Africa and Australasia
Red Kite *(Milvus milvus)*	24″ (61cm)	19½″ (495mm)	Europe, north-west Africa, Canary and Cape Verde Islands
Whistling Kite *(Haliastur sphenurus)*	21″ (53cm)	16″ (406mm)	Australia except Tasmania, New Guinea, New Caledonia
Brahminy Kite *(H. indus)*	18-20″ (46-51cm)	15″ (381mm)	Southern Asia, E. Indies, New Guinea, N. Australia, Solomons

	Length	*Wing*	*Distribution*
White-bellied Sea Eagle *(Haliaeetus leucogaster)*	30-34" (76-86cm)	22" (559mm)	Southern Asia, Australia, New Guinea
Sanford's Sea Eagle *(H. sanfordi)*		22" (559mm)	Solomon Islands
African Fish Eagle *(H. vocifer)*		22" (559mm)	Africa
Madagascar Fish Eagle *(H. madagascariensis)*		20" (508mm)	Madagascar
Pallas' Sea Eagle *(H. leucoryphus)*	30-33" (76-84cm)	22½" (571mm)	Central Asia, south to northern India
Bald Eagle *(Haliaeetus leucocephalus)*	34-43" (86-109cm)	20-27" (508-685mm)	North America
White-tailed Sea Eagle *(H. albicilla)*	27-36" (69-91cm)	22-28" (559-711mm)	Greenland and northern Eurasia
Steller's Sea Eagle *(H. pelagicus)*	42-45" (107-114cm)	22-27" (559-685mm)	Eastern shores of the northern Pacific
Lesser Fishing Eagle *(Ichthyophaga nana)*		14-19½" (355-495mm)	South and south-east Asia, Borneo and Sulawesi
Grey-headed Fishing Eagle *(I. ichthyaetus)*		16½-20" (419-508mm)	South and south-east Asia, Borneo and Philippines
Palm Nut Vulture *(Gypohierax angolensis)*		16½" (419mm)	Africa south of the Sahara
Egyptian Vulture *(Neophron percnopterus)*	23-26" (58-66cm)	19½" (495mm)	Southern Europe, Middle East, Africa and India
Lammergeier *(Gypaetus barbatus)*	40-45" (102-114cm)	30-36" (762-914mm)	Mountain ranges of Europe, Asia and Africa
Hooded Vulture *(Necrosyrtes monachus)*		18½" (470mm)	Africa
Indian White-backed Vulture *(Gyps bengalensis)*		22" (559mm)	India, Burma, Laos, Cambodia and Vietnam
African White-backed Vulture *(G. africanus)*		22½" (571mm)	Africa
Indian Griffon *(G. indicus)*		26" (660mm)	India and south-east Asia
Ruppell's Griffon *(G. ruepellii)*	37-42" (94-107cm)	25" (635mm)	Africa
Himalayan Griffon *(G. himalayensis)*		31" (787mm)	Himalayas
Griffon Vulture *(G. fulvus)*	38-41" (97-104cm)	28" (711mm)	Southern Europe, Central Asia, north-west Africa
Cape Vulture *(G. coprotheres)*		27" (686mm)	South Africa
Lappet-faced Vulture *(Torgos tracheliotus)*	39" (99cm)	30" (762mm)	Africa and occasionally in Israel
Indian Black Vulture *(Sarcogypos calvus)*		24" (610mm)	India, Burma, Thailand and Laos
European Black Vulture *(Aegypius monachus)*	39-42" (99-107cm)	31" (787mm)	Eurasia
White-headed Vulture *(Trigonoceps occipitalis)*		25" (635mm)	Africa
Short-toed Eagle *(Circaetus gallicus)*	25-27" (66-69cm)	20-24" (508-610mm)	Southern Europe, Asia and Africa
Brown Snake Eagle *(C. cinereus)*		19-22" (482-559mm)	Africa south of the Sahara
Southern Banded Snake Eagle *(C. fasciolatus)*		15" (381mm)	East African coast from Kenya to Natal
Smaller Banded Snake Eagle *(C. cinerascens)*		15" (381mm)	West savannah regions of Central Africa
Bateleur *(Terathopius ecaudatus)*	24" (61cm)	19-21" (482-533mm)	Africa south of the Sahara
Philippine Serpent Eagle *(Spilornis holospilus)*		13" (333mm)	Philippines
Celebes Serpent Eagle *(S. rufipectus)*		13-15" (333-381mm)	Sulawesi (Celebes)
Crested Serpent Eagle *(S. cheela)*		11½-19" (292-482mm)	Tropical Asia, East Indies, and Philippines
Nicobar Serpent Eagle *(S. klossi)*		10-11½" (254-292mm)	Great Nicobar Island
Andaman Serpent Eagle *(S. elgini)*		14½" (368mm)	Andaman Islands
Congo Serpent Eagle *(Dryotriorchis spectabilis)*		12" (305mm)	West and central Equatorial Africa
Madagascar Serpent Eagle *(Eutriorchis astur)*		12" (305mm)	Madagascar
African Harrier Hawk *(Polyboroides typus)*	25" (64cm)	17-19" (432-483mm)	Africa south of the Sahara and north of the Zambesi
Madagascar Harrier Hawk *(P. radiatus)*		14½-16½" (368-419mm)	Madagascar
Crane Hawk *(Geranospiza caerulescens)*		11-13" (279-333mm)	Central and South America
Spotted Harrier *(Circus assimilis)*	21-23" (53-58cm)	15-18" (381-457mm)	Australia and eastern East Indies
Marsh Harrier *(C. aeruginosus)*	20" (51cm)	15-17" (381-432mm)	Most of the Old World except the far north
African Marsh Harrier *(C. ranivorus)*		13-15½" (333-393mm)	Eastern and southern Africa
Black Harrier *(C. maurus)*	19½" (50cm)	13-14½" (333-368mm)	South Africa
Hen Harrier *(C. cyaneus)*	17-20" (43-51cm)	13-16" (333-406mm)	North America and Eurasia
Cinereous Harrier *(C. cinereus)*		12-14½" (305-368mm)	Southern America and Falkland Islands
Pallid Harrier *(C. macrourus)*	18" (46cm)	13-15" (333-381mm)	East Europe & USSR wintering in Africa and southern Asia
Montagu's Harrier *(C. pygargus)*	16-18" (41-46cm)	13-15" (333-381mm)	Europe and USSR, wintering Mediterranean, Africa, India
Pied Harrier *(C. melanoleucus)*		13-15" (333-381mm)	East central Asia, wintering in south-east Asia
Long-winged Harrier *(C. buffoni)*		14½-18" (368-457mm)	South America

	Length	*Wing*	*Distribution*
Dark Chanting Goshawk *(Melierax metabates)*	20-22″ (51-56cm)	12-13″ (305-333mm)	West and central Africa, Arabia
Pale Chanting Goshawk *(M. canorus)*	21-25″ (53-64cm)	13-15″ (333-381mm)	East and southern Africa
Gabar Goshawk *(M. gabar)*	12-14″ (30-36cm)	8″ (203mm)	Africa south of the Sahara and south-east Arabia
Doria's Goshawk *(Megatriorchis doriae)*		11-13″ (279-333mm)	New Guinea
Red Goshawk *(Erythrotriorchis radiatus)*	20-24″ (51-61cm)	14-16½″ (355-419mm)	Northern half of Australia
Goshawk *(Accipiter gentilis)*	19-26″ (48-66cm)	12½-15″ (318-381mm)	Northern hemisphere of Old and New Worlds
Henst's Goshawk *(A. henstii)*		11-12½″ (279-318mm)	Madagascar
Black Sparrowhawk *(A. melanoleucus)*	18-23″ (46-58cm)	11-13½″ (279-342mm)	Africa south of the Sahara
Meyer's Goshawk *(A. meyerianus)*		11½-13½″ (292-343mm)	Moluccas to Solomons
Burger's Sparrowhawk *(A. buergersi)*		11½-12½″ (292-319mm)	Eastern New Guinea
Ovampo Sparrowhawk *(A. ovampensis)*	13-15″ (33-38cm)	8-10″ (203-254mm)	Africa south of the Sahara
Madagascar Sparrowhawk *(A. madagascariensis)*		6½-9″ (165-228mm)	Madagascar
Japanese Sparrowhawk *(A. gularis)*	10-12″ (25-30cm)	6½-8″ (165-203mm)	Eastern Asia and Japan
Besra *(A. virgatus)*	12-14″ (30-36cm)	5½-7″ (140-178mm)	Himalayas to south-east Asia and East Indies
Celebes Little Sparrowhawk *(A. nanus)*		6-7″ (152-178mm)	Sulawesi (Celebes)
Vinous-breasted Sparrowhawk *(A. rhodogaster)*		6½-8″ (165-203mm)	Sulawesi (Celebes)
Moluccan Sparrowhawk *(A. erythrauchen)*		6½-8″ (165-203mm)	Moluccas
Collared Sparrowhawk *(A. cirrhocephalus)*	13-15″ (33-38cm)	6½-10″ (165-254mm)	Australia, New Guinea, eastern East Indies
New Britain Sparrowhawk *(A. brachyurus)*		6½-8″ (165-203mm)	New Britain
Sparrowhawk *(A. nisus)*	11-15″ (28-38cm)	7-10″ (178-254mm)	Eurasia and North Africa
Rufous-breasted Sparrowhawk *(A. rufiventris)*	13-16″ (33-41cm)	8-9½″ (203-241mm)	Africa south of the Sahara
Sharp-shinned Hawk *(A. striatus)*	10-14″ (25-36cm)	6½-9″ (165-228mm)	North and South America, Caribbean
Red-thighed Sparrowhawk *(A. erythropus)*		5½-6½″ (140-165mm)	Africa south of the Sahara
African Little Sparrowhawk *(A. minullus)*	9-12″ (23-30cm)	5½-6½″ (140-165mm)	Africa south of the Sahara
Chestnut-bellied Sparrowhawk *(A. castanilius)*		6-7″ (152-178mm)	West Africa
African Goshawk *(A. tachiro)*	14-15″ (36-38cm)	8-10″ (203-254mm)	Africa south of the Sahara
Crested Goshawk *(A. trivirgatus)*	16″ (41cm)	7-10½″ (178-267mm)	Southern Asia, Philippines and Borneo
Celebes Crested Goshawk *(A. griseiceps)*		6½-8″ (165-203mm)	Sulawesi (Celebes)
Spot-tailed Accipiter *(A. trinotatus)*		6-6½″ (152-165mm)	Sulawesi (Celebes)
Blue and Grey Sparrowhawk *(A. luteoschistaceus)*		7½-8½″ (190-216mm)	New Britain
Australian Goshawk *(A. fasciatus)*	16-22″ (41-56cm)	9½-12½″ (241-318mm)	Australia, New Guinea, Flores, Timor, Christmas Island
Gray's Goshawk *(A. henicogrammus)*		8½-9½″ (216-241mm)	Moluccas
Variable Goshawk *(A. novaehollandiae)*	13-20″ (33-51cm)	7-12″ (178-315mm)	Australia, New Guinea and islands from Ceram to Solomons
Grey-throated Goshawk *(A. griseogularis)*		8-10″ (203-254mm)	Moluccas
Black-mantled Accipiter *(A. melanochlamys)*		8½″-10½″ (216-267mm)	New Guinea
Imitator Sparrowhawk *(A. imitator)*		7-10″ (178-254mm)	Solomon Islands
Pied Goshawk *(A. albogularis)*		8-10½″ (203-267mm)	Solomon Islands
New Caledonia Sparrowhawk *(A. haplochrous)*		7½-9½″ (190-241mm)	New Caledonia
Fiji Goshawk *(A. rufitorques)*		7½-9½″ (190-241mm)	Fiji
New Guinea Grey-headed Goshawk *(A. poliocephalus)*		7½-8½″ (190-216mm)	New Guinea
New Britain Grey-headed Goshawk *(A. princeps)*		10-11″ (254-279mm)	New Britain
Grey Frog Hawk *(A. soloensis)*	12-14″ (30-36cm)	7½-10″ (190-254mm)	China and Korea, wintering in Philippines and Sulawesi
Levant Sparrowhawk *(A. brevipes)*	13-15″ (33-38cm)	8½-9½″ (216-241mm)	Balkans and Middle East
Shikra *(A. badius)*	12-14″ (30-36cm)	6½-10½″ (165-267mm)	Asia and Africa south of the Sahara
Nicobar Shikra *(A. butleri)*		7″ (178mm)	Nicobar Islands
France's Sparrowhawk *(A. francesii)*		6-7″ (152-178mm)	Madagascar
American Collared Sparrowhawk *(A. collaris)*		6-7″ (152-178mm)	South America
Tiny Sparrowhawk *(A. superciliosus)*	8-11″ (20-28cm)	5-6″ (127-152mm)	South America
Gundlach's Hawk *(A. gundlachi)*		9½-10½″ (241-267mm)	Cuba
Cooper's Hawk *(A. cooperii)*	14-20″ (36-51cm)	8½-11″ (216-279mm)	North America
Bicoloured Sparrowhawk *(A. bicolor)*	14-18″ (36-46cm)	8-11″ (203-279mm)	Central and South America

	Length	*Wing*	*Distribution*
-**bellied Goshawk** *(A. poliogaster)*	17-20″ (43-51cm)	9-11″ (228-279mm)	South America
tailed Hawk *(Urotriorchis macrourus)*		11½″ (292mm)	West Africa
hopper Buzzard *(Butastur rufipennis)*	16-18″ (41-46cm)	11½-14″ (292-355mm)	Africa south of the Sahara
s-winged Buzzard *(B. liventer)*	16″ (41cm)	10½″ (267mm)	South-east Asia and East Indies
-eyed Buzzard *(Butastur teesa)*	16″ (41cm)	11-12½″ (279-318mm)	India to Burma
faced Buzzard *(B. indicus)*	17″ (43cm)	13″ (333mm)	East Asia; winters south to Philippines, East Indies
l Buzzard *(Kaupifalco monogrammicus)*	13-15″ (33-38cm)	8-9½″ (203-241mm)	Africa south of the Sahara
coloured Hawk *(Leucopternis schistacea)*	15-17″ (38-43cm)	11½″ (292mm)	Amazonian rainforests
beous Hawk *(L. plumbea)*		9″ (228mm)	Eastern Panama and northern South America
d Hawk *(L. princeps)*		14½″-15½″ (368-393mm)	Costa Rica to Ecuador
-faced Hawk *(L. melanops)*	16″ (41cm)	8-9½″ (203-241mm)	Amazonian rainforests
-browed Hawk *(L. kuhli)*		8-9½″ (203-241mm)	Amazonian rainforests
-necked Hawk *(L. lacernulata)*		12″ (305mm)	Brazilian rainforests
lumbeous Hawk *(L. semiplumbea)*		6½-9½″ (165-241mm)	Central America and north-west South America
Hawk *(L. albicollis)*	19-22″ (48-56cm)	13-15½″ (333-393mm)	Central America and northern half of South America
backed Hawk *(L. occidentalis)*		13-14½″ (333-368mm)	Ecuador
ed Hawk *(L. polionota)*		14-16″ (355-406mm)	Eastern Brazil to northern Argentina
non Black Hawk *(Buteogallus anthracinus)*	18-22″ (46-56cm)	15½″ (393mm)	Southern U.S.A. to northern South America
rove Black Hawk *(B. subtilis)*		13½″ (333cm)	Pacific Coast of Central and northern South America
s Crab Hawk *(B. aequinoctialis)*	18″ (46cm)	12½″ (318mm)	Northern South America
Black Hawk *(B. urubitinga)*	20-24″ (51-61cm)	15½″ (393mm)	Central and South America
Solitary Eagle *(Harpyhaliaetus solitarius)*	26-28″ (66-71cm)	19-20½″ (482-521mm)	Central America and north-west South America
ned Solitary Eagle *(H. coronatus)*		21½″ (546mm)	Southern South America
nah Hawk *(Heterospizias meridionalis)*	20-25″ (51-64cm)	15-16½″ (381-419mm)	Eastern Panama south to northern Argentina
g Buzzard *(Busarellus nigricollis)*	18-20″ (46-51cm)	14-16″ (355-406mm)	Central and South America
-chested Buzzard-Eagle *(Geranoaetus* *noleucos)*	24-27″ (61-69cm)	18-22″ (457-559mm)	South America
s Hawk *(Parabuteo unicinctus)*	19-22″ (48-56cm)	12-15½″ (305-393mm)	Southern U.S.A., Central and South America
Hawk *(Buteo nitidus)*	15-17″ (38-43cm)	9-10½″ (228-267mm)	Southern U.S.A., Central and South America
side Hawk *(B. magnirostris)*	14-16″ (36-41cm)	8-11″ (203-279mm)	Central and South America
s-thighed Hawk *(B. leucorrhous)*	14-15″ (36-38cm)	8-10″ (203-254mm)	South America
vay's Hawk *(B. ridgwayi)*		8½-9½″ (216-241mm)	Hispaniola
houldered Hawk *(B. lineatus)*	18-24″ (46-61cm)	13″ (333mm)	North America and northern Mexico
l-winged Hawk *(B. platypterus)*	14-19″ (36-48cm)	9½-11½″ (241-292mm)	North America and Caribbean
-tailed Hawk *(B. brachyurus)*	17″ (43cm)	11-13″ (279-333mm)	Southern U.S.A., Central and South America
son's Hawk *(B. swainsoni)*	19-22″ (48-56cm)	14½-17″ (368-431mm)	West N. America, north Mexico; winters Argentina
agos Hawk *(B. galapagoensis)*	22″ (56cm)	14½-17″ (368-431mm)	Galapagos Islands
-tailed Hawk *(B. albicaudatus)*	23-24″ (58-61cm)	15-18″ (381-457mm)	Southern U.S.A., Central and South America
acked Buzzard *(B. polyosoma)*		14-17½″ (355-445mm)	Western and southern South America
ey's Buzzard *(B. poecilochrous)*		17½″ (445mm)	Western and Southern South America
tailed Hawk *(B. albonotatus)*	18-22″ (46-56cm)	15-17″ (380-438mm)	Southern U.S.A., Central and South America
ian Hawk *(B. solitarius)*		10½-12″ (264-308mm)	Hawaii
ailed Buzzard *(B. ventralis)*		14-17″ (351-427mm)	Southern Chile and Argentina
ailed Hawk *(B. jamaicensis)*	19–25″ (48–63cm)	13-17″ (333-431mm)	North and Central America
non Buzzard *(B. buteo)*	20-22″ (51-56cm)	13½-16½″ (343-419mm)	Eurasia, some wintering Africa, southern Asia
n Mountain Buzzard *(B. oreophilus)*	18-20″ (46-51cm)	13-14″ (333-355mm)	Mountains of East and southern Africa
gascar Buzzard *(B. brachypterus)*		12½″ (317mm)	Madagascar
h-legged Buzzard *(B. lagopus)*	20-24″ (51-61cm)	15½-19″ (393-482mm)	North and Arctic of Eurasia and North America
legged Buzzard *(B. rufinus)*	20-26″ (51-66cm)	16½-19½″ (419-495mm)	South-east Europe, North Africa, Central Asia
d Buzzard *(B. hemilasius)*		17½-20″ (445-508mm)	Central and eastern Asia; winters southern Asia
ginous Hawk *(B. regalis)*	23-24″ (58-61cm)	17″ (431mm)	Western North America
n Red-tailed Buzzard *(B. auguralis)*	21-23″ (53-58cm)	14″ (355mm)	West and Central Africa

	Length	*Wing*	*Distribution*
Jackal Buzzard *(B. rufofuscus)*	18-21″ (46-53cm)	15½-18½″ (393-467mm)	Africa south of the Sahara
Guiana Crested Eagle *(Morphnus guianensis)*	32-34″ (81-86cm)	17-19″ (431-482mm)	South America
Harpy Eagle *(Harpia harpyja)*	34-37″ (86-94cm)	21½-24″ (546-610mm)	Central America south to northern Argentina
New Guinea Harpy Eagle *(Harpyopsis novaeguineae)*		14½-19″ (368-482mm)	New Guinea
Philippine Eagle *(Pithecophaga jefferyi)*		23½″ (597mm)	Philippines
Indian Black Eagle *(Ictinaetus malayensis)*	27″ (69cm)	20½-22½″ (521-571mm)	Southern Asia and East Indies
Lesser Spotted Eagle *(Aquila pomarina)*	24-26″ (61-66cm)	17½-20″ (445-508mm)	Central and eastern Europe, India and Burma
Greater Spotted Eagle *(A. clanga)*	26-29″ (66-74cm)	19½-21½″ (495-546mm)	North-east Europe, Central Asia and Siberia
Tawny Eagle *(A. rapax)*	26-31″ (66-79cm)	19-22″ (482-559mm)	Eastern Europe, Asia and Africa
Imperial Eagle *(A. heliaca)*	31-33″ (79-84cm)	22½-26″ (571-660mm)	Spain and southern Europe, Central Asia
Wahlberg's Eagle *(A. wahlbergi)*		15½-17½″ (393-445mm)	Africa south of the Sahara
Gurney's Eagle *(A. gurneyi)*		21″ (533mm)	Moluccas and New Guinea
Golden Eagle *(A. chrysaetos)*	30-35″ (76-89cm)	22½-28″ (571-711mm)	Northern Hemisphere of New and Old Worlds
Wedge-tailed Eagle *(A. audax)*	36-40″ (91-102cm)	23-26½″ (584-673mm)	Australia
Verreaux's Eagle *(A. verreauxi)*	31-38″ (79-97cm)	22-25″ (559-635mm)	Africa south of the Sahara, in mountainous areas
Bonelli's Eagle *(Hieraaetus fasciatus)*	26-29″ (66-74cm)	16-22″ (406-559mm)	Eurasia and Africa
Booted Eagle *(H. pennatus)*	18-21″ (46-53cm)	14-17″ (355-431mm)	Southern Europe, North Africa and southern Asia
Little Eagle *(H. morphnoides)*	18-20″ (46-51cm)	13-16″ (333-406mm)	Australia, excepting Tasmania, New Guinea
Ayres' Hawk-eagle *(H. dubius)*	18-23″ (46-58cm)	13-16½″ (333-419mm)	Africa south of the Sahara
Chestnut-bellied Hawk-eagle *(H. kienerii)*	20″ (51cm)	15-17″ (381-431mm)	Southern Asia and East Indies
Black and White Hawk-eagle *(Spizastur melanoleucus)*	22-24″ (56-61cm)	13½-16½″ (343-419mm)	Central and South America
Long-crested Eagle *(Lophaetus occipitalis)*	21-23″ (53-58cm)	14-16″ (355-406mm)	Africa south of the Sahara
Cassin's Hawk-eagle *(Spizaetus africanus)*		13″ (333mm)	West Africa
Changeable Hawk-eagle *(S. cirrhatus)*	27″ (69cm)	14-19½″ (355-495mm)	Southern Asia and East Indies
Mountain Hawk-eagle *(S. nipalensis)*	26″ (66cm)	16½-20½″ (419-521mm)	Southern continental Asia
Java Hawk-eagle *(S. bartelsi)*		14½″ (368mm)	Java
Celebes Hawk-eagle *(S. lanceolatus)*		14-16½″ (355-419mm)	Sulawesi (Celebes)
Philippine Hawk-eagle *(S. philippensis)*		13-15½″ (333-393mm)	Philippines
Blyth's Hawk-eagle *(S. alboniger)*	21″ (53cm)	13½″ (343mm)	South-east Asia
Wallace's Hawk-eagle *(S. nanus)*	18″ (46cm)	12″ (305mm)	Malaya, Borneo and Sumatra
Black Hawk-eagle *(S. tyrannus)*	25-28″ (64-71cm)	14-17½″ (355-445mm)	Central and South America
Ornate Hawk-eagle *(S. ornatus)*	23-25″ (58-64cm)	13½-15½″ (343-393mm)	Central and South America
Crowned Eagle *(Stephanoaetus coronatus)*	32-36″ (81-91cm)	17½-20½″ (445-521mm)	Africa south of the Sahara
Isidor's Eagle *(Oroaetus isidori)*	25-29″ (64-74cm)	18-20½″ (457-521mm)	Andes
Martial Eagle *(Polemaetus bellicosus)*	31-33″ (79-84cm)	22-26½″ (559-673mm)	Africa south of the Sahara

Family **Sagittariidae:**

Secretary Bird *(Sagittarius serpentarius)*	50-59″ (127-150cm)	25″ (635mm)	Africa south of the Sahara

Family **Falconidae:**

Yellow-throated Caracara *(Daptrius ater)*	17-19″ (43-48cm)	12½″ (318mm)	Northern half of South America
Red-throated Caracara *(D. americanus)*	19-22″ (48-56cm)	14″ (355mm)	Central America and northern South America
Carunculated Caracara *(Phalcobaenus carunculatus)*	20-22″ (51-56cm)	15″ (381mm)	Andes of Ecuador and Colombia
Mountain Caracara *(P. megalopterus)*	19-21″ (48-53cm)	15½″ (393mm)	Andes
White-throated Caracara *(P. albogularis)*	19-21″ (48-53cm)	14½″ (368mm)	Andes, Patagonia, Tierra del Fuego
Forster's Caracara *(P. australis)*	21-23″ (53-58cm)	16″ (406mm)	Falkland Islands and islands off Cape Horn
Crested Caracara *(Polyborus plancus)*	20-24″ (51-61cm)	14-16″ (355-406mm)	Southern U.S.A. to Tierra del Fuego
Chimango Caracara *(Milvago chimango)*	15-17″ (38-43cm)	12″ (305mm)	Southern half of South America

	Length	*Wing*	*Distribution*
Yellow-headed Caracara *(M. chimachima)*	16-18" (41-46cm)	10½-12" (267-305mm)	Panama and South America
Laughing Falcon *(Herpetotheres cachinnans)*	18-22" (46-56cm)	10-12" (254-305mm)	Central and South America
Barred Forest Falcon *(Micrastur ruficollis)*	13-15" (33-38cm)	6½-8" (165-203mm)	Central and South America
Sclater's Forest Falcon *(M. plumbeus)*	12-13" (30-33cm)	7" (178mm)	Colombia and Ecuador
Slaty-backed Forest Falcon *(M. mirandollei)*	14-16" (36-41cm)	9" (228mm)	Costa Rica to northern South America
Collared Forest Falcon *(M. semitorquatus)*	18-24" (46-61cm)	10-11" (254-279mm)	Central and South America
Traylor's Forest Falcon *(M. buckleyi)*	14-16" (36-41cm)	8½" (216mm)	Ecuador and Peru
Spot-winged Falconet *(Spiziapteryx circumcinctus)*	11" (28cm)	6-7" (152-178mm)	Argentina
African Pygmy Falcon *(Polihierax semitorquatus)*	11" (28cm)	4½" (114mm)	Eastern and southern Africa
Fielden's Falconet *(P. insignis)*	10-11" (25-28cm)	5½" (140mm)	South-east Asia
Red-legged Falconet *(Microhierax caerulescens)*	7½" (19cm)	4" (101mm)	India and South-east Asia
Black-legged Falconet *(M. fringillarius)*	6" (15cm)	4" (101mm)	South-east Asia, East Indies
Bornean Falconet *(M. latifrons)*	6" (15cm)	4" (101mm)	Borneo
Philippine Falconet *(M. erythrogonys)*		4½" (114mm)	Philippines
Pied Falconet *(M. melanoleucus)*	7½" (19cm)	4½" (114mm)	South-east Asia
Lesser Kestrel *(Falco naumanni)*	12" (30cm)	9½" (235mm)	Southern Europe to Central Asia, winters Africa, India
Greater Kestrel *(F. rupicoloides)*	13½-14½" (34-37cm)	9½-11½" (241-292mm)	East and South Africa
Fox Kestrel *(F. alopex)*	16-17" (41-43cm)	10½-12" (267-305mm)	Central Africa
American Kestrel *(F. sparverius)*	10½" (27cm)	6½-8" (165-203mm)	The entire New World except the far north
Common Kestrel *(F. tinnunculus)*	13-14" (33-36cm)	8½-11" (216-279mm)	Europe, Asia and Africa
Madagascar Kestrel *(F. newtoni)*		7½" (190mm)	Madagascar
Mauritius Kestrel *(F. punctatus)*		6½-7½ (165-190mm)	Mauritius
Seychelles Kestrel *(F. araea)*		6" (152mm)	Seychelles
Moluccan Kestrel *(F. moluccensis)*		8-9" (203-228mm)	East Indies
Nankeen Kestrel *(F. cenchroides)*	12-14" (30-36cm)	9½-11" (241-279mm)	Australia and New Guinea
Grey Kestrel *(F. ardosiaceus)*	14" (36cm)	8-10" (203-254mm)	Africa south of the Sahara
Dickinson's Kestrel *(F. dickinsoni)*	11-12" (28-30cm)	9" (228mm)	Southern half of Africa
Madagascar Banded Kestrel *(F. zoniventris)*		8½" (216mm)	Madagascar
Red-footed Kestrel *(F. vespertinus)*	12" (30cm)	8½-10" (216-254mm)	Central Europe and Asia, wintering in Africa
Red-headed Falcon *(F. chicquera)*	12-14" (30-36cm)	7½-9½" (190-241mm)	India and Africa south of the Sahara
Merlin *(F. columbarius)*	10½-13" (27-33cm)	7½-9" (190-228mm)	Northern hemisphere of New and Old Worlds
Brown Falcon *(F. berigora)*	18-20" (46-51cm)	12½-15½" (318-393mm)	Australia and New Guinea
New Zealand Falcon *(F. novaeseelandiae)*		9-12" (228-305mm)	New Zealand
European Hobby *(F. subbuteo)*	12-14" (30-36cm)	9½-11" (241-279mm)	Europe and north central Asia
African Hobby *(F. cuvieri)*	12" (30cm)	8-10" (203-254mm)	Africa south of the Sahara
Oriental Hobby *(F. severus)*	10" (25cm)	8½-10" (216-254mm)	South Asia, East Indies, New Guinea, Solomons
Australian Hobby *(F. longipennis)*	12-14" (30-36cm)	9-10½" (228-267mm)	Australia
Eleanora's Falcon *(F. eleanorae)*	15" (38cm)	12-14½" (305-368mm)	Mediterranean islands, wintering in Madagascar
Sooty Falcon *(F. concolor)*	13-14" (33-36cm)	10-11½" (254-292mm)	North Africa and Near East; winters E. Africa, Madagascar
Bat Falcon *(F. rufigularis)*	9-12" (23-30cm)	7-9" (178-228mm)	Central and South America
Aplomado Falcon *(F. femoralis)*	15-18" (38-46cm)	10-12" (254-305mm)	South-west U.S.A., Central and South America
Grey Falcon *(F. hypoleucos)*	14-17" (36-43cm)	10½-13½" (267-343mm)	Australia
Black Falcon *(F. subniger)*	17-22" (43-56cm)	14½-16½" (368-419mm)	Australia, not including Tasmania
Lanner Falcon *(F. biarmicus)*	16-18" (41-46cm)	12-15" (305-381mm)	South-east Europe, Middle East, Africa
Prairie Falcon *(F. mexicanus)*	15½-19½" (40-49cm)	11½-14" (292-355mm)	North America
Laggar Falcon *(F. jugger)*	16-18" (41-46cm)	12-14½" (305-368mm)	India and Burma
Saker Falcon *(F. cherrug)*	18" (46cm)	13-16½" (333-419mm)	Central Europe and Asia, wintering N. Africa, S. Asia
Gyr Falcon *(F. rusticolus)*	20-24" (51-61cm)	13½-16½" (343-419mm)	Arctic of Old and New Worlds
Orange-breasted Falcon *(F. deiroleucus)*	13-15" (33-38cm)	10-11½" (254-292mm)	Central and South America
Taita Falcon *(F. fasciinucha)*	11½" (29cm)	8½" (216mm)	East and Central Africa south to the Zambezi
Peregrine Falcon *(F. peregrinus)*	14-19" (35-48cm)	10½-15" (267-381mm)	Whole world, except high Arctic and Antarctic

Reading List

The single most important reference work on raptors remains the monumental *Eagles, Hawks and Falcons of the World* by Leslie Brown and Dean Amadon. Published in 1968 by *Country Life*, this two-volume work is now to be obtained only on the second-hand market, but is generally available in good libraries. It covers every species in the fullest possible detail, and although our knowledge of some species has increased greatly since 1968, there are still many for which the information available is the same now as it was then. Another very comprehensive work, published four years earlier, is *Birds of Prey of the World* by Mary Louise Grossman and John Hamlet. This book deals with owls as well as day-active birds of prey in a single volume. Some additional works, many of them still available, are listed below by alphabetical order of the author's name.

General Works

Brown, L. 1976: *Birds of Prey; their biology and ecology.* Paul Hamlyn, London.
A readable yet erudite general survey.

Ferguson-Lees, I.J. (in press): *Raptors; an Identification Guide.* Christopher Helm, Bromley.
A vital recognition guide to the world's raptors.

Newton, I. 1979; *Population Ecology of Raptors.* T. & A.D. Poyser, Berkhamsted.
An in-depth, scholarly study of raptor ecology.

Regional Works

Gensbøl, B. 1984: *Birds of Prey of Britain and Europe.* William Collins, London.
A photographic identification guide.

Hollands, D. 1984: *Eagles, Hawks and Falcons of Australia.*
Thomas Nelson, Melbourne.
Illustrated with superb photographs.

Porter, R.F. *et al.* 1981: *Flight Identification of European Raptors* (3rd ed.) T. & A.D. Poyser, Calton.
Flight recognition explained with line drawings and photographs.

Steyn, P. 1983: *Birds of Prey of Southern Africa.* Croom Helm, Beckenham.

Monographs

Cade, T. 1982: *The Falcons of the World.* William Collins, London.
Study of the Falconidae, beautifully illustrated by R. David Digby.

Newton, I. 1986: *The Sparrowhawk.* T. & A.D. Poyser, Calton.
Ratcliffe, D. 1980: *The Peregrine Falcon.* T. & A.D. Poyser, Calton.
The two preceding works both feature studies of pesticide damage.

Tubbs, C.R. 1974: *The Buzzard.* David & Charles, Newton Abbott.

Walter, H. 1979: *Eleonora's Falcon. Adaptions to Prey and Habitat in a Social Raptor.* University of Chicago Press, Chicago.
A detailed scientific investigation of an exceptionally interesting species.

Watson, D. 1977: *The Hen Harrier.* T. & A.D. Poyser, Berkhamsted.

Index

Page numbers in italics refer to illustrations.
Map numbers are printed in bold.